£30

£7.
ART
24/11

SPODE

I China: Antique Shape double icepail with Butterfly embossment. Height, 12¾in. Marks 5b, 10 and '4004'. (*R.S.Copeland Esq.*)

SPODE

A HISTORY OF THE FAMILY, FACTORY AND WARES FROM 1733 TO 1833

LEONARD WHITER

BARRIE & JENKINS
LONDON

© Leonard Whiter 1970, 1978

First published 1970
Second edition 1978

Published by Barrie and Jenkins Limited
24 Highbury Crescent, London N5 1RX

ISBN 0 214 20476 6

Photography by Harold Holdway
Photoset in Monotype Plantin
Printed in Great Britain by
W.S.Cowell Limited
Butter Market Ipswich
Colour plates by
Colour Workshop Limited
Mimram Road Hertford
Designer: John Sutherland-Hawes

TO THE MEMORY OF SIMEON SHAW

A debt acknowledged
& a compliment returned

Contents

NOTE: Throughout the book three-digit numbers refer to sources of information. Explanatory notes are numbered 1–89.

List of illustrations

Monochrome Plates

NOTE: The index to pattern names and numbers at the end of the book gives references to the plates in which they are illustrated.

Monochrome Plates *continued*

Monochrome Plates *continued*

Other illustrations

Acknowledgments

The notes and references display my debts to other authors and provide a bibliography, but the greatest debt of all I owe to Harold Holdway, Art Director of the Spode Factory. Providing me with all but a few of the photographs used in this book was a task of several months, but sharing with me his vast and expert knowledge of Spode has been the patient work of years.

This book would not have been possible without the full co-operation and help of William Whatmore, Managing Director of W.T.Copeland & Sons Ltd, and his fellow directors; to all of whom I give my sincere thanks.

To my wife I owe much for practical help but even more for her encouragement. It has been my good fortune to have had as a tutor Reginald Haggar, whose example and help have been invaluable, and to have been within easy reach of the often needed assistance of Norman Emery and his staff at Hanley Reference Library. Robert Copeland generously provided the fruits of his own research and gave welcome help with indexing. Geoffrey Godden gave me valuable advice and information and four choice photographs. For my knowledge of references to Spode among the Wedgwood MSS I am almost entirely indebted to J.K. and Una des Fontaines, and for permission to quote—and other help— to Josiah Wedgwood and Sons Ltd, Barlaston. Special thanks are due to William Algar, a descendant of Henry Daniel, who made the Daniel MSS freely available to me.

I have often needed an expert opinion from my colleagues: Cyril Allen, ceramicist; Tom Barlow, master modeller; Frank Boothby, master engraver; Paul Holdway, engraver and Stan Nicholls, potter. Others who have given help are Paul Wood, who did the sketches, Edward Baker, Miss Jean Bettaney, Harold Cheshire, Miss Iris Hackney, and Mrs Muriel Radford.

For providing pieces for photography, I have to thank the directors of W.T.Copeland & Sons Ltd and R.Spencer Copeland, Robert Copeland, Major A.J.Bather and Nigel Bernard.

My thanks are also due to: Geoffrey de Bellaigue, Mrs Joyce Hanson, Bevis Hillier, Mrs Molla Kraft, Miss Jane Langton, Mrs M.B.Moore, Arnold Mountford, John Yates, the Burns Club of Dumfries, the Guildhall Library, the Hudson's Bay Company, the National Army Museum, the Royal Artillery Institution and Richard Newton.

Author's preface

The Spodes, father and son, claim notice on account of the pots they made. By these they will be judged, whatever is written about them, and from this their admirers may derive satisfaction and their chroniclers reassurance. The increasing interest in what one of their severest critics was moved to describe as their 'wonderfully diverse and well-made wares' and the desire to share a little knowledge, gleaned these last ten years in and about the place where they were made, must be this book's justification.

LEONARD WHITER

Spode Works, Stoke-on-Trent, Staffordshire
March 1970

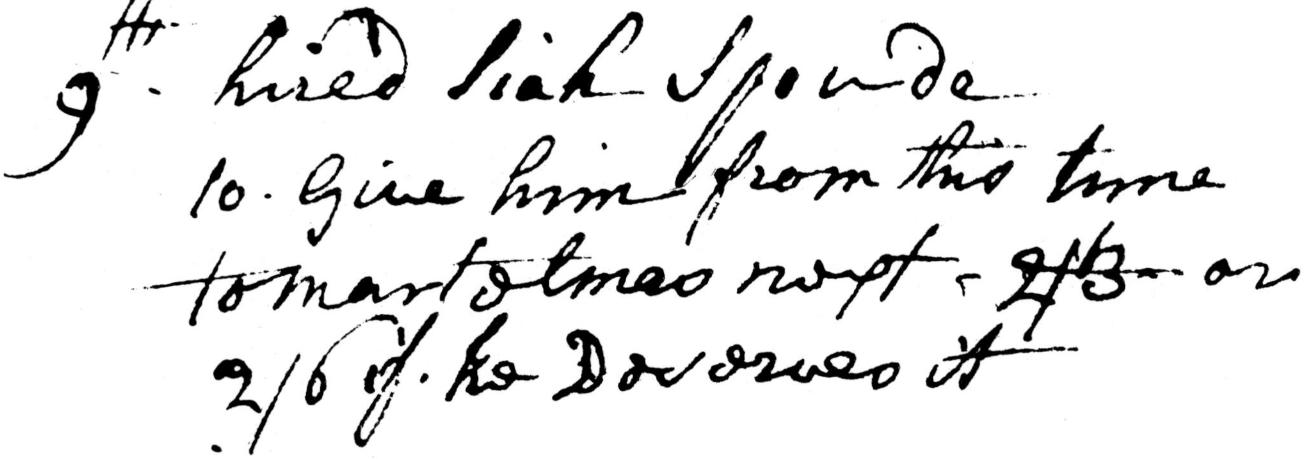

9th: hired Siah Spode
10. Give him from this time
to martlemas next — 2/3 — or
2/6 if he Deserves it

Entry dated 9th April 1749 in Thomas Whieldon's notebook

1 Spode 1

Lane Delph in the eighteenth century was a small collection of houses located between Stoke and Lane End, about a mile from the centre of each. It preserved its separate identity well into the next century although always properly belonging to Fenton, sixth of the Pottery Towns—the one Arnold Bennett forgot. It was here, in 1733, that Josiah Spode was born. We call him Josiah Spode 1, intending no disrespect to his father of the same name.

Spode 1 spent his entire life within sight of his birthplace, his remotest venture taking him no farther afield than Shelton, not two miles away. In Lane Delph, or within half a mile of it, his father and his mother died, his eldest son found his wife, and Samuel, his younger son, spent his entire adult life. Writing of Spode 1 in 1843, a mere forty-six years after his death, John Ward commented 'few particulars are known to us'$_{282}$* and the intervening years have brought but a scant supplement. Only two stark facts are known concerning the earliest part of his life: in 1739 his father died and was buried in a pauper's grave. To have a father who was a pauper and then to have no father at all, at the age of six, is an unlucky start to life anywhere at any time—but particularly unlucky in eighteenth century England. We can only speculate on the tribulations of the widow, Ellen Spode. Spode 1 was her only son, but there were other children.

If a boy had to face the world penniless and fatherless in the 1740s there were worse places than the Potteries, where a great industry was taking shape. The rapid establishment of tea as a national beverage, even before the middle of the century, was an unexpected social and economic phenomenon which provided a continuing stimulus; and this very favourable external circumstance was matched by the efforts of the Staffordshire potters themselves. In the first fifty years of the century they accomplished a succession of technical breakthroughs, and their wares—from being indistinguishable from those of any village potter in England—through the introduction of flint and West of England clays and the double method of firing, biscuit and glost, assumed the character of the English earthenware which was to command world markets for two centuries. The use of plaster of Paris moulds and new methods of manipulation and decoration enabled them to diversify their wares as well as to increase their capacity for producing them. The pewterers, in the direct line of fire, lost ground rapidly;[1] even the silversmiths must have had momentary misgivings. Yet always

---

* Throughout this book three-digit numbers refer to sources of information which appear on pages 236 to 239. Explanatory notes are numbered 1 to 89 and appear on pages 228 to 235.

more important than the near monopolising of traditional markets were the constantly developing new ones, among different social classes at home and other nations abroad, and these new markets were as much created as they were captured by Staffordshire's products.

Years ago, Lane Delph was consumed in the Potteries' seven-mile sprawl which, even in 1795, struck the confused Aikin as 'but one town although under different names'.[154] He was a stranger to the district, however, and a local man could still describe Lane Delph in the 1840s as 'little more than a large village . . . favourably situated, on two sides stretches of beautiful country and pleasant walks in abundance'.[195] Although in the middle of the eighteenth century it may have been 'a chief place in the Southern part of the district',[244] in 1738, when the entire population of the Potteries was estimated at four thousand and that of the whole of Fenton at two hundred,[273] the little place, only a part of the latter, must have been small indeed. Even so, Simeon Shaw, the Potteries' first historian who wrote in 1829, observed that the number of old houses there 'shew it to have been long one of the seats of manufacture',[237] and as such it was a place holding opportunities even for a pauper's son. In the Potteries, at least, skill and enterprise could win a rich reward without privilege; and when capital was needed to supplement them, there were those who would trade it for knowledge.

Adjacent to Lane Delph was Little Fenton, where Thomas Whieldon worked. Accorded to be both the best and the most successful potter of this particular time, he produced a wide range of wares. By 4th April 1749, Spode I was working for him. Whieldon's notebook, which records the fact, is so disorderly that it is impossible to be sure of the period of time it covers; but since it contains no entries earlier than 1749, it is possible that Spode I was there before this date. Whether he was working for Whieldon or not, he would have been working for someone before the mature age of sixteen. Given the need to earn money, no difficulty was presented by age in the early industrial society of the time.

The entries relating to Spode I in Whieldon's book are as follows. Martelmas was Martinmas, 11th November, the traditional hiring time:

		£	s	d
1749, April 9th				
Hired Siah Spoade, to give him from this time to Martelmas next, 2s.3d., or 2s.6d. if he Deserves it.				
2nd. year .	. . . .		2	9
3rd. year .	. . . .		3	3
Paid full earnest .	. . . .		1	0

1752, February 22nd

Hired Josiah Spoad for next Martlemas,			
per week		7	0
I am to give him earn		5	0
Paid in Part		1	0
Paid do		4	0

1754, February 25th

Hired Siah Spode, per week		7	6
Earnest	1	11	6
Paid in Part		16	0 [2]

In the first entry, the 2s.3d. has been scored through by Whieldon, so it appears that Spode I did deserve and get 2s.6d, (see p. 1). Although he is usually referred to as having been apprenticed, it is possible that the distinction between apprentice and worker was not very clear to him or his master; but it was clearly made by Arthur Young nearly twenty years later, in 1770: 'In general the men earn seven shillings to twelve shillings; Women five shillings to eight shillings. Boys, chiefly apprentices, but two shillings a week for the first year, and a rise of threepence per annum afterwards. Before they are apprentices two shillings and ninepence per week, as they then learn nothing. But few girls'.[297]

It is hard to believe that boys earned more before being apprenticed in consideration of learning nothing. In 1751, Whieldon was paying a boy called Samuel Edge 1s.3d. a week; and in 1749, Ann Blowr's boy was getting 2s. a week for 'treading ye lathe'. For very young boys wages were paltry. According to Simeon Shaw, John Mitchell paid his seven-year-old lathe treaders fourpence a week for their arduous and purely mechanical task, the rate for which was still only sixpence in 1766.[240] In 1801, Spode II paid William Shaw, who was properly apprenticed to him for six years,[3] exactly what Spode I was promised by Whieldon, but these rates seem very generous compared with the one shilling a week which Aaron Wood received through the first three years of his six-year apprenticeship to Dr Thomas Wedgwood, which began in 1731.[239] When J.Fletcher was apprenticed to the Taylor brothers for six years, some time in the 1740s, he received the same rates as Spode I, but these were 'The highest wages then given, and paid him because he had already acquired considerable knowledge of different parts of the business'.[249]

The payment of wages to an apprentice was in itself contrary to the custom of apprenticeship and in 1744 was declared illegal in London. But by the end of the eighteenth century it had become so widespread that provision was being made for the entry of wages on the standard printed indenture forms. By the middle of the century, the Elizabethan Statute of Artificers of 1562, which governed the hiring of apprentices and most matters relating to them, was being breached as often as it was observed. This was particularly so where no strong local guild existed to enforce its provisions: unlike the cutlers of Sheffield, the Staffordshire potters had none, potting having remained a widespread, country-type craft rather than a town-based manufacture until a time well after the guilds had passed their heyday of power and usefulness.[162]

Although the first entry for Spode I is the only one in the notebook which concerns a hiring as long as nearly three years, this is still excessively short compared with the apprenticeship terms of six years which seemed more usual in the district. John Turner's abortive apprenticeship to Daniel Bird was to last for only five years;[201] but this was, by any standards, an apprenticeship proper for it began with a payment by Turner senior of £20, and after such a handsome fee—more than Spode I earned in the whole of his term—there would have been no room for argument about whether his son was primarily a pupil or a producer. The position of the scion of a middle class family was not to be compared with that of Spode I.

Whatever his exact initial status, by 1752 he had graduated to journeyman. His wage of seven shillings a week compared with the eight shillings which Whieldon paid George Bagnall as a fireman and Elijah Simpson as a turner. Disappointingly, there is no reference to any particular trade for him, but this is mainly the case in the notebook's entries.

Just as the connection with Whieldon could pre-date the first entry in 1749, so it could post-date the last one in 1754; but there are entries for later years, up to 1760, and it seems likely that on 25th February 1754, the year that Josiah Wedgwood joined Whieldon as a partner,[213] Spode I hired himself to him for the last time. The following month he reached his majority, and six months later he was married. On 8th September 1754, described as an 'Earth Potter', he signed the Stoke marriage register in an unsure hand. His bride, Ellen Finley, was unable to do the same and made her mark below. She was eight years older than her husband and by 1772, perhaps well before, was conducting her own business in Stoke as a haberdasher.[4] Both these facts may be significant in relation to a marriage which marked the beginning of a more flourishing phase in Spode I's career.

For what little information we have concerning the next twenty years we must be grateful to Simeon Shaw—grateful also that the few facts available from other sources are supplementary rather than contradictory to his account. He tells us that 'Of the four apprentices to Mr Whieldon, three commenced business and were eminently successful'.[242] One of the three was Spode I.

After (the first) Mr. Josiah Spode left the employment of Mr. Whieldon at Fenton, he was employed along with the late Mr. Charles Harvey, in the manufactory of

Mr. Banks (who resided at Stoke Hall) on White Stone Ware and for Cream Colour. Scratched and Blue Painted$_{253}$ [and elsewhere] About 1756, Mr. R. [sic.] Bankes, and the late Mr. John Turner, made White Stone Ware at Stoke, on the spot part of the premises of Josiah Spode, Esq.$_{245}$

Presumably, Spode I had lived with his mother in Lane Delph or Lower Lane when he was a bachelor; but that he moved to Stoke on or shortly after his marriage is shown by this being given as his town in the register entry for the baptism of his first child, Josiah, on 25th May 1755.[5] In 1758, he appears to have acquired his own property, building a house and shop directly by Banks' factory, where he was then working.[6] Perhaps the shop saw the beginning of Ellen's haberdashery business.

Banks was probably already in partnership with John Turner when Spode I joined him. Turner had originally been apprenticed at the age of fifteen to Daniel Bird, who potted only two hundred yards from Banks' factory, at Cliff Bank.$_{234}$ Bird met with an accidental death in November 1753,$_{202}$ before a year of the apprenticeship term had elapsed, and Turner seems to have descended the hill to join Banks as a partner at the remarkable age of fifteen with virtually no potting experience.[7] Between them, at a date unknown, they purchased the factory which, up to then, must have been held on lease.$_{100}$

Although he only says 'about', it is just possible that Shaw's date of 1756 for Turner joining Banks is strictly correct, another stage intervening between Turner losing his master, Daniel Bird, and the beginning of the partnership. This would also explain why Turner is not mentioned by Shaw as being with Banks when Spode I went to work for him. The only suggestion of this which can be discovered is the unlikely one made by Henry Wedgwood in 1879 that he went off to Shelton to pot by himself.$_{202}$ It is easier to believe that young Turner represented something of a windfall to Banks, in much the same way that Thomas Mountford did to Spode I some years later. Turner senior, a successful lawyer, would have been able to provide his son with something to recommend him to the Stoke potter in addition to the doubtful assets of extreme youth and ten months' experience. Such an influx of capital may well have accounted for the employment of Spode I and Charles Harvey and made possible the expansion and purchase of the site.

The site occupied by Banks and Turner was large and the lawyer's description as impressive as an estate agent's: 'All those Pot houses Workhouses Warehouses Ovens Hovels Buildings Pot works Yards Lands and Hereditaments'.$_{100}$ In fact, it was mainly meadowland and would probably have been the small intimate establishment to be expected at a time when the most important potter of the day, Whieldon, could only boast a 'Small range of low buildings, all thatched'.$_{241}$ Even though Shaw tells us William Banks lived at Stoke Hall, the

II Earthenware and other wares: Left to right and top to bottom: (1) Basket with pierced lid in unglazed cane ware. Mark 3. (2) Matchpot in coloured earthenwares. Height, $4\frac{1}{8}$in. Mark 2a. (3) Griffin candlestick in red ware and basalts. Mark 2b. (4) Bow-handled basket in stoneware. Mark 3. (5) Mug in stoneware. Mark 3. (6) Covered jar in jasper-type stoneware. Mark 3. (7) New Shape jar in earthenware with lustre decoration. Mark '3747' only. (8) Matchpot in green glazed earthenware. Mark 4. (9) Jug in glazed cane ware, Mark 2a.

local big house, the two partners with Charles Harvey, Spode I and a few lads could well have been the entire complement. It is a perfectly legitimate fancy that Spode I, a fully proficient workman, five years older than John Turner, played an important role in the instruction of the man whose taste and proficiency were later to distinguish him, perhaps above all others, as a potter's potter.

Such a second-hand claim to fame would have been all that Spode I achieved if, with the vast majority of his anonymous contemporaries, he had been content to continue in paid employment. The first opportunity to go into business on his own appears to have opened up for him in Shelton, half a mile or so from where he was working.

> But Messrs. Baddeley and Fletcher discontinuing making Porcelain, at Vale Lane, Shelton, Mr. Spode commenced manufacturing the pottery most in demand— Cream Colour and Blue Painted, White ware; and his productions were of tolerable excellence. His family remained resident at Stoke.[253]

Fortunately, it is now possible to find out a great deal more about Messrs Baddeley and Fletcher than Shaw seems to have done. The discontinuance of porcelain-making at Shelton, which apparently marked Spode I's move there, probably took place in 1761.[8]

Shaw's account—the only source of information on this first self-employed venture of Spode I—is too circumstantial to be lightly suspected, pinpointing as it does the occasion which made the premises available and describing the wares manufactured. So far in the story, outside sources have revealed him a faithful guide. The mention of Spode I continuing to reside in Stoke, an odd circumstance at a time when a house for the master was part of every factory, could perhaps mean that Mrs Spode had already established her haberdashery business and it was making a contribution to family funds not to be jeopardised by her husband's first independent command. It does give a certain air of impermanence to the venture, which seems to have been short-lived.

If 1761 or 1762 is taken as the year in which Spode I left for Shelton, then he left Banks after John Turner had already broken up the partnership by going to Lane End. This makes odd reading of Shaw's continuation of his story, unless it is remembered that, although Turner may have left in 1759, Shaw believed that he did not go until 1762.[9]

> And Messrs. Banks and Turner separating and Mr. Banks relinquishing business in a short time afterwards, Mr. Spode engaged the manufactory, (which subsequently he purchased), and there manufactured also Black printed, and Black Egyptian.[253]

Banks must have relinquished business before early 1764, for on 26th

B

February of that year he sold his factory and part of the adjacent land, known as Madeley's Meadow, to Jeremiah Smith.[100] On 27th August 1766, Smith acquired from Banks the remainder of this meadow which is commemorated to this day by a piece of stubborn nomenclature, one of the Spode Factory's modern tunnel ovens still bearing the inherited and now unlikely title of 'The Meadow Oven'.[10] The Meadow embraced the Factory from the north and, the presence of so much adjacent land proving a great convenience, in later years it became completely occupied by buildings and the other paraphernalia of a constantly expanding business. At this early date it was complete with cowsheds, and in July 1777 Spode I paid part of a bill for the carriage of coals in hay, presumably mown on it.

Jeremiah Smith, High Sheriff of Staffordshire in 1762, was a man of substance and diverse business interests,[152] but potting does not appear to have been one of them and his only use for the premises must have been to let them, presumably as quickly as possible. If Spode I was his first tenant, he must have transferred his business in Shelton to the scene of his former labours in Stoke as early as 1764. He took the ultimate steps on 29th February 1776, when he purchased the whole of the premises, including all the Meadow.[100]

Shaw makes no mention of Spode I's partners, and yet two are known: William Tomlinson and Thomas Mountford. The partnership with Mountford, which began in 1772,[4] has every indication of being, for Spode I, strictly a means of getting the funds for conducting a business. It is a fair assumption that the one with Tomlinson, which had begun earlier, had a similar basis. Only towards the end of his career is there any evidence of Spode I having substantial capital at his disposal, and the purchase of the Stoke factory in 1776 was only made possible by a mortgage of £1,000 from his wealthy landlord.[100]

Thomas Mountford provided £500, all the money necessary for their joint venture at Shelton, and in return was to be 'honestly and faithfully instructed' by Spode I in the 'whole art and mystery' of the potter's trade. Whether he was an inept pupil, the art proving too mysterious for him, or whether some other circumstance intervened is unknown, but no fruit survives by which we may judge the honest and faithful instruction which should have been lavished on this princely provider.

Spode I's other partner, William Tomlinson, also seems to have left no trace of his subsequent activity.[11] About the partnership practically nothing is known. It was due to finish on 11th November 1774,[4] but when in fact it began and ended is not recorded. It was certainly in being in November 1772, since it is expressly reserved from Mountford and Spode I's mutual undertaking not to involve themselves in any other potting enterprise. An invoice survives from Spode and Tomlinson made out to Josiah and Thomas Wedgwood, which

is given in Appendix III. It is dated 7th September 1771, and, most unfortunately, gives no address. But there cannot be much doubt that this would
have been from the Stoke Factory and that it was there that Tomlinson was in
partnership with Spode I, perhaps ever since he returned from Shelton—or
even earlier, since Spode I would almost certainly have needed a partner for his
very first venture at least as much as he did later.

The partnership with Mountford was a quite separate affair. It began on
11th November 1772; and so, for the second time (if Shaw is to be believed),
Spode I found himself in business in Shelton. He still continued to live in
Stoke, however, as we should expect: the living quarters at the Shelton factory—
which was rented from Elizabeth Mountford, a widow—were to be occupied
by his partner.

Half of Mountford's £500 was lent to Spode I at interest so that they should
each be able to contribute equally to the purchase of the necessary 'clay, flint,
lead, colours, pots, pot boards and other wood wares, utensils and things'.
Mountford was to have 4 per cent per annum interest on the £250 he put into
the joint stock; but this was more than balanced by a weekly wage of twelve
shillings which Spode I was to draw 'as an adequate compensation for his
superior skill and attendance in the management and carrying on of the said
joint trade and for the necessary instructions to the said Thomas Mountford'.
Any profits over and above were to be divided equally.

It is not known if this venture in Shelton continued until the partnership
had run its full seven-year course. If it did, 11th September 1779 should mark
the end of Spode I's involvement in anything but his Stoke Factory.

It is to be hoped that one day fresh evidence will come to light which will
remove the need for the uncomfortable amount of speculation and guesswork
which cannot be avoided in trying to trace the activities of Spode I between 1754
and 1776. Until it does, the following précis of the foregoing account of what
could have happened is offered with diffidence:

1754 to 1761 After marrying, resides in Stoke and is employed by Banks and
              Turner; later, Banks alone.
1762 to 1764 Self-employed in Shelton, perhaps with a partner.
1764 to 1772 In partnership with Tomlinson at Banks' old factory in Stoke,
              which they rent.
1772 to 1774 Partnership with Tomlinson continues at Stoke. In quite
              separate partnership with Mountford at Shelton.
1774 to 1779 Continued independently at Stoke and after 1776 is owner of
              the factory. Partnership with Mountford continues.
1779 et seq. Continues at Stoke alone.

As early as 1846, the date of the beginning of Spode I's proprietorship of his factory in Stoke had become uncertain and was being stated as 'about 1770'.[128] No better date could have been chosen, falling, as it does, exactly midway between the date when he probably first 'engaged the manufactory' and the date when he definitely became its owner.

It must be regretfully accepted that we shall never know when we hold a piece of ware made by Spode I before he became firmly established at his own Stoke Factory. Indeed, the problem of identifying his productions even after that point is a very severe one. This cannot prevent a certain satisfaction that all the evidence points to his having been concerned with every important species of ware associated with eighteenth-century Staffordshire. It is no accident that these wares have for so long excited such interest and opened wide so many purses for, as a class, they are the biggest original contribution made by Britain to ceramics. As a youth, Spode I must have played a part in the manufacture of the superbly potted wares, with their exciting, coloured glazed decorations, that are associated with Whieldon's name. When a young man, Banks employed him on 'White Stone Ware and for Cream Colour. Scratched and Blue Painted'.[253] If white stoneware means salt glazed—which it probably does—Banks was making the best of both worlds, and Spode I became acquainted with this well-established product of the district at the same time he was introduced to the new, and potentially all-important, cream coloured ware.

The products which, according to Shaw, were most in demand at the time Spode I began business on his own account and which, therefore, he made were 'Cream Colour and Blue Painted, White ware'.[253] On returning to Stoke, he there manufactured 'also Black printed and Black Egyptian'. Even without any account, it could be imagined that this selection would most likely have represented his early range. Black Egyptian (which Josiah Wedgwood, ever the salesman, dubbed Basalts) and its companion body, Red Egyptian, were the two most popular self-coloured wares of the time and it is unlikely that the second one, of terracotta colour, was not made by him as well as the first, although it is not specifically mentioned by Shaw. In origin, it was probably even older than the Black, going back at least to the time of the Elers and being virtually endemic in Staffordshire, since it was the colour to which one of the most abundant local clays fired—without the addition of a stain. Both bodies were only suitable for ornamental wares, teapots, jugs and sugar boxes. For the bulk production of table wares, the new earthenware body, rapidly being perfected, was the prime product of the whole district. This was inevitably made by Spode I, as Shaw recounts. When he refers to 'white ware'—as opposed to 'white stone ware'—he undoubtedly means the normal earthenware of the period but glazed white instead of yellow and, in this guise, usually now termed pearl ware.

According to Shaw, Spode I decorated his tableware. The white ware was 'blue painted' and 'black printed'. No marked example black printed in the eighteenth-century fashion has, as far as I know, ever been found; but a piece of blue painted pearl ware, which has the marks of being of early date, is illustrated in Plate 105. The decoration is not to be confused with hand-painted Chinese landscapes done as matchings for existing services. The style is chinoiserie, not Chinese, and it is no matching piece. It belongs to the very extensive class of blue painted patterns of this kind, produced in a similar style by many English potters on both pearl ware and cream coloured. This class of decoration was doomed by the printer's press, an early introduction by Spode I: 'About 1784, he introduced the manufacture of Blue Printed into Stoke; on the improved methods successfully adopted by Mr Ralph Baddeley of Shelton'.[253]

The painters of the district 'employed every artifice'[253] to prevent the success of the new blue printing method, but in vain. It was destined to sweep all before it: to make fortunes for many potters and reputations for a few.

Printing on thin paper, impressions transferred to the fired ware, and paper washed off.

2   Father and son

The marriage of Spode I and Ellen Finley was fruitful. Their first son, Josiah, was born in May 1755 and their second, Samuel, in October 1757. Five daughters followed, the last in 1777 when her mother was fifty-one years old.

For the sake of their biographers, fathers should not give their sons their own christian names. The practice is an invitation to confusion, particularly when the son is only twenty-two years younger than the father. More than one writer has been trapped by the inconsiderate juxtaposition of the two Josiahs but, with care, it is possible to trace fairly clearly the separate course of Spode II during the years when his father was alive. One of his obituarists begins a brief account of his life by stating that he was 'from his earliest years remarked for intelligence and attention. When taken from school, his father employed him occasionally to superintend every branch of the manufacture in which his services could be available'.[131]

A major mystery in the life of his father is how he managed to get any schooling at all; a minor one in that of the son is where he received his. That Spode II attended the Free Grammar School at Newcastle-under-Lyme (where he was to send his own son) is not unlikely, but there is no evidence of this. The life which awaited him on completing his education sounds not unlike that of a present-day management trainee.

In July 1775, at the early age of twenty, he married Elizabeth Barker of Lane Delph, whose father, John Barker, was one of the three 'successful apprentices' of Whieldon mentioned by Shaw, the other two being Spode I and Robert Garner. The marriage is another indication of the close association which the three of them seem to have preserved in later life, Robert Garner actually going into partnership with Barker.[246]

The obituary already quoted says 'neither interest nor ambition had part' in the union; but a dowry of £500 which Shaw mentions Spode II received with his bride was a not unhelpful gesture on the part of his father-in-law, who, with Spode I, agreed that they had been provided with 'a proper opportunity to establish a regular London business, alike advantageous to themselves and to the newly married pair, the younger Mr Spode therefore commenced as a Dealer in Earthenware; and subsequently also of Glass and Porcelain'.[254]

This great adventure did not begin immediately after the marriage. Their first child, William, was baptised on 8th March 1776, and their second, Josiah III, on 24th August 1777, both in Stoke. It was not until the following year that

Spode 11 became a freeman of the City of London, a recognised prerequisite to opening a shop there—for although some merchants and bankers may have avoided the status, which was not without onerous obligations, retail trade in the City was kept an exclusive preserve for freemen.[168] The way to become one was to be admitted to one of the City Livery Companies, and by this date it did not matter which. There never has been a City Company of Potters or Pot Sellers, the nearest approximation being the Glass Sellers who sold both and which Miles Mason appropriately joined in 1783.[179] John Turner's partner, Abbot, however, joined the Carpenters[203] and Spode 11's choice was equally incongruous: the Worshipful Company of Spectacle Makers, whose court recorded in its minute book: '11th March 1778. Free per redemption. Josiah Spode Son of Josiah Spode of Stoke in Staffordshire Potter, was this day admitted per Redemption and Sworn. No. 29 Fore Street—Potter'.

His membership imposed not the slightest optical obligation. He had paid his money (redemption) and was now free to conduct his business in pottery and take his apprentices—although, when he did so, he had to be careful to describe himself as 'Josiah Spode Esquire and Spectaclemaker'. In 1783, William Ward, a potter of Lower Lane, Stoke, sent his son Richard to join him; and possibly William Copeland joined him as an apprentice in much the same way,[12] probably well before 1790, in which year he signed an order for Spode addressed to Wedgwood's London Rooms.[13] First of a line destined to carry on Spode's business for four generations, William Copeland was an expatriate of Staffordshire during Shaw's life there—which explains why, not knowing him, Shaw did not refer to him by name, terming him in his one brief mention a 'confidential servant'.[255] By 1843, however, when John Ward was writing, the Copelands were firmly re-established in their home district, and Ward tells us more:

> In conducting the London business Mr. Spode [11] found it necessary to engage a resident Partner and connected himself with William Copeland, a native of the parish of Stoke, who, whilst quite a young man had been recommended to the elder Mr. Spode, for his warehouse department and for many years before he was admitted Partner, superintended the London establishment.[284]

William Copeland was baptised on 8th December 1765. His father was a farmer at Hollybush Farm, not much more than half a mile south of Lane Delph and only five hundred yards west of Longton Hall.[185] Here he died, in 1776, a man of modest substance, described by the fast-vanishing title of Yeoman.[100] It is not clear from Ward's account which 'warehouse department' he means— the Factory's or the one at London. He would have been of much more use in London after a period of time spent at the Factory; and a spell in the warehouse was, until very recently, the approved beginning to a sales career in the pottery trade. It still is, with some manufacturers. The recommendation to Spode I may have come from one of William Copeland's relatives. His father had a half-brother named John, and a John Copeland witnessed his will. In 1782, Spode I acquired a tenant of this name for one of his houses and made a note of it in his receipt book.$_{100}$

When William Copeland died in 1826 he left an estate which, when finally liquidated, amounted to more than £86,000. The stamp duty paid was alone equivalent to his father's total fortune of £750.$_{100}$ He died ten years too soon to see his own son, William Taylor Copeland, become Lord Mayor of London. An unaccountable statement by Jewitt in 1877 that, before his association with Spode II, William Copeland 'travelled in the tea trade', lavishly embroidered since, has for too long robbed the Potteries of its own two-generation version of the Dick Whittington story.[14]

There is no good reason to believe that, from the outset, the business established by Spode II in London was not strictly his own. Spode II's retail resources in London were never monopolised by his father's wares, although they may have formed his principal merchandise—particularly at the beginning, when his stock was limited to earthenware only. As late as 1795, according to Shaw, he christened Cheatham and Woolley's new dry body for them, naming it 'pearl', and it is hard to explain his being accorded such a privilege unless he was acting as the agent for its sale.$_{260}$ Certainly from the start he would have been expected to sell the products of his father-in-law, John Barker. Spode I may, as Ward relates, have received his son into partnership several years prior to his death.$_{283}$ From the evidence of Spode II's activity in Stoke this seems certain, but we are probably misled by any implication that the strictly mercantile venture in London was a joint one. Throughout the Spode Period, for only one brief span of years, from 1797 to 1805, can the Factory and the London business be regarded as an integral whole, owned by one and the same man (see Appendix II).

If Spode II ever had cause to regret his move to London, it would have been for personal rather than business reasons: in 1782, by which date his family had been augmented by three daughters, his wife Elizabeth died of fever. He was never to re-marry. The business seems to have been successful from the start. Fore Street, Cripplegate, was perhaps not quite the same as Greek Street, Soho, where Josiah Wedgwood's palatial London premises had been located since 1773. There is no record of Fore Street being blocked with the carriages of the fashionable world as their eager owners packed into No. Twenty-nine[15] but

> The assiduity he manifested, to gratify the varying tastes and wishes of purchasers in kinds, quality and shapes of the various articles, soon gained him extended

connections, while the excellent Blue Printed pottery (recently introduced), supplied by the father, obtained such preference as to produce a considerable increase of business.[254]

This account does not make it clear that Spode II's business was of a predominantly retail nature, but at this time it was inevitable that it should be. It was only with the growth of the large, and subsequently powerful, china dealers in London during Victoria's reign that any rigid distinction appeared between wholesaling and retailing in the pottery trade; even in the early nineteenth century Flight, Barr and Barr of Worcester were able to conduct the whole of their business on a strictly private basis, avoiding retailers altogether.[172]

In the three entries in the Cripplegate Register for the baptisms of his daughters, Spode II is variously described as a 'Hardwareman' in 1778, a 'China man' in 1780, and a 'Warehouse-keeper' in 1781. The clerk responsible seems to have given him steady promotion, and the first entry for Spode II's business in a London directory in 1785 names his premises 'The Staffordshire Warehouse'—a name which it retained from then on. No doubt his trade developed rapidly, but these descriptions indicate no change in its nature. Even in 1765, someone who was impatient with this genteel euphemism was asking, 'Have we now any Shops? Are they not all turned into Warehouses?'[160] Although Spode II certainly dealt with other 'China men' in London, it is likely that his dealings direct with the public always remained a substantial, even if ever-decreasing, proportion of his trade.[16] A servant girl in one of Thomas Hood's comic poems mentions 'Wedgwood's and Mr Spode's' in much the way that someone might currently refer to two well-known London stores whose names are household words.[17]

The retailing of the Potteries' products had naturally kept pace with the expansion of the industry and the increase in public demand. The days of the itinerate pot-sellers were far from numbered and their undignified calling persisted well into the nineteenth century, even in the metropolis.[18] But that established retail outlets existed, even before the eighteenth century, of a character which would be easily recognised today, is apparent from a protest made by the Glass Sellers in 1691. They complained that these pedlars were 'So presumpteous as to cry and proffer both glasses and Earthingware before the very dores and Shops of these that are legall sellers'. Unfair competition to retailers 'Dealing in commodities yt take up a great deale of Roome, oblidge them to hire great houses and sitt at great Rents'.[163] The rapid development of pottery retailing in the next century kept pace with the growing popularity of tea, coffee and chocolate. Daniel Defoe, incensed by the increase in trade for commodities which he regarded as effete and trivial, made an eloquent and sarcastic protest against it in 1713:

It is impossible that Coffee, Tea, and Chocolate can be so advanced in their Consumption, without an eminent Encrease of those Trades that attend them; whence we see the most noble Shops in the City taken up with the valuable Utensils of the Tea-Table. The China Warehouses are little Marts within themselves. . . .[134]

The 'China or Earthenware men' and other dealers in 'Baubles and Trifles' who were at one time 'Found only in Lanes, and Allies or Back-Streets and By-Places, and are fittest for such places' continued their decadent and successful careers and by the time Spode II arrived in London were a long-established and conspicuous part of the scene. A trend to 'Warehouses' specialising in the goods of one manufacturer became more firmly rooted later, reaching its zenith in the late nineteenth century.

Concrete evidence of the success of Spode II's business is provided by the ever-increasing size of his premises. Beginning in 1778 at No. Twenty-nine Fore Street, by 1785—the year in which he first appears in Lowndes London Directory—he had moved to the slightly larger No. Forty-six. Three years later came another move, next door to No. Forty-five, which was more than twice the size and had three times the frontage of the original No. Twenty-nine.[19] In 1790, to supplement the main premises, he rented a warehouse in Moor Lane, a few yards away.[100] Finally, in 1796, he left Fore Street for good and moved to Portugal Street, by Lincolns Inn Fields. He thus acquired not only a better address, finding himself for the first time listed in Boyle's Court Guide among 'All who move in the fashionable circle', but premises of truly staggering size: nothing less than a converted theatre.[20]

Although he was making his fortune in London, Spode II seems never to have thought of himself as a Londoner. He took care that the baptisms of his three London-born daughters should be entered in the register of his home parish; a not unknown practice, but these entries are the only ones of their kind in the Stoke Register. Although Spode I disposed of the Stoke Factory in his will as though it were entirely his, it was 'Josiah Spode the younger of Fore Street in the Ward of Cripplegate London, Potter' who, in 1787, finally paid off the Factory's mortgage[100] and 'Josiah Spode the Younger of the City of London, Potter' who, in 1790, took a leading role in forming what was probably the first potters' joint stock coal company, known initially as Harrison Spode and Company and later as the Fenton Park Colliery.[100] Spode II joined partnership with two Stoke potters, one in Fenton, four pottery firms in Lane Delph, four in Lane End, an enameller and one experienced collier in the 'Trade and business of coal masters'. The lands in which they could 'dig, delve, search, sink, tunnel and mine upon at their wills and pleasures' were leased from the Fletcher and Armistead families and were conveniently situated for all of the

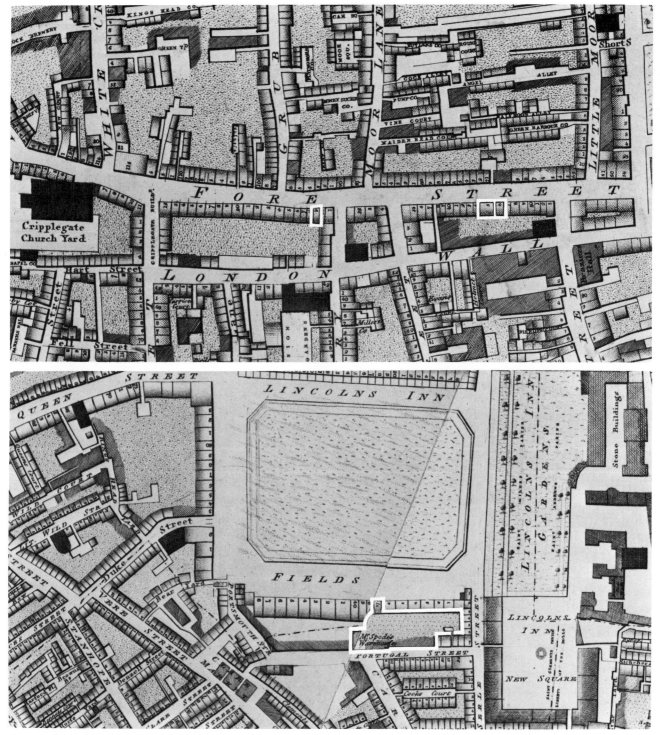

From R. Horwood's Plan of London. Published 24th May 1799

Fore Street, and Cripplegate from an engraving by J. Tingle

partners at Fenton. Spode II never forsook his interest in this enterprise and saw it become one of the foremost collieries in the district.

By this date, Spode II had demonstrated the aptness of John Ward's description of him as 'a Man of Energy, Promptitude, Decision and great Aptitude for Business'.[283] Ward, a well-to-do solicitor, writing after the Spode family was extinct in the district, could afford more scope to his critical faculties than the impecunious and necessarily discreet Simeon Shaw. He adds 'to Mr Spode's decision of character, may be attributed a demeanor, somewhat arbitrary among his servants, from whom he exacted scrupulous obedience, respectful behaviour, and strict punctuality'.[284] His description of Spode I is almost a complete contrast: 'Mild, modest, and unobtrusive; averse from participating in general society, or public business, but sedulously devoted to his own particular pursuits'.[282] The son's record is not that of a mild man and it is much to be doubted if he was modest. Hardly unobtrusive, he built himself the largest mansion Stoke was ever to see, not forgetting to acquire a coat of arms at the same time,[100] and he participated in general society to such an extent that a Jubilee celebration he gave in 1809 was still recalled with awe eighteen years later.[131] No public business in Stoke, from rebuilding the church to commanding the Yeomanry, seems to have been without the benefit of his participation; and his particular business pursuits included—in addition to potting and retailing and wholesaling his own and other people's ware—coal mining, property development and transport.

Apart from seeming never to let pass an opportunity for a wise investment in house purchase, Spode I appears to have been little concerned with what happened outside his own factory's gates. He found £200, in 1792, for a mortgage for the Tittensor-Talk Turnpike Road which passed directly outside them,[103] but the major step of ensuring the factory a cheaper supply of coal was left for his son to take. In 1795, the Newcastle Canal was cut. It passed between his factory and that of Thomas Wolfe, his neighbour. Both were prepared to demolish certain buildings to make way for it, since the advantage of having a link with the Trent and Mersey Canal to Liverpool was obvious and substantial; but although the new canal company had no fewer than forty-two proprietors (shareholders), neither Spode I nor Wolfe feature among them.[122] Since few subjects touch a potter's heart as much as an increase in freight charges, it is no surprise to find him, in 1785, adding his name to a protest against a proposed one on the canals;[102] but it is almost a shock to find it, a month before his death, appended to a purely political declaration in support of the government, and there is a temptation to guess that its presence there is more an exhibition of family solidarity with his two sons, who were also signatories, than anything else.[135]

The drive and rapid success of the son in London would have reflected directly and beneficially on the factory in Stoke. As expressed much later, 'each essentially promoted the other'. Although the scale of Spode I's manufacturing was never to approach that of his son's, later, it does not appear to have been trivial, even before the beginning of the London business. A clue to its extent, at the very start of his ownership of the Stoke factory, can be found in his receipt book.[100]

This book provides a complete record, from January 1777 to Spode I's death in 1797, of his payment of poor levies, chief rent and taxes—obligations which he met promptly. Any satisfaction at finding him to have been a model citizen in this respect is more than outweighed by disappointment that he only used the book for business transactions during the first year, and even then spasmodically. The first ten entries are as follows:

1   Received, 10th January, 1777, 11s.4½d. for the poor levies for the Meadow and pot work, which is in full for the year 1776 for the third rate by me, George Henney.

2   Received, 20th January, 1777, of Josiah Spode £24.18s.6d. which is in full for carriage of Brundwood Coals to 23rd December, 1776 (included) by me, James Yates.

3   Received, 3rd February, 1777, of Josiah Spode £1.3s.6d. which is in full for cording by me for father, John Smith.

4   Received, 6th March, 1777, of Mr. Spode £22.3s.9d. for white lead on account by Thomas Smith.

5   Received, 20th March, 1777, of Josiah Spode 11s.4½d. for poor levies, for Madeley Meadow and the pot works for the fourth rate for the year 1776 by me, George Henney.

6   Received, 2nd April, 1777, of Josiah Spode £17.12s.0d. which is in full for carriage of coals to 28th March, received by me, John Sarjeant.

7   Received, 3rd April, 1777, of Josiah Spode £5.10s.0d. for carriage of forty-four crates to Winsford, marked J.S. Donovan No. 1 to 44 for Mr. James Donovan, Dublin which is in full for all account by me, Robert Yates (?) Junior.[21]

8   Received, 2nd July, 1777, of Josiah Spode £33.18s.0d. for carriage of Brundwood coals and being in full to 21st June included by me, James Yates.

By hay and cash	£13	12s.	0d.
By cash from [indecipherable] . . .	£20	6s.	0d.
	£33	18s.	0d.

At the same time paid Mr. Yates two guineas for carriage of fourteen Stacks which is in full for carriage of coals for the month of June included.

9   Received, 7th July, 1777, of Josiah Spode 11s.4½d. for poor levies for Madeley Meadow and pot works adjoining. Being for the first rate for this present year 1777 and 15s. 0d. for the Highways being in full for this year by me, George Henney.

10 Received, 29th September, 1777, of Josiah Spode a bill value £23.0s.0d. which is in full for carriage of coals and on all account by me, James Yates.

The eighth entry reveals that he paid for his carriage at the rate of 3s.0d. a stack. A stack appears to have weighed twenty-five hundredweight.[22] Brund-wood will refer to the type of coal, not the district of origin, and is likely to have been the type better known as Burn Wood.[231] The coals would probably have arrived at the Factory in the way described in an interesting passage quoted by Simeon Shaw, borne by pack horses 'along lanes extremely dirty and roads scarcely passable', each horse carrying about two and a half hundredweight, its services charged at the rate of 1d. a mile. If Spode 1's payments were based on this rate, the coal must have been coming from more than three miles away and, since the coal itself seems to have cost about 6s.0d. a stack, we have some idea of the exorbitant cost of carriage resulting from the lack of good communication.[23] Since coal was the potter's main raw material, when the Factory started to use it from Fenton Park—less than two miles away and brought by cart—it must have made a noticeable improvement in its economy.[24] It is not surprising that in the 1790 Fenton Park Colliery agreement the Stoke partners had a clause included that the Company would 'make one or more good and sufficient road or roads of the width of twenty-four feet for the accommodation of all persons residing in Stoke-on-Trent aforesaid resorting to the said collieries and mines'. In fact, a good road had been built before the agreement came into effect.

Spode 1 paid his carriage bills every quarter, and they total £101.10s.6d. for the year from September 1776 to September 1777. Although there can be no guarantee that some relevant transaction has not been omitted, or even that the carriage rate was constant, it is impossible to resist the temptation to do some simple arithmetic based on his carriage payments in an attempt to arrive at some estimate of the coal consumed and, thus, provide a clue to the size of his output at this period. Taking the carriage charge as a constant 3s.0d. a stack, he must have had 677 delivered. If each stack weighed 3000 lb,[22] this was equivalent to just over 906 present-day English tons. The quantity may seem paltry compared with the much higher consumption achieved by potteries in the next century— upward of 200 tons a week at the Spode Factory in 1819 (see Chapter V) and 180 tons a week at Minton's in 1837[177]—but it must be remembered that probably none of Spode 1's productions required more than two fires, a biscuit and a glost. An average monthly use of seventy-odd tons could produce a fair

quantity of ware of this kind: in 1833, the Spode Factory's costing book estimated that one ton of coal fired an average of seven hundred and twenty blue
printed dinner plates.[24] In 1806, when the Turner Factory was put up for sale,
it was described as one 'Where the making of Porcelain, and Earthenware, in
all its branches, has been carried on to a great extent, for a great number of
years', but a coal consumption of only forty tons a week was mentioned and this
may have been an exaggeration as the advertiser was intent on demonstrating the
large savings in cost which would be enjoyed because of the factory's proximity
to its source of supply.[204]

An indication that Spode I's management was not only successful but
progressive is provided by a statement by Aikin in 1795:

> At this place [Stoke-on-Trent] a gentleman of the name of Spode established a
> few years ago the first steam engine to grind burned flint for potters' use; which, it
> is said, answers the expectation.[155]

This is contradicted by Simeon Shaw who, in a very detailed account, gives the
credit to Spode I's next-door neighbour, Thomas Wolfe, and the date as shortly
after 1792.[234] This is confirmed by Ward.[285] Wolfe certainly had 'an engine'
in 1795 since his water supply for it was expressly safeguarded in the Act of
Parliament for the Newcastle Canal, which was not allowed water from the
spring he used for it.[122] The apparent contradiction may be resolved if we can
accept that Aikin meant a fire engine and not steam engine. There is evidence
that Spode I possessed one of these precursors to the steam engine, which he
used at an early date to raise water to work a wheel for grinding flint.[267] If
Aikin did confuse the two, then it was an error repeated in 1819 by John Hassell
who mentioned that the Factory had two steam engines, 'the oldest of which has
been erected nearly forty years'.[194] Spode II introduced a fully-fledged steam
engine from Boulton and Watt in 1802.[268]

Spode I's receipt book and a few other sources contain evidence that by 1780
he was moving a long way from his earlier impecunity. He seems to have sub-
scribed to the view that there is nothing as safe as houses and by this year had
acquired at least three above his own needs, which were producing £9.10s.0d. a
year in rent. At the end of 1783, a year of hunger and hardship for the Potteries,[281] he purchased from a certain James Turner another twelve, directly
opposite his own factory; and in 1786 he began paying taxes for substantial
additional property in Bucknall, near Stoke. In 1793, he further increased his
property holdings directly by the Factory by purchasing more land fronting
Stoke High Street, where six houses were subsequently built.

He provided a house in Newcastle-under-Lyme for his married daughter,
Sarah;[100] and the one he built for his second son, Samuel, at the Foley, Lane

III Earthenware: Blue Printed. This selection shows the main shades of blue encountered on Spode wares. The sixteen inch dish in 'Two Figures' and the comport, top left, in 'Forest-Landscape, First' are characteristic of the earliest wares. The coffee pots in 'Tall Door' and Blue Italian are representative of the later, finer blue, and the Castle plate is representative of the light blue sometimes used.

End, was notable for its 'excellence of construction and elegance of appearance'.[238] More important for Samuel was that his father provided him with a factory to go with it; both, according to Ward, on the occasion of his marriage.

The date of Samuel's marriage to his wife, Sarah Garner, remains for us to discover; but their first child died an infant on 10th December 1784, and on 2nd April 1785, Spode I paid 4s. 3d. window and house tax for his son at the same time that he paid his own. An almost complete mystery surrounds Samuel's potting activities. He has been given the title of 'the last of the salt glaze potters', but with what justification is not clear.[25] An entry of about 1813 in a recipe book of Spode II's enameller, Henry Daniel, gives an underglaze brown colour described as 'same as used at Mr Samuel Spode's'.[101] The only detailed documentation relating to him which survives concerns an unsavoury dispute he had with three of his workmen in 1791. It shows him in a bad light but reveals nothing about his products.[26]

On the 18th August 1797, Spode I died suddenly. His will, which was made on his deathbed, was hurriedly put together and sparse in its detail.[100] It was an unbusinesslike oversight, of a kind of which it would be hard to imagine his son, Josiah, being guilty: but then, when he died in his turn, although his virtues were more widely recorded, no one thought of using the two adjectives 'amiable and endearing' to describe them.[144]

Spode I's receipt book: entries of house rents paid

3 The crucial years, 1797–1806

The second generation of English industrialists must have been a formidable band. Spode II was perhaps representative. His father's success was adequate to provide him with an education and a good but not soft start to life. The fruits of that success were not so great that the son ran any danger of the kind against which Miss Meteyard so primly warned, 'The possession of large fortunes at that period of youth when energy, self-denial and industry should build up character, is, in too many instances, an evil rather than a good'.[218] Neither were Spode I's achievements of such a brilliant nature that they could overawe his son or rob him of that 'unquietness of spirit' which Josiah Wedgwood deliberately endeavoured to instil in his sons. Poverty and hard times were far enough in the past to leave him uninhibited by any first-hand taste of them, but not so remote that they could not engender a certain toughness and provide a distant motivation. To this extent, circumstances had allied themselves with what natural talents he possessed to ensure that he made his way in the world and, in 1797, at the age of forty-two, he could fairly call himself a very successful man. According to Shaw, 'In one year prior to the demise of his father, the clear profits of the London business alone exceeded £13,000'.[27] At this point in his career, his father's death required from him a major decision. His alternatives were clear: to return to Stoke or to remain in London; to become primarily a manufacturer or to remain primarily a merchant. He came back home.

The close connection he had always preserved with Stoke; his partnership in the Factory with his father; the fact that his second son, Josiah III, had been brought up by his grandparents and 'As soon as his youth permitted, initiated in the business of a Potter, under his grandfather'[141]—all these make his decision seem natural and inevitable. But even on his deathbed, Spode I had no clear idea of what his son's choice would be, stressing in his will that if Spode II did not take the Stoke Factory his brother Samuel should be given the chance of acquiring it. At this point in time, it is very doubtful if the Stoke Factory represented as substantial an asset as Spode II's London business and, whatever opportunities he may have seen for himself in manufacturing, he could never have devoted himself to it and moved back to Stoke without the assurance that his London business would not be neglected in his absence. Here he was fortunate. William, his eldest son, was twenty-one and William Copeland, his right-hand-man, was thirty-two: both were old enough and experienced enough to be left in control and ultimately, in 1805, have the London business completely relinquished to them. With affairs in London so satisfactorily arranged, Spode II found a suitable residence in Fenton Hall, not half a mile from the Factory, which now began to receive the greater part of his energy and attention.[28]

The cat was among the pigeons. The expression calls for an immediate apology, since it implies less respect for Spode II's contemporaries than is felt. The Potteries were filled with able manufacturers and London with successful merchants: it was the combination of the two talents and areas of experience which was rare, if not unique. We cannot really visualise the Staffordshire potters, as a whole, fitting Shaw's description of an earlier period, when they sat 'on the ale benches at home' discussing the origin of cream coloured ware as a matter of purely domestic interest while Josiah Wedgwood made arrangements in London to monopolise all the credit, causing them 'to cogitate on their own listlessness and indifference'.[248] But Stoke was still a long way from London, even in 1797, and the average Staffordshire potter must have been by training inadequately equipped for, and by circumstances largely prevented from, studying his markets at first hand.

Spode II was not the only merchant in charge of a pottery. Miles Mason had for many years conducted a business in London which could not have been dissimilar to Spode II's, and in 1800 he established himself as a manufacturer in Lane Delph, after an earlier brief potting venture in Liverpool with experienced partners.[180] His knowledge of potting, however, must have been of very recent acquisition—as was that of Thomas Byerley, who had been left in day-to-day control at Etruria since the death of Josiah Wedgwood in 1795.[219]

Not only did Spode II combine wide and up-to-date marketing expertise with sound early training and some later experience as a manufacturer and industrialist, but he also had complete control of the sale and distribution of his products in London, their main market. His flourishing London business had also provided him with large funds with which to finance any new venture or expansion on which he might wish to embark.

In the well-established earthenware products of his factory, for which it had an acknowledged reputation, Spode II must have recognised potential enough; but more exciting was that which lay in an entirely new product—china. One of the reasons advanced for the break-up of the Whieldon-Wedgwood partnership was that the older man 'was satisfied, and was unwilling to commence the manufacture of kinds of Pottery then in embryo'.[250] Like Wedgwood, Spode was a different breed:

> About 1800,[3] Mr. Spode commenced the manufacture of Porcelain, in quality superior to any previously made in England, and in imitation of that made at Sèvres, which it equalled, if it did not surpass, in transparency. For entering on

this manufacture with every reasonable prospect of success, Mr. S. was well capacitated, by the extensive knowledge he possessed relative to those subjects apparently best adapted for public demand, and which seem calculated to ensure quick and profitable returns. At this period, the London Dealers were supplied from Worcester, Derby and Caughley, with the best British Porcelain; having rich embellishments upon most beautiful patterns of the various Articles. He therefore now incited the ingenuity of his modellers and other plastic artisans, to produce varied shapes of the Articles already in use; and to design other new Articles for the approbation of persons of taste. The bone body Porcelain which is very transparent, he brought to considerable perfection.[255]

In this passage, it is regrettable that Simeon Shaw has more to say about the non-technical than the technical ramifications of Spode II's venture. It could be guessed that he would know exactly what shapes, articles and patterns were required by the market since, according to Ward, before his return to Stoke, his London premises contained 'an unrivalled stock of earthenware, china and glass' which 'attracted the notice of all the higher classes of Society of the metropolis'.[283] The china he had been purchasing from 'other houses'. These could have been any or all of the three mentioned by Shaw—Worcester, Derby and Caughley—but there is no reason why this part of his merchandise should not have been imported. Thomas Flight, the Worcester manufacturer, bought large quantities of French porcelain for resale in his London rooms in Coventry Street,[169] and no doubt many others did the same when it became available cheaply after a commercial treaty with France, in 1787, which reduced the rate of duty from 80 per cent to 10 per cent. Miles Mason, who was tempted to manufacture china in Staffordshire at about the same time as Spode II, had previously been, in London, 'a principal purchaser of Indian [oriental] Porcelain, till the prohibition of that article by heavy duties'.[180]

That Spode II should know what forms and decorations should be given to his china once he had obtained it is not surprising, but we are left wondering how, almost suddenly, he started to produce a 'Porcelain, in quality superior to any previously made in England'. The only clue given is the mention of the 'bone body'. There is a strong tradition that the very origin of bone china is to be found in the body that Spode II introduced as the last century began. Such traditions do not depend entirely on the written word—but to the extent that this one does, it depends on the word as written by Simeon Shaw in the first and last sentences of the passage quoted.[29] Elsewhere, he credits William Littler with being the first potter to make use of 'calcined bone earth', and yet he flatly states 'I am not aware of the person by whom was made the first bone china'.[229]

What are we to make of these apparently contradictory statements by Shaw? The confusion may be in our minds rather than his. To use bone in potting,[30] even porcelain making, is one thing; to make bone china is another.

The use of bone in porcelain probably first took place at Bow, possibly as early as 1749. It seems subsequently to have been widely understood and valued. Chelsea, Lowestoft, and Chaffers and Pennington in Liverpool all used it to a greater or lesser extent, the proportion of the total ingredients being in some cases as high as 48 per cent.[288] Derby were certainly using bone in their body at the end of the eighteenth century: in 1791 they were having difficulty in obtaining the right quality and quantity.[170] Even across the Atlantic, Bonnin and Morris, the proprietors of the short-lived porcelain factory at Southwark, Philadelphia, advertised in 1770 for bones of every kind and in any quantity.[200] In all these porcelains, however, bone was being combined with ingredients like soap stone, lime and sand, producing a variety of wares all known by the generic name of soft pastes. None of these would have been recognised in Simeon Shaw's day, or our own, as 'bone china'.[31]

There is no such thing as *the* formula for bone china. Variations are endless and have always been so, but the idea pervading them all is that to the two classic ingredients of hard paste porcelain—fine, white burning clay and part-decomposed granite stone, combined in proportions which can be quite varied— should be added their own weight, or somewhat less, of calcined bone. Early formulae often included quite large quantities of flint and ordinary ball clay, of the kind employed in earthenware. The clay and stone required for their porcelain were known to the Chinese as kaolin and petunse. The English source for both is Cornwall, although the latter is found in a much impurer form than in China. They are known respectively as Cornish Clay (or China or Growan Clay) and Cornish Stone (or China, Moor or Growan Stone). They first started to be employed in Staffordshire shortly after 1775. In that year, a parliamentary fight—led by Josiah Wedgwood and John Turner, and headed by Lord Gower —to prevent Richard Champion retaining under Cookworthy's patent a complete monopoly of their use, ended in success for the Staffordshire potters.

The involved and interesting story behind this success is well documented by Jewitt.[206] Victory came at the eleventh hour in the form of two new clauses to the bill then before the House of Lords. The first obliged Champion to enrol his current specification of body and glaze, and the second made it clear that the patent did not extend to the use of the two materials 'except such Mixture of Raw Materials, and in Such Proportions as are described in the Specification'.[121] In this specification for his porcelain body, Champion claimed to use only china clay and stone in the ratios of sixteen of clay to one of stone and one of clay to four of stone 'and every proportion intermediate'.[123] This is as scientific an attempt at formulation as sticking two pins in a list of numbers. It was, of course, designed to embrace any possible combination of the two substances which could result in porcelain, and still leave a wide margin of safety.

From Simeon Shaw's day on, it has been stated that for the next twenty years the renewed patent effectively prevented anyone from using the materials for manufacturing a translucent body, thus preventing any activity of this kind in Staffordshire.[251] But the wording of the patent reveals a possible loophole for any one using them for this purpose in combination with an entirely different material. It could have been this difference rather than any question of trans-lucency—nowhere mentioned in either the Specification or the Parliamentary Act—which legitimised the new, improved earthenware formulae, incorporating china clay and stone, which began to be used and which aided a further expansion in trade for the Potteries' staple product. It may have been this continued and increasing success with their long-established product, rather than any Staffordshire convervatism or un-Staffordshire respect for the spirit or letter of the law of patents, which made the potters shy of china. Like sensible men, they may have been content to make earthenware and profits while poor Champion just made porcelain.

A survey of the history of china making in the Potteries up to this year, 1775, would not have encouraged any potter tempted to try his hand at the esoteric art. The enterprising William Littler had failed to make a living at it at Longton Hall or elsewhere; and although John Baddeley's bankruptcy in 1761 cannot be attributed to his manufacturing porcelain, it is noticeable that in his subsequent successful partnership with Fletcher he contented himself with the traditional Staffordshire products. There had been others in the district, but the fact that virtually nothing is known of them is in itself a pointer to their end.

These early Staffordshire experimental ventures had all been with artificial soft paste porcelains of a type made elsewhere in the United Kingdom. When Champion came into the Potteries looking for partners, he could offer the true hard paste formula and a thirteen-year corpus of knowledge concerning its manufacture acquired at Bristol and, before that, at Plymouth. The company he formed in 1781, Hollins Warburton and Company, later New Hall, meant that china making was at least re-established in the area by the time Spode II returned from London; and there is evidence, particularly in the early translucent products of Neale of Hanley, that it was an activity being pursued elsewhere in the district.

In retrospect, it seems inevitable that it should have occurred to someone in Staffordshire at the end of the eighteenth century to combine Champion's materials with calcined bone. China clay and stone were by then thoroughly familiar to every potter in the area and the use of calcined bone there was nothing new. As early as 1759, John Baddeley of Shelton had purchased a large quantity of bone which, remarkably, was delivered to his factory already calcined.[32] The identity of the potter who took the first tentative step in a direction which now seems so obvious will probably always remain a mystery; but whoever he was, he must spare some credit for Spode II, whose energy and resources ensured the initial success and longevity of what Solon called 'this evergreen Bone China'.[266]

If Spode II's name is the first to come to mind in conjunction with bone china, it is not just because he made it nor even because he made it supremely well but because he firmly established it in the market. If he 'perfected' it,[29] then the manufacturing and marketing implications of that perfection are each of them at least equal in importance to the chemical one. Obtaining the correct body was almost the minor part of such an undertaking. Starting from nowhere on an earthenware factory, implementing its production and obtaining the necessary new shapes, new styles and methods of decoration, all sufficiently good to compete successfully with the long-established chinas from abroad and other parts of England—these were, if anything, even more formidable tasks.

There is a temptingly tidy misconception that progress in potting is a matter of formulae and the possession of precious scraps of paper. The sad words of Bernard Palissy, master potter extraordinary, written nearly four hundred years ago, serve as a warning:

> Had I employed a thousand reams of paper in writing for you all the accidents that have occurred to me upon my search, you may assure yourself that, however clever you might be, there would occur to you a thousand other crosses which could not be taught by letters and which, even if you had them written, you would not believe until you should have been thrust by experience among a thousand troubles.[228]

The prerequisite for bone china was not the discovery by some chemical genius of an exact combination of substances which would give the desired result. Wide differences in the various proportions were acceptable and, given the underlying idea of bone china, success depended not so much on nicely calculated less or more as on the methods of making and firing and the development of an appropriate glaze. Paramount among these was the method of firing, and it is here that bone china appeared in its most practical and obliging light. For half a century, Staffordshire potters had been expert at a two-fire process in which they fired their biscuit ware higher than their glost. This was the very reverse of hard paste porcelain manufacture—although not of the various eighteenth-century English soft pastes. The fact that bone china could be fitted in with this traditional earthenware firing sequence meant that its production could be accommodated on an established earthenware pot bank with nothing like the turmoil and adaption which might have been expected.

Equal in importance to any precise formula finally selected was the quality and treatment of the ingredients. Even in the present age of quality controls, laboratory testing and well-behaved suppliers, potters can experience nightmare moments due to variation in their raw materials. How much worse in times when they could have been warned about virtually all of their purchases in the way they were about bones:

> The best that can be used are the leg bones of oxen and cows but on no account horses bones as they are open and spongey whereas the former are solid. . . Let great care be taken in picking them over before grinding so as to get rid of all iron and other impurities in which they frequently abound, from a large proportion being collected by bone collectors who sell them by weight and to make them heavy frequently thrust spikes of iron up the hollow parts . . .[33]

Whatever difficulties stood in the way in the very early years of the century, Spode II achieved his objective. This was not to establish a reputation as a ceramicist or deliberately lay the foundation of what later became a new industry.[34] It was, quite simply, to produce a china as near as possible in appearance to Sèvres soft paste, loveliest of all western porcelains and then, as now, a standard of perfection. The nearer he approached this goal the more assured he could be of his market. At the same time, his factory, like that of every English potter, was not the plaything of an indulgent monarch or an eccentric aristocrat. If the new product was to be sold at the right price and in the right quantity, it had to show an economically low level of loss in manufacture and be made from materials which were readily available and, if possible, familiar. From such practical and commercial considerations came a new kind of china which, however emulative in its conception, from its birth commanded judgment in its own right. It received its first accolade at the Spode Factory in 1806.

In September of that year, the Prince of Wales, later to become George IV, and the Duke of Clarence, later William IV, finally arrived at Trentham, just south of the Potteries, after an extremely leisurely peregrination from London. They were the guests of the Duke of Sutherland, but found time to do more than attend the coming-of-age party of one of his sons. On the twelfth of the month, they appeared in Stoke.

> On Friday morning their Royal Highnesses, accompanied by the Marquis of Stafford, Lord Harrowby, Lord Crewe, Lord Gower, Lord Petersham, Lord Granville Leveson Gower, the Lord Chief Baron, Mr. Vernon, Mr. MacDonald, The Rev. Archdeacon Woodhouse, Col. Leigh, Mr. Wilbraham, Major Bloomfield, Mr. Heathcote etc. etc. proceeded to Stoke-upon-Trent, when they were received under arms by the Stoke, Penkhull and Fenton Volunteers, commanded by Lieut. Col. Whalley, and immediately visited the extensive manufactory of Mr. Spode. After going through the principal warehouse (a room 117 feet long) which was fitted up with much taste and judgment, and exhibited such a splendid

assemblage of finished goods as did great credit to the manufacturer, and drew down the high encomiums of the whole party; they proceeded through the working part of the manufactory, where their Royal Highnesses examined the different branches with the most marked attention and expressed themselves to be much gratified with the process and various modes adopted. Their Royal Highnesses signified that the whole was new to them and nothing could exceed their affability and condescension to all ranks of persons. As a mark of his approbation the Prince of Wales was graciously pleased to allow Mr. Spode the distinguishing privilege of considering himself 'Potter and English Porcelain manufacturer to His Royal Highness'. We cannot but remark that in France the porcelain manufactory always possessed the high sanction and patronage of the Princes of the Blood, and we doubt not but that, under the auspices of our Princes and Nobility, English China will rival the most finished productions of foreign countries, and give to our own manufacturers the whole of this important and valuable trade.[35]

In his account, Shaw stressed that 'the appearance and demeanour of the working classes drew forth repeated eulogiums' from the royal pair. Well prepared and doubtless with more than an inkling of what was at stake, they rose to the occasion, resplendent in their best bibs and tuckers—'Mr Spode had so arranged that all the persons employed, of both sexes, were in their best attire, to manifest their respectful and loyal attachment to the Heir Apparent'.[257] Having conferred the hoped-for honour on Spode II and his 'English Porcelain', the Prince proceeded to Etruria and his new potter's most formidable rival, Wedgwood.

It must be recognised that Spode II's rapid success in these early years, and later, was in great measure due to the leading firm in the Potteries no longer being as formidable a rival as it could have been. It is hard to imagine that he would have been allowed to reach such a dominant position quite so quickly if the great Josiah Wedgwood himself had been alive and in control of his old empire. But the mantle of the lion had fallen on a mouse: in place of Josiah Wedgwood was his nephew, the hard-working but inadequate Thomas Byerley.

In August 1802, having got wind of unrest among his workers, which may have been encouraged by his own inept handling of a dispute with one of them over a book of recipes, Byerley wrote to Josiah Wedgwood Junior:

I think it not improbable that something is brewing, to use John Beardmore's expression. I know that Spode has endeavoured to get some of our men, and he may think such a party as this [Hackwood, the modeller] may be of considerable importance to him. He is very anxiously endeavouring, I believe, to get into the same tracks that we are in, and to improve his articles by our models, and I do not think he will be very scrupulous in the means.[223]

He added, rather pathetically, 'Do you think I should ask Hackwood about this?' It is impossible not to feel sorry for Byerley, so anxious to do the right thing, writing to his partner for advice on matters which an experienced potter would have taken in his stride. Miss Meteyard's diagnosis was that 'his natural place was the counting house not the studio or workshop', and her retrospective remedy 'securing an active working partner like Spode, Turner or Adams'.[219] For the management of a complex and world-famous pottery, Byerley seems not to have been qualified by artistic judgment, mercantile ability or practical potting experience. One feels for him among the shrewd Staffordshire craftsmen he employed—a breed quick to exploit weakness if they find it where they can legitimately look for strength.

John Wedgwood might comment on the serious state of the clay making process—'Mr Byerley not knowing anything at all of the manipulations, he is of no use but to fall into passions and get laughed at'[224]—but his two brothers and he himself, to a large extent, continued to find preoccupations away from their factory. These three able men were no wastrels, but their inherited fortunes enabled them to choose their interests. If he ever had time to learn of them, Spode II must have been delighted to hear of Thomas Wedgwood's interesting experiments towards photography in London and Josiah Wedgwood Junior's successful cultivation in Dorset of the Swedish turnip.[220]

It was not until 1807 that Josiah Wedgwood Junior moved back to Staffordshire and an active part in his factory's affairs, and by that time Byerley was complaining not of others endeavouring 'to get into the same tracks as we are in' but of how Wedgwood designs were 'halting after others'.[225] The old giant of Etruria must have turned in his grave. There is no evidence that Spode II's quality was lower than theirs at this period—but his prices were, and of this they were constantly reminded:

> Mr. Spode has also imitated the blue flowers . . . I could not learn the price exactly but was given to understand they were much cheaper than ours. (In 1810)[109]

> Mr. Spode's prices of blue printed are so low that Mr. Bateman can get no orders for blue ware. (In 1811)[110]

> The price [of incense vases] is objected to—we are told Mr. Spode sells them at 11/–d. each which we charge at 15/–d. and 18/–d. (In 1811)[111]

> I believe Mr. Spode undersells us in Incense Vases, and he copies all our shapes. (In 1812)[112]

Josiah Wedgwood had never been afraid of being undersold, and copying was as endemic to the trade as absenteeism after pay day; but his high prices had gone hand in hand with impeccable quality and, just as important, a leading place in every new development in technique and taste. Not until 1805 did his successors enter the enormous and profitable market for underglaze blue printed wares.[147] In 1810, Miles Mason condescendingly offered to make bone china for them, but after another two years their own finally drifted on to the market— and a few years later drifted off again.[36] In 1814, their chief traveller informed his head office 'that the newly introduced Stone China of Spode and Mason was much in demand'. He had the effrontery to add 'I presume you know what it is'.[113] Their own reached the market six years later.[146]

In contrast, Spode II seems never to have let pass a marketing opportunity, and his successes in this direction naturally required an equal attention to the industrial aspects of his business. The major addition of china to the Spode Factory's established range of products and a general increase in the scale of its production must have resulted in substantial alterations and additions to the building and plant inherited from Spode I. 'He very considerably enlarged the size of his Works',[283] and the adjacent meadow provided an obvious and ample site for this extension. The only land Spode II ever purchased adjacent to the Factory were two small sites, acquired in 1797 and 1800, at the far west corner. These were used for houses, not industrial purposes.[100]

In November 1802, Spode II purchased a steam engine from Boulton and Watt.[268] Although steam engines were not uncommon in the district by then and were widely used in the Staffordshire collieries, he may have been one of the first potters to use one to provide power for his throwers' wheels and turners' lathes. The conventional use was for grinding raw materials, and it was whilst Spode II's new engine was so engaged that there occurred what may be the earliest recorded accident due to machinery in the pottery industry. The victim was not a poor uncompensated workman but his own son, Spode III.

> A lamentable accident occurred to him in 1803. His father had just completed the erection of a steam-engine and mill-work, for the grinding of materials required in the manufacture of pottery and porcelain. Mr. Spode was inspecting the operations, when a crown wheel struck his hat; and, in lifting his arm to protect himself, the hand passed between the cogs of the wheels, and immediate amputation became indispensable.[141]

The Factory's main supply of coal seems to have remained the Fenton Park Colliery, in which Spode II's interest never lessened. In 1813, when the coal company's main lease was renewed for thirty years, only he and Thomas Wolfe remained of the original fourteen partners. Thomas Minton and his partner, William Pownall of Liverpool, were among the eight new ones who had appeared in the previous twenty-three years.[100] In 1827, at his death, instead of

his original one-fourteenth, Spode II owned three-sevenths of the company—
a share valued at £6,000. The extent of his holding points to an interest in coal
not confined to the needs of his own factory, and a draft lease of 1802 survives[100]
which indicates very strongly that he had become a coal master in his own right.
The lease, which was for twenty-one years, was between him, acting entirely
on his own behalf, and the absentee landlords of the land at Lane Delph, where
the mines were situated. Among these was Thomas Fenton Grosvernor of Leek,
not to be confused with the Thomas Fenton who later married Spode II's sister.
It was agreed that a minimum of ten thousand tons a year should be raised. Like
all the mines in the district, clay and marl abounded, being excavated with the
coal. These were ideal for saggar making and brick manufacture and Spode II
reserved the right to make and fire bricks at the colliery, as well as the right to
grind 'Colours, Flints, Glazes or other material' with any fire or steam engine
he erected there.

In the then all important matter of canal transport, the Factory's needs had
been satisfied in an ideal way in 1795. Not only did the Newcastle Canal pass
right along one of its boundaries and provide a direct link by water to Liverpool,
but its use up to where it joined the main Trent and Mersey Canal was free. This
was a concession made by the proprietors in consideration of Spode I having
sacrificed 'Two certain Pieces of Building, part of the Pot Works' to allow the
construction of the new waterway.[122]

The canal alone separated Spode II's factory from that of his good neighbour,
Thomas Wolfe. From 1790 on the two men collaborated in obtaining supplies of
coal from Fenton Park and nine years later they joined forces to ensure their
supplies of Cornish Clay and Stone. In 1799 they succeeded in obtaining the
lease of clay setts on Carloggas Moor in Cornwall, in the face of lively competition from, among others, Wedgwood, Derby, Coalbrookdale, and New Hall.
The last were the sitting tenants and seem to have accepted their defeat with bad
grace, since their refusal to co-operate with their successors during the transition
period prompted a veiled complaint to the landlord, Lord Camelford.

The Carloggas lease envisaged that the setts would yield annual quantities
of approximately three hundred tons of clay and twelve hundred of stone. Such
an output resulted in a rent of about £900 a year, based on a figure of over £2 a
ton for the clay and about 2/– a ton for the stone. This appears to have been
achieved regularly during the time that the partnership continued—nearly
twenty years—but would, hardly, alone, have been sufficient for the needs of
the owners. By 1816 the two potters were together in another enterprise, holding
a third share each in the Cornwall Clay and Stone Company. The remaining
third was divided between three Cornish merchants.

Spode II and Thomas Wolfe must have found each other congenial part-

ners.[37] Short choruses were more to be expected than long duets when Staffordshire potters combined. But that Spode II had no objection in principle to joining
a larger combination is shown by a letter he wrote in 1804 to Thomas Byerley:

Buxton, 22nd May, 1804

I was so unfortunate as not to get your letter till this day—having left home on
Saturday morning very unwell. I left orders with my son to open my letters and
any that were particular to send to me here, he had the caution to send your letter
down to Mr. Minton, who returned it and for answer he would see about it in the
morning, my son being poorly. Miss Spode enclosed your letter with others to
me here, and from your wishing an answer by Monday's post, anything I could
write into the country would be too late.

When your son called upon me to say there had been no meeting at Hanley—I
had previously told him whatever Mr. Wedgwood and the majority of the meeting
agreed to I would join, but the fewer the more agreeable to me. I again told him
I would make one in the proposal you mention in your letter, had I been in health
I certainly should have took an active part in your absence. I have seen several
potters and spoke to them on the business but did not find any one anxious but
Mr. E. Mayer—I rather think Pike has been busy amongst them with samples of
his clay (which certainly burns very white) and has poisoned the minds of several
against the partnership. I really don't know at present four in the pottery likely
to join, they all seem blind to their own interest, and if you endeavour to explain,
they think you are doing it to serve your own purposes, however should any steps
be taken to secure it, I will gladly make one of six, nine or twelve.

Should this not be the case, could any plan be proposed to secure from Messrs.
Pitt & Calcraft a certainty of a given quantity of good clay yearly for ourselves, I
would take 300 tons a year—and to let the other potters who seem so indifferent,
to treat for themselves. As I am likely to stay here a few days, I should be happy
to receive a few lines from you at this place.

I am, Dear Sir, very truly,
Your Obedient Servant,
JOSIAH SPODE[119]

The success of Spode II's ambitious approach to manufacturing is indicated
by his purchase in 1802 of the freehold of the Portugal Street premises in
London, which twenty-five years afterwards were valued at £8,000. In 1804, in
his grant of Arms, he was still described as a merchant; but the following year
he made a decision which indicates that the factory which had been his main
preoccupation for seven years was now a markedly improved asset. In 1805,
although he retained the ownership of the premises, he completely relinquished
the London business to his eldest son William and William Copeland, who
became co-partners (see Appendix II). By then, Spode II had become a very

wealthy man—able, in November of that year, to provide a marriage settlement of £8,000 for Elizabeth, the first of his three daughters to marry.[100]

Elizabeth married an ex-major of the 21st Light Dragoons. The match may have been pleasing to her father, who was himself a former sparetime cavalryman with the rank of captain, commanding the Pottery Troop of Volunteers. These volunteer groups had been formed all over England early in 1798 when a French invasion seemed imminent, and nowhere did the patriotic fervour which this threat produced become more evident than in the Potteries. Spode II's corps was one of several in the district, but since each of its seventy-odd men was mounted and equipped at his own expense it must have been one reserved for the well-to-do.[276]

Fenton Hall, the residence he was renting, seemed hardly to reflect Spode II's ever-growing importance in the district and in September 1803 he took the first step in building the Mount—a splendid mansion which was to bear 'acknowledged pre-eminence' in the borough. The seventeen-acre site selected was acquired from the assignees in bankruptcy of John Harrison, the potter, and was located at Penkhull, only half a mile from the Spode Factory. Spode II had already shown an interest in this pleasant little village, the oldest and without doubt the most salubrious part of Stoke. In 1800 he leased a farm there, and by 1803 had purchased at least three separate parcels of land on which he built a total of forty-eight houses, twenty of them in a square at the very heart of the village.[100] They were built to a low standard and were obviously designed for his poorest work people.[151] Even after his own house was complete, he continued to buy land for housing development in the area, no doubt because it was situated so conveniently near to the Factory.

The site of his future home was occupied already by a building known as Tittensor's House, which had to be demolished. The work must have gone fast since the new building appears to have been ready for occupation in the following year.[28] John Ward described the Mount as 'An oblong building of stone, with a semicircular entrance on the west-front; an elegant and lofty dome, which lights the stair-case, gives an exterior air of grandeur to the structure'.[286]

Shaw stressed its ideal situation, 'enjoying a prospect almost unbounded, over the vicinity and the adjacent counties', and the 'extensive gardens and pleasure grounds' which surrounded it.[235] These were not limited to the original seventeen acres, for by 1827 the site had been surrounded by a fifty-acre ring fence acquired at various times.[100]

Stoke's most prominent citizen had acquired a worthy setting. Ward called it 'a local and lasting trophy of his success in the pursuit of trade'—and lasting it has proved. The houses he built for his workers in the nearby village lasted nearly as long.[38]

This Indenture, made the 11th Day of November in the Year of our Lord, One Thousand, *Seven hundred & Ninety Nine. Between Will.m Shaw Son of John Shaw of Buerton* in the Parish of *Audlam* ———————— and County of ~~Stafford~~ *Chester* of the first Part, the said *John Shaw* of the second Part, and *Josiah Spode* of *Stoke* ———— aforesaid, Potter of the third Part Witnesseth that the said *Will.m Shaw* of his own free Will, and by and with the Consent of *John Shaw — his father* hath put, placed and bound, and by these Presents DOTH put, place and bind himself Apprentice unto the said *Josiah Spode* ———— to learn that Branch of the Potter's Art or Business, called *Handling & pressing* of Earthen Ware, *in China* and *he* to serve after the manner of an Apprentice from the day of the date of these presents, for and during and unto the full end and term of *Six Years* ——— from thence next ensuing and fully to be complete and ended, during all which said time the said Apprentice shall and will faithfully, diligently and honestly serve his said Master as a good honest and faithful Apprentice ought to do; And the said *Josiah Spode* doth hereby covenant for *himself* or *his* Executors and Administrators, to and with the said *William Shaw* Executors and Administrators, that *he* the said *Josiah Spode* shall and will teach and instruct the said *Will.m Shaw* ———— or cause him to be taught and instructed in that Branch of the Potter's Art or Business, called *Handling and Pressing* ——— in the best manner *he* can, during the said term; And also shall and will pay or cause to be paid unto the said *Will.m Shaw* weekly and every week during the said term the following wages, namely for every weeks work within the first year of the said term the sum of *two Shillings & 3 pence* for every weeks work within the second year *two Shillings & Six pence* for every weeks work within the third year *two Shillings and Nine pence* for every weeks work within the fourth year *three Shillings* ———— for every weeks work within the fifth year *three Shillings and three pence* for every weeks work within the sixth year *three Shillings & Nine pence* ~~for every weeks work within the seventh year~~ and after the same rate in each year for less than a weeks work, which shall be deducted according to the days he shall be absent; And lastly the said *John Shaw* ———— doth hereby covenant for himself, his Executors and Administrators, that the said *John Shaw* ———— his Executors or Administrators shall and will find and provide the said *Will.m Shaw* with sufficient meat, drink, washing, lodging and cloaths at all times during the said term.

IN WITNESS whereof the said parties have hereunto set their Hands and Seals the
(23 Day ~~and Year first above~~ of *Feb.ry in the year* 1801 ————

SEALED and delivered (being first duly   *W.m Shaw*
Stamped) in the presence of

William Smith

Josiah Spode Jun.r   *John Shaw*

                                              Josiah Spode

SMITH—PRINTER—NEWCASTLE-UNDER-LYME.

William Shaw's Indenture. See Note 3. Spode III signed as a witness.

4 Henry Daniel and the decorators

That Spode II was a master merchant, rather than a master potter, when he returned to Stoke was perhaps his greatest single advantage. His prime concern for the previous twenty years had been to establish himself first as a merchant of pottery and subsequently of pottery, china and glass. It was this background which, in Shaw's view, gave his entry to china manufacture every reasonable prospect of success. His experience had taught him a great deal about the business of manufacturing but he was shrewd enough to be aware of his limitations and did not hesitate to bring into his firm specialists with technical knowledge and ability that he could not, himself, command. Such a man was Henry Daniel.

Henry Daniel was Spode II's enameller. The fact is well known but has been little regarded. A number of papers relating to the Daniel family, discovered in 1965,[101] enable a clearer idea to be formed of this man's contribution to the Spode Factory during the period for which he was responsible for the enamelling.

The term 'enameller' is rarely heard now in the pottery industry. When it is used, it refers to a paintress. The earlier meaning of the word was far different, and in the case of Henry Daniel it described a function which is shared today between an art director, a decorating manager, a colour manufacturer and a works chemist. We may form some idea of Daniel's responsibility if, as an exercise in imagination, we can visualise Spode's wares stripped to the white: deprived of their rich ground colours; all painting absent, and untouched by the gilder's brush. Through nearly two decades, the recruitment, training and superintendence of the layers of grounds and the painters—of flowers, landscapes, birds, figures and arms—was Daniel's sole charge, and the invention and manufacture of the very materials they used was his labour. In this specialist area, Spode II needed a partner; but that this was not a partnership in any legal sense is made clear by a document, reproduced on pages 40 and 41, which shows the nature of the arrangement between the two men when, in August 1822, they severed their connection.

Clearly, Daniel was operating a factory within a factory: an odd arrangement to modern eyes. The end of it is established beyond all doubt, since the footnote makes it clear that Daniel was not being supplanted by another enameller: Mr Spode would be hiring his men for the future. It would be good to know how many of Daniel's staff remained with Spode II and how many left with him. A study of entries c. 1822 in the surviving Spode pattern books reveals no change

IV China: Dish and twig-handled comport with Flower embossment in Pattern 1926. The scene on the dish is described as 'Builders Abbey, Shropshire' (an error for Buildwas Abbey) and that on the comport as 'Bassingwerk Abbey, Flintshire'. Mark 10 on both pieces, with pattern number.

in either the hand which made them or the kind or style of patterns being entered.

The beginning of the association between Spode and Daniel has not been ascertained as precisely as its finish, but it was certainly in being in 1805. In 1846, John Hancock wrote to the *Staffordshire Mercury* to establish his claim to the invention of lustre and stated that he first put it into practice 'at Mr Spode's manufactory for Messrs Daniel and Brown'.[143] His hiring agreement to Daniel and his partner has survived and is illustrated on page 42. It shows that he engaged himself to them as 'an enameller and layer of grounds of various sorts on china and earthenware' for two years commencing 12th August 1805, at a weekly wage of 30s.0d. for each year; he agreed to serve at 'their manufactory at Hanley or Stoke Upon Trent'.[101] The Daniel and Brown partnership was dissolved the following year:

> Notice is hereby given that the partnership between the undersigned Henry Daniel and John Brown as Potters, Enamellers and Gilders, at Hanley and Stoke Upon Trent, in the Staffordshire Potteries, was on the 4th day of June instant, dissolved by mutual consent. The manufactory at Hanley will be carried on in future by the said John Brown on his own separate account to whom all persons indebted to that concern are to pay their debts and by whom all just demands thereon will be discharged. The manufactory at Stoke Upon Trent, will be carried on in future by the said Henry Daniel, on his own separate account. Dated this 7th day of June, 1806.[39]

It seems from Hancock's description that the establishment in Stoke was the one within the Spode Factory. This appears to have been a specialist branch of activity, catering exclusively for Spode 11's requirements and under the direct management of Henry Daniel, whose earliest surviving book of colour recipes contains several entries, *c.* 1805, in which Spode is mentioned by name. John Brown presumably managed the establishment in Hanley, in which Henry's father, Thomas, may also have been concerned, and this would have catered for a number of other manufacturers in the way of a general trade. It is noticeable that in trade directories of 1802 and 1805, Hanley is the only address given for the firm. It is also the only address which appears for them in the account books of Chamberlain of Worcester, one of their customers. The kind of goods they supplied to Chamberlain—earthenware (which Chamberlain did not make) and blue printed wares[40]—suggests that the Hanley branch's activity was more broadly based than the Stoke/Spode one since there is no evidence that Henry Daniel was ever responsible for the printing of the long established Spode underglaze blue ware.

At what point in time before 1805 Daniel established himself at Stoke may never be discovered, but it was probably not much before that date—if at all.

Dr   Mr. Henry Daniel in a/c. with Jos...

			£	s	d
1822					
March 25	To 1 years rent of Land near Commercial Buildings		9		
June 24	To 3½ years rent of Goldpan at 15£ ⅌ year		52	10	—
	To ½ years rent of a House, Chandler's shop &c in Mr Thos Daniel's		27	12	6
July 7	To ½ years rent of House in Mr. Henry Daniel's possession		12	10	
August 10	To Two Weeks rent of Enamelling Work shops		8	—	—
	To Grinding 13℔. of Color		—	13	
	To discount on Goods Enamelled		31	6	3
	To Commission for Cash on said Goods		—	8	—
	To Cash lent on 13 April 1816 and Interest due thereon		223	6	3½
			£365	6	0½
	To Balance Brought down		151	10	3½
	To Balance due to Mr. Henry Daniel		848	9	8½
			1000	0	0

Examin...

...ode Esqr   Cr

2   £ s d
4 3   By Goods Enamelled as p Bill 208 15 9
      By a lot of Goods Damaged ....   5 — —
      By balance due to Josiah Spode .... below 151 10 3½

                                                          £365 6 0½

      By the whole stock of Enamelld burnished and other goods —
      Enamelling Kilns, Tools, Benches, Utensils, Fixtures, Bricks of all —
      kinds, Materials, Goods, and other Effects now belonging to
      Henry Daniel and remaining upon the premises at the Work-
      shops, and Manufactory of Mr Spode including the benefit —
      of the future Services of the Servants & Apprentices in Mr.
      Henry Daniel's Employment which are now given up to   } 1000. 0. 0
      Mr Spode's own use & also including an account claimed
      by Mr Henry Daniel for some Colours furnished by him
      to Mr Spode and in respect of all which Articles before
      mentioned Mr Henry Daniel has agreed to accept one
      thousand pounds as a full compensation for the same

                                                          1000 0 0

      Final Balance coming to Mr Henry Daniel 848 9 8½

Morres 1822 August Seventeenth

                    Henry Daniel
                        Willm Outrim for
                            J Spode ____ 0

NB. If any of the men employed by Mr Henry Daniel
    do not hire themselves to Mr Spode Mr Henry Daniel
    will be at Liberty to engage them for his own service —

                        Henry Daniel
                        Willm Outrim for
                            Josh Spode _____

MEMORANDUM of an AGREEMENT made and entered into by and between the undersigned *John Hancock Senr.* of the one Part, and the undersigned DANIEL and BROWN, of the other Part, as follows:— The said *John Hancock Senr.* in Consideration of the Wages to be paid him as hereinafter mentioned, hereby engages himself to the said DANIEL and BROWN, as a *Enammiller & Layer of Grounds of Various Sorts*

in China and Earthenware, for the Term of *Two Years* commencing from *August 12th* *1805* —during all which Term the said *John Hancock Senior* undertakes and agrees, faithfully and diligently to serve the said DANIEL and BROWN, in the said Branch or Capacity, at their Manufactory at *Hanley* or *Stoke-upon-Trent*, to attend and work there the regular and usual working Hours,

to do and perform his Work in a good, perfect, skilful, and workmanlike Manner, to the best of his Skill and Ability, and not in any wise to communicate, divulge, or make known to any Person or Persons, the Patterns, Shapes, Arts, or Methods of Manufacturing, practised and used at the said DANIEL and BROWN's Manufactory,—but in all things to promote the Advantage of his said Masters to the utmost of his Power, and to serve them during all the said Term as a good and faithful Servant ought to do:—And the said DANIEL and BROWN hereby agree to receive the said *John Hancock Senior* into their Service and Employ, in the Capacity aforesaid, for the Term aforesaid; and in Consideration of such good and faithful Service, undertake and agree to pay to the said *John Hancock Senior* the weekly Wages or Sum of *Thirty Shilling pr Week for each Year*

Nevertheless it is the true Intent and Meaning of this Agreement, and of the said Parties, and they do hereby expresly declare, that such Wages are only to be paid, and to be due and payable for such Time only as the said *John Hancock Senr.* shall actually work at the said DANIEL and BROWN's Manufactory, in Conformity to his said Engagement, and not otherwise.—As witness their Hands the *June 26th* Day of *1805*

John Hancock
Henry Daniel
John Brown

Witness to the signing hereof

James Ellis
Henry Carr

John Hancock Senior's Indenture

The employment of John Hancock Senior together with three others (see opposite and p. 55)—all beginning in 1805, although at various times—may mark the year as the start of the new, expanded establishment located at the Spode Factory. This was a move which would have been justified by the success of the new bone china and the consequent increase in the volume of enamelled decorations; this success could also explain why Daniel broke with Brown in 1806.

There is no reason to suppose that, when Henry Daniel left Spode to become a pottery manufacturer on his own account, the close working connection between the two men had not proved mutually satisfactory and that they did not part good friends. Daniel continued for many years to rent from Spode the house in which he lived[41] and was one of the main mourners at the funeral of his son, Spode III, in 1829. The 1822 balance sheet indicates how they had conducted their affairs. Daniel owned, as could be expected, all the tools, benches etc. which were used in the decorating process. Rather surprisingly, he also owned the kilns in which the wares received their decorating fires—and these, at this period, would have been substantial constructions, quite incapable of being dismantled or moved in any way. He rented the gold pan, the use of which he must surely have monopolised, and paid by weight for his colours to be ground. Both operations would have depended on the Factory steam engine. He also rented the workshops which housed his decorators, but they were *his* decorators and their future services formed part of the assets for which Spode paid. Particularly interesting is the invoicing of decorated goods back to Spode. The £5 credit 'by a lot of goods damaged' even suggests that Spode invoiced him with the goods in their undecorated state and subsequently had them re-invoiced back to him finished.

Although one may have depended entirely on the other for his employment, the relationship was emphatically that of one businessman with another rather than employer and employee, and this is strongly brought out by the way in which they preserved secrets from each other. John Hancock's invention of lustre was of great value to his employer, Henry Daniel, who had no intention of revealing the significant use of platinum, a material not hitherto used in the Potteries and the basis of the superior sorts of silver lustre. Apparently, at this early date he was not renting the gold pan but was paying for the use of Spode's grinding facilities at so much a pound, as he still was for colours in 1822. This presented him with the problem of how to enter in the record the grinding of platinum, the very mention of which would tell too much. No such secrecy was necessary for 'pale gold' (which Daniel made in the proportion of half an ounce of prepared gold to 12 grammes of prepared silver), and in his colour book he noted 'November 11th 1805 half pound platina entered by the name pail gold in Mr S—book'.[101] Spode II seems to have been equally close. Daniel, no doubt with an eye to the future as much as to his general education, was not above making entries in his books about matters which did not directly concern him; but when, about 1817, he noted a bone china formula (given in Chapter VIII) he could not be sure he had it right and wrote 'I believe this to be Mr Spode's New China Body for Teaware and Ornaments as good as French'. It can be supposed that the last thing to do was ask Mr Spode himself for confirmation.

If the arrangement which existed between Spode and Daniel seems strange to us, it is because we forget by how much the art of potting pre-dates that of enamel decoration in Staffordshire. Shaw, following an account of the improvements made in cream colour in 1751 by Mrs Warburton, gives a valuable account:

> The Pottery differing in quality and glaze to any before manufactured, trial was made of the adequacy of its glaze to bear fine designs of the enameller. This was first practised by some Dutchmen, in Hot Lane; who, to preserve their operations secret, had their muffle in a garden at Bagnall, the property of Mr. Adams. Mr. Daniel, of Cobridge, was the first native who practised enamelling. Workmen were soon employed, from Bristol, Chelsea, Worcester, and Liverpool, where Tiles had long been made of Stone Ware and Porcelain; and who had been accustomed to enamel them upon the white glaze, and occasionally to paint them under the glaze. For some years the branch of Enamelling was conducted by persons wholly unconnected with the manufacture of the Pottery; in some instances altogether for the manufacturers: in others on the private account of the Enamellers; but when there was a great demand for these ornamented productions, a few of the more opulent manufacturers necessarily connected this branch with the others. At first, the enamellers embellished merely the tasteful productions, figures, jars, cornucopiae, &c., and the rich carved work on the vessels; then they painted groups of flowers, figures, and birds; and at length they copied upon their breakfast and dessert sets, the designs of the richest Oriental porcelain.[247]

We have a picture of potters taking their ware for enamelling in rather the way that a housewife of the time would have taken a goose to the local baker. A potter in a large enough way of business could have monopolised the output of even a substantial enamelling establishment, and the arrangement made between Daniel and Spode would be a perfectly logical development from a situation like this. More than most products, pottery benefits from a minimum of bulk handling: provided the mountain were large enough, Mohammed could be brought to it. Shaw tells how Hollins Warburton and Company employed outside enamellers when they first began making porcelain under Champion's patent but that this activity was soon transferred to the main factory.[232]

Today, all manufacturers, whether opulent or not, 'necessarily connect this branch with the others', although so many other branches, such as the grinding of flint, the calcining of bone and even saggar making, all of which they once accepted as part of their craft, are now regarded as the legitimate preserve of specialist companies. Yet colour making, a skill essential to any enameller in the early nineteenth century, has survived as a separate entity and become, if anything, more specialised.

With the growth of the manufacture of bone china and the universal preponderance of enamelled decorations, the fate of enamellers as a notable, independent species was sealed. They either lost their identity, becoming absorbed completely by the potteries they served or, like Daniel, Elijah Mayer and John Aynsley, became manufacturers themselves. A few small enamelling establishments survived into this century, catering for the impecunious; but these, serving the undistinguished without distinction, were mere shadows of the trade's former glories at a time when an enameller like Daniel treated with a potter like Spode as an equal.

Whatever other enamellers were available to Spode II, Henry Daniel was an aristocrat in his craft. In the passage quoted above, 'Mr Daniel of Cobridge' (between Burslem and Hanley) is credited with being the first native to practise enamelling. Eight years later, in 1837, chauvinistically ignoring the Dutchmen previously noted but having allowed ample time for the descendant of any other native claimant to register a complaint, Shaw repeated the assertion, placing 'Mr Thomas Daniel, glaze enamelling' in his impressive and well-known list of pottery firsts, immediately following 'Mr Warner Edwards, biscuit painting'.[229] From this, it sounds as though Mr Daniel of Cobridge and Thomas Daniel are one and the same[42]—Henry Daniel's father, whose introduction to the art Shaw recounts in detail:

> At that time the various kinds of pottery with lead ore glaze, were made at a small manufactory, (which now is that belonging to Messrs. Ridgway, at the bottom of Albion Street Shelton,) by Mr. Warner Edwards, whose secret partner was the Rev. Thomas Middleton, the Minister of (Old) Hanley Chapel. Mr. Edwards's chemical ability exceeded that of all other persons in the district; for he could make the various kinds of Pottery then in demand, and prepare and apply the different colours, to ornament them. He was a careful, shrewd, and very intelligent man, and when he was attacked, in 1753, by the sickness which proved fatal, he presented to the late Mr. Thomas Daniel, (who had been his apprentice, and was then his only private assistant), a Drawing Book, embellished with many elegant Patterns; and on the first leaf is written, by himself—'Werner Edward's Art of making Enamel Colours in a plain manner'. On the blank sides of the leaves, Mr. T. D. wrote, from Mr. Edward's dictation, the minute instructions and requisite information concerning the several processes, and components for preparing of the different colours; and the prices of the several chemical preparations and minerals, with the names of the persons in London, Manchester, and Liverpool,

from whom they could be obtained of the best quality and at the lowest price. Thus the old gentleman rendered more useful to himself, the practical skill in the manipulations already acquired by Mr. D. while he rewarded in the best manner his industry and integrity. This Drawing Book, which we recently inspected, had been surreptitiously copied by some of the colour makers of the district, when it was recovered by the owner's son, Mr. H. Daniel, of Stoke, justly celebrated thro' the trade an Enameller of the greatest ability.[43]

Thomas Daniel lived to a considerable age. His son Henry was appointed administrator to his estate in April 1825,[101] indicating that he had died in that year or just before. His birth date has not been ascertained positively, but among the Daniel Papers there is a reference which suggests 1742, although it is more likely that it was 1739.[44] Either of these makes Shaw's date of 1753 in the passage above seem a little too early. Although, at his death, Thomas Daniel was described as a colour maker, he may not have been actively engaged in his profession at such an advanced age; but his two surviving notebooks show that he was so engaged up until at least 1813.[45] Both of these books are very small, and the entries—which are random and untidy—only provide a glimpse of his activities during two brief periods of his long life. The earlier of them has a few notes on colour making processes and some recipes, including one named 'the mixture for Tobys coats' and another 'the large Flower pott Green'; but there is evidence from two entries, one for a dozen blue printed cups and saucers and another for a dozen enamelled ones, that he was engaged in more than colour making. He noted that he 'commenced with Mr Wilson' on the 30th August 1787, and he received regular monthly payments from him of two guineas in September and October and one guinea a week throughout November—whether as wages or payments on account for goods supplied is not clear. In 1789, he noted the sale of two pounds of cobalt to Mr John Mayer at thirty-four shillings a pound. Entries in the Chamberlain account books in 1798 and 1799 show that his colours were going as far afield as Worcester, and he seems to have been associated with Richard Dyer, a former apprentice of Nicholas Sprimont of Chelsea.[46]

The next notebook contains more colour recipes and processes and some notes of business transactions. Between 1808 and 1811, he supplied colours of various sorts and in varying quantities to Mollard (twelve pounds of cobalt at ninety shillings a pound), David Wilson, Wedgwood and Byerley (many different colours but brown in the largest quantities), Greatbach (mainly blue and brown), Minton,[47] George Poulson, Whitehead, Keeling and Hackwood, and George Ridgway (mainly rose colour). By far the largest transactions recorded were with Shorthose and Heath for cobalt and calx. Two notes of unpriced quantities of raw cobalt under this name are so large they suggest that, although they were potters, they were in fact supplying Thomas Daniel with this expensive commodity. One of the entries shows that in the three months September to November of one year (not stated but probably 1808) his dealings with them involved two hundred and ninety-six pounds of common cobalt and two hundred and fifty-three pounds of the best sort. The only staff he employed at this period was a boy, Sam Morley, who received six shillings a week. In view of the high prices of the principal commodity in which he dealt in such large amounts, it seems he was still obtaining a comfortable living from the skills which he had been practising so long and which, by this date, he had long since passed on to his son.

Henry Daniel's immediate antecedents had provided the best imaginable background for his trade. Testimony to his competence can be read on the wares which made Spode II his fortune and in the ode on pages 48 to 50, which was written in his praise by one of his painters. This poem is the happiest survival among the Daniel Papers. It provides, in an excellent copperplate hand, the only contemporary description from the inside of the Spode Factory at this period which is ever likely to be discovered. To express any regrets concerning it would be ungrateful, but its author neither signed nor dated it. Although his full name may never be learnt, the last couplet of Stanza 15 leaves no doubt concerning J.D.'s occupation—and he was at least obliging enough to write on paper which was clearly water-marked with the date 1812. The indications are that he wrote a few years after that.

Stanzas 30 to 33 contain references to Henry Daniel's family. The baptisms of his four children were all, oddly but conveniently, entered on the same day, 13th August 1807, in Stoke Parish Register. Their births were better spaced: Thomas was born on 4th May 1798; Richard on 23rd March 1800; John on 30th May 1802; and Ann on 29th December 1805. Thomas was apprenticed to his father as an enameller and gilder of earthenware on his fourteenth birthday in 1812,[101] and Richard later became his father's partner in the firm H.&R. Daniel, which they began after the break with Spode.[48] These are the two who, in the poet's words, were 'in the band' at the time he was writing. The one who was nearly forgotten and who narrowly missed the 'benefit of rhyme' was John, the youngest. From Stanza 32, it is clear that he was also expected to join his father later, when he had finished his studies. This is not what happened in fact, for in 1820 he went to join Mr Threlfall, a Banker and Merchant of York Street, Liverpool, on a three-year engagement. This was not successful and he subsequently entered the pottery trade, appearing as the proprietor of China Rooms in Nottingham in 1829.[49]

All this must have been in the future when the Ode was being written and John was presumably then still at school, persevering in his 'studies great'. Even

Progress of Enamelling by Henry Daniel—an Ode

1   Assist Apollo give thy sovreign aid,
O come Euphrosyne celestial maid;
And tune my Soul new wonders now to tell,
The happiness that's found in doing well;
Oh may I speak with freedom in this cause,
And to the world give its deserv'd applause.

2   Come then thou true philanthropist and kind,
Let's open to the world thy gen'rous mind,
Thy feelings so pathetic sense so fine,
Thou always wast attended by the nine;
Thy plans so various in doing good,
The means whereby thou findest poor men food.

3   When first thou took'st to great Apollo's line,
Thy heart seem'd dead till thou didst them refine;
Thy penetration was so wond'rous keen,
Thou soon discover'dst what none else had seen;
Thy pencils blended with thy chymic skill,
They soon produc'd good pieces from the kiln.

4   Still thou wast not content with what was good,
Thou hadst not clear'd the water from the mud;
In which thou know'dst of pearls of greatest price,
And many thoughts that thou wast over nice;
Since then unto the world thou hast it shewn,
That there was precious treasures yet unknown.

5   Thy mind was yet continually on move,
Thou wast so much determind to improve;
The studies of our much beloved art,
That it might find its way to ev'ry mart;
Thy soul's so great that it cou'd never bear,
To see us conquer'd by rich foreign ware.

6   With servants three or four to thy own praise,
Thou decoratedst ware in diff'rent ways;
Then soon appear'd a small but neat showroom,
Thy colours all appear'd with such rich bloom;
That they astonish'd all at the first sight,
And thus thou brought'st the buried gems to light.

7   But still the mind continually did soar,
Thou soon hadst servants more than half a score;
Thy perseverance yet could not here cease,
If not improving thou wast ne'er at peace;
By this thou brought'st to bear such wond'rous things,
But still they were not fit for Lords and Kings.

8   The factory increases by degrees,
And each one seems content with his own fees;
Now artists are so various at each seat,
And each one strives to make the art complete;
Tis wonderful for strangers to behold,
The diff'rent forms that they will pencil gold.

9   But yet thy genius could not here abate,
Thou would'st have artists still of greater rate;
Of which I'll mention when it is their turns,
But yet with other things my bosom burns;
I cannot mention just at my own will,
Therefore for a short time they must be still.

10   Thy business so increas'd such great demands,
Thou now employ'st more than a hundred hands;
But none thou trusts with thy unrival'd skill;
Thou seem'st to manage all at thy own will,
Thy secrets are so wonderfully fine,
There's no admittance only for the nine.

11   The Gold thou'st brought to grind upon large mills,
And calculated all thy standing kilns;
Thou'st brought them to such a colossal size,
With towers majestic pointing to the skies;
Such things as these they ought to be admir'd,
In ancient times by other means they fir'd.

12   Come then Euphrosyne and bring thy best,
I feel as if I'd had sufficient rest;
Give me thy power these artists for to praise,
And shew their glorious works in different ways;
They'll be so wond'rous tedious to unclue,
They cannot all be seen at our first view.

13 Now all the factory it seems complete,
It is so stored with Artists of first rate;
The greatest things seem them not to controul,
Such wond'rous things they've done shews their
  great soul,
Yet constantly they seem for to improve,
The science of the Art they firmly love.

14 Here's Sherwin, Hancock, Burgess and some more,
I could not enter in my verse before;
Great Artists of fair Floras flow'ry reign,
From which the Factory receives great gain;
The first Pomona in wreath'd flowers enclose,
From which the Prince of Wales's order rose.

15 The Ornamental Gilders they have charms,
The Herald Painters practise nought but arms;
The Landscape Painters they are fix'd in herds,
Here's others that do nothing paint but birds;
For figure painting there's but little call,
By this you see my case is worst of all.

16 There's numbers more than yet here cant be pen'd,
If all were mention'd we should scarce e'er end;
All worthy Artists not of the first rate,
So various their employment yet not great;
But like the lever to the engine true,
All play their parts for what they have in view.

17 There's numbers more too tedious to be nam'd,
Fine daughters of the brush but yet not fam'd;
All useful in their diff'rent branches ply,
With cheerful countenances full of joy;
Nor need they study as the first I've pen'd,
So soon they bring their parts unto an end.

18 But yet not half thy bus'ness is unfurl'd,
Such wond'rous things thou'st spread about
  the world;
Kings, Princes, Nobles, men so high renown'd,
All, all agree thy judgment it is sound;
Such frequent purchases so often bought,
And from thy penetration they are wrought.

19 Oh then my Muse help me for to aspire,
And swelling Gratitude in numbers higher;
For goodness render'd to synonymous name,
No wonder then in speaking of his name;
My heart beats fervent at each Muse's call,
To pay the Gratitude I owe for all.

20 Come then Pegasus raise me on the wing,
Still help my soul with harmony to sing;
To unravel all the wond'rous things he's done,
And how he's toil'd beyond the setting sun;
In flaming Caverns like a Cyclop slept,
When wearied nature from its home was kept.

21 Sometimes in dead of night when all at rest,
Prepar'd for chymistry and on thy vest;
Thou'lt vessels from the rattling furnace draw,
If a beholder it would strike with awe;
To see the fluid fire in torrents run,
Like Etna's rivers dazzle in the sun.

22 How shall I then speak of the Chymists praise,
Who from the dross divides the golden rays;
His calx so numerous so fine his hues,
His purples, greens and all his various blues;
Besides a number that I can't name,
But so well known they've rais'd the country's fame.

23 How should it that such studies could be plan'd,
Was't thou not help'd by the Almighty hand;
Such penetration often they require,
Tis wonderful to see thee raise them higher;
So matchless thy productions when once seen,
Thy matted blues, japans and ever greens.

24 Now see him in the Compting House he's plac'd,
While all the Factory still, his crafts are trac'd;
Large volumes now in silence he turns o'er,
And views each line that he has wrote before;
To regulate a difference if there be,
But all his works they generally agree.

25 The pattern room is wonderful to view,
    They all bespeak thy animation true;
    All hobbies call a fictious name for great,
    No matter whether it be tea or plate;
    Some they're suspended on the lathy strings,
    Like birds in air with plumage on their wings.

26 While some on steppy shelves their beauty shew,
    Numerous Tea Sets spread the bench below;
    The centre table forms still richer glow,
    While spangling orders all the ground bestrew;
    With mathematic marks each piece is grac'd,
    But speak the number soon they find your taste.

27 Now view his pensive look that is not stain'd,
    With misery but still with study pain'd;
    His soul for business now seems not in tune,
    But yet he visits singly every room;
    To give directions from his last nights skill,
    Then ev'ry thing is done to his own will.

28 As bow that's always bent is not so strong,
    Sometimes thou tak'st relax but this not long;
    Soon as thy nerves have gain'd their former power,
    Thou something new bring'st forward ev'ry hour;
    To see the charming things thou'st done before,
    How great our wonder when thou bring'st us more.

29 To hear the sweetness of thy partners voice,
    Thyself a Momus o'er the cups of life;
    Thy arguments so firm thy tone so strong,
    Thy judgment so refin'd for to prolong;
    The cheerful hours that seem to glide away,
    Nor are we weary till the break of day.

30 No wonder then thy Sons should be inclin'd,
    To the fine arts and such exalted mind;
    Thy daughter too is of Apollo's reign,
    To hear her oftener oh then I could fain;
    Such charms of music sweet they are in sound,
    They lift the drooping spirits from the ground.

31 Oh may they all be blest with health and peace,
    Thy daughter, sons and all thy noble race;
    Till all the science of the arts they know,
    And not a thing escape them here below;
    And when they die to heaven may they ascend,
    This, this the wish of thy beloved friend.

32 There's yet one more I first think of in time,
    He must not miss the benefit of rhyme;
    In studies great he seems to persevere,
    When he is perfect he will soon be here;
    To join his loving brothers in the band,
    And take his comely sister by the hand.

33 See here ye spendthrifts of the British land,
    The way to wealth is here already plan'd;
    Throw by your revels you will find it good,
    Try his example then you'll not him grudge;
    Of the great wealth that he in peace enjoys,
    With his sweet wife, one girl, three lovely boys.

34 Now if this had been wrote by some divine,
    Thou might'st have [obliterated] beauty [obliterated]
    But as its by a miserable wretch,
    Perhaps a second reading it wont fetch;
    I pray thee judge it fair then this first time,
    And I will trouble thee no more with rhyme.

J.D.Scripsit hoc

if his education was more protracted than that of his brother Thomas, we are left with 1820 as the very latest date for the composition of the poem; and if it was proposed that John should join at fourteen, like his brother, then it was up to four years before this. Ann, who had an admirer in the poet, was only eleven years old in 1816 and the reference to her brother taking her by the hand in Stanza 32 may have been strictly, not figuratively, descriptive: this was probably the way the painters were used to seeing her accompanied when she visited their workrooms as a child.

Parts of the poem provide supplementary background to the balance sheet of 1822. No mention is made anywhere of any process other than decorating and, throughout, 'the factory' means Daniel's establishment within the Spode Works. A study of some old maps of the Factory, and even its present layout, leads to the conclusion that this was located on the north west side of the site. The decorating kilns mentioned in Stanza 11 survived to within living memory. There were three of them, shaped more like skittles than bottles. Although smaller than the ovens used for firing the biscuit and glost ware, they were nearly as tall and their more rakish proportions did make their towers majestic. From the 1822 balance sheet we know that Daniel owned them, and the poem suggests that he actually built them—to a specification grander than that usual for the time. Included in the items Spode II purchased from him in 1822 were 'bricks of all kinds'. Another survival at the Spode Factory until recent times was the gold pan, also mentioned in Stanza 11, which was rented at £15 a year. Not unnaturally, nowhere in his eulogy does J.D. mention Spode II, any more than he mentions his surrounding works. The sense of Stanza 29, the weakest in the work, is hard to fathom; but from the sweetness of the voice, the partner referred to must mean Daniel's wife, Elizabeth, who could have felt justly aggrieved had she been left out altogether.

J.D. had probably been with Henry Daniel many years, for he begins with a description of a start from very small beginnings. 'Servants three or four' could hardly have coped with the whole of Spode II's enamelling, even in 1805; and it is difficult to see what use there could have been for the small showroom mentioned in Stanza 6, except at the Hanley premises of Daniel and Brown, before 1806. 'More than a hundred hands' would have been needed by the second decade of the century. The Derby decorating establishment in 1832 was given as ninety-one: nine painters, nine paintresses, forty-one gilders and thirty-two burnishers.[186] Derby only produced china, but even so the balance looks odd for their class of wares: too many burnishers and not enough paintresses. Daniel's establishment was certainly differently proportioned. Although due allowance must be made for the needs of rhyme, one class of painters alone, for landscapes, was 'fix'd in herds'. There would have been an even greater number of paintresses. No printers are mentioned, and there is no evidence that this process, established long before Daniel's arrival, was one of his responsibilities. It was something in which he was intimately concerned, however. His surviving colour books show that he produced the printing colours and oils needed by Spode II, and his own girls would have filled in the enamelled decorations on the underglaze outline-printed wares.

The hierarchy of the painter's world in Staffordshire was established almost from the start: it is clear in the poem, and it remained unchanged for well over a century. At the top, the established specialist men painters; next, their aspiring apprentices; then the women, producing slight decorations and, at the bottom rung of the ladder, filling in printed outlines. Keeping them all fully employed was not an easy task. On 12th September 1820, Henry wrote to his son John, 'the women work all overtime the men but short at present'.[101] The specialist men painters were, like poor J.D, often hard hit by a swing in taste away from their particular subject and could rarely adapt to others without difficulty.

The answer to the frequently asked question on why painters were not allowed to sign their work lies not so much in the employer's desire to claim their credit as the hard economic facts of running a decorating establishment. Some painters are better than others. If we imagine, for example, three landscape painters, X, Y and Z, all allowed to sign their work, which is of uneven quality, X's being the best, we can also imagine that it will only be a matter of time before orders arrive stipulating 'must be painted by X'. Before long, he will have a backlog of work, while his two colleagues sit idle and the total production of landscape painting by the factory dwindles. Further, he will start to get ideas of his own importance or, just as bad, the factory's competitors will. For a variety of reasons the signing of work became general at the end of the nineteenth century—and some of the difficulties experienced through the practice were exactly those outlined. The anonymity of the painters of Spode's china must, therefore—no matter how frustrating to collectors—be understood if not forgiven.

Unfortunately, the Spode pattern books, unlike Derby's, provide no names. The Factory practice, as revealed later, seems to have been to enter the artist's name not by the pattern but in the accompanying price fixing books and these, except for those from *c.* 1840 on, are missing from the Spode archives. Derby collectors are doubly fortunate because Haslem, a most competent chronicler with a professional eye, appeared early to record details of his former colleagues, the Derby painters. In the absence of any other information, the names of the three top flower painters, Sherwin, Burgess and Hancock, given in Stanza 14, are precious new possessions.

Another painter's name discovered for the period is that of John Wood, a landscape painter, whose name appears in an entry for a colour recipe made by Henry Daniel at some time before October 1820, 'indian ink colour for John Wood's full landscapes'. Another entry of the same period is noted as being for J.Leigh. John Leigh was still at the Factory in 1835, for a colour book of that period$_{100}$ has an entry for 'brown to match a foreign landscape coffee cup done by John Leigh, August 1835'. Other names which appear among Daniel's recipes *c.* 1820 and which may refer to painters are Phillips and Masery (the spelling of the last is not clear). There is always the hope that signed pieces of privately executed work will be discovered and provide a key to the identification of their work for Spode.

Sherwin, whom the poet credits with the Prince of Wales' order (presumably the first following the visit of 1806 and, from the description given, consisting of fruit and flowers), is the only artist whose name appears in the Spode pattern books. A tattered working copy which remains has written for the centre of Pattern 3449 'Sherwin's fruit and flowers in centre'. The pattern is given in full in the master copy of the books and is reproduced in Plate 207. I have never seen a piece of this pattern, but if one is discovered it must not be automatically assumed that it was painted by Sherwin in person: centres and borders were frequently called after their originators, long after they were being executed by other and often lesser men. Several Spode patterns have fruit and flowers in this style, and two which are particularly similar are numbers 1995 and 1412. A John Sherwin of Burslem, described as a china painter, was married at Burslem on the 27th November 1803, and this may be the same man. Two designers and engravers of the same name, who may have been relatives of his, Henry and Elijah, are recorded after 1830; and a contemporary Sherwin, Ishmael, is noted as an ornamental gilder at Flight Barr and Barr in Worcester.$_{173}$

There is less to be discovered about the name Burgess and almost too much about that of Hancock, who would very likely have been a member of the family of John Hancock Senior, discussed later. A china painter called Joseph Burgess was married, like John Sherwin, in Burslem and in the same year—6th March 1803. A small book of Henry Daniel's colour recipes, dated 1812, begins with one headed 'Burgess rosé plates lined with this brown'. This is immediately followed by another recipe for brown, using the same ingredients but in different proportions, and headed 'Hancock rose plates'. Very shortly afterwards, another is annotated 'this is the colour 18 plates was painted with by Burgess'. The recipe for this colour would have produced a sepia, which suggests that Burgess may have been responsible for some of the lovely rose painting which can be found in several Spode patterns in this unusual colour for the subject. One of these, number 2088, is *c.* 1812 but the others are much earlier.

Since the 1822 statement of account specifically allowed Daniel to hire any of his men who did not hire themselves to Spode II—and since some, perhaps most, would have preferred to stay with their old employer—the names of some of the decorators at Henry Daniel's own factory soon after he left Spode are of interest. Four are mentioned by his son and partner Richard in an enthusiastic sales report on what appears to be his first selling trip to London:

> My dear Father,
>
> If you can by any means get four or six good flower painters, do, I conjure you. I sold eight of the very best Desserts yesterday to Daniel and Palmer, besides lower-priced ones, the whole order will come to £400. I have today sold Mr. Phillips seven rich Dessert Sets and eight lower-priced ones, besides a large quantity of Gadroon Tea and Breakfast ware. Daniel and Palmer pay cash as soon as goods come to hand, allowing them $2\frac{1}{2}\%$. They would have ordered twelve table services if I had them. They will keep their stock low until ours comes out: Phillips wants table ware badly.
>
> Have made sixty or eighty dozen larger Gadroon Desserts. Do get some good flower painters if possible. I have now sold more than Pegg and Brammer and Ellis will do for six months. I have just done with Phillips and have not time to say more. I will tomorrow write more fully.
>
> Take no more common painters or gilders, we must have the very best only. You may venture on another ground layer. I have sold nothing else. Don't let Bagguley leave.
>
> Now is the time or never. Everybody says they never saw such goods before. John Ridgway says we cut up his trade and John Rose sends out the goods so bad everybody complains.
>
> I remain dear father,
Your loving son, Richard.
>
> I hope you will not inform Thomas what I am doing. Mr. Yates is nothing in this market. Ann is very well and sends her love. In the morning I go to see Tom Duffolk (?).[50]

The identity of Pegg remains a mystery. At this date, the deservedly famous flower painter Quaker Pegg, of Derby, was only forty-eight; but Haslem, his biographer, states that he painted at Derby from 1813 to 1820 and then left to take a little shop, where he remained the rest of his life.[188] I have certainly never seen a Spode piece which could be identified as his work, and the thought that he may have been working for Daniel and, before that, for Spode has to be reluctantly dismissed. The Peggs were a Staffordshire family. Quaker Pegg himself was born there and educated at Shelton, and Pegg is still a common name in the Potteries.

Nothing is known of Brammer. But if the other flower painter, Ellis, is

V China: Two Bell Shape chocolate cups and stands. Height, 4½in. Bottom: cup and stand, Mark 10 and '711'. Top: stand, Mark 10 and '3613' with a Copeland and Garrett printed mark. (*N.Bernard Esq.*)

James Ellis, then he was certainly with Daniel throughout the period when he was connected with Spode. He witnessed John Hancock's hiring agreement in 1805, was named as one of Henry Daniel's executors in his will in 1812 and was still with him in 1825, when his name appears again as a witness in hiring agreements.[51] Bagguley may have been another man who had worked with Daniel for many years at the Spode Factory and left it with him. He combined colour making with ground laying, which was usual, and twelve recipes headed 'Baggeley colours' are in one of Daniel's note books, c. 1816. Another entry, made before November 1805, is annotated 'blue as made by Bageley for Derby china manufactory to gild upon. Hancock's blue the same'. This does not necessarily mean that he was ever employed at Derby, although it is not unlikely: he may have sent colours there when he worked independently before joining Daniel. A Thomas Baggaley, described as an enameller of Old Hall Road, Hanley, is listed in a trade directory of 1802.[157]

Hiring agreements survive for three other men who joined Daniel and Brown at roughly the same time as John Hancock Senior. His son, John Hancock Junior, was engaged on 11th November 1805, as an 'enameller and layer of grounds of various sorts' for two years, commencing at a salary of 27/- a week. Heber Marsh was engaged in the same trade on 10th August 1805, for three years, at a weekly wage of 21/-, with a present of three guineas at the commencement of each year. Joseph Turner, 'enameller and gilder', was engaged to start on 6th May of the same year for a period of three years, at a weekly wage of 18/- for the first, 21/- for the second and 22/- for the third year.[101]

A colour recipe, entered by Daniel, c. 1821, has the name J. Turner written by it—but this may be James Turner (not Joseph), whose name appears by another one, c. 1816. Heber Marsh's name occurs in the recipe books many times, c. 1805 and again c. 1821. A Hebba Marsh was one of six ground layers employed at Minton in 1834.[176]

The Hancock family is fortunately and, in view of its great importance, justly well documented by John Haslem. Its head, John Hancock Senior, served his apprenticeship at Derby but left very shortly after its completion and spent most of his life in the Potteries. Simeon Shaw stated, 'Mr John Hancock was, for some time prior to 1800, employed by Messrs Turner, of Lane End; and while there he introduced the method of gilding with burnished gold'.[52]

Shaw credits him with being the first to make this very important advance in decorating, and it is the earliest indication of the technical ability which, by his death in 1847 at the age of ninety, had earned him the title of 'father of the Potteries'.[189] He may have remained with the Turners longer than Shaw suggests, and the reason for his joining Daniel and Brown at the Spode Factory in 1805 could have been the imminent failure of the Lane End business. The other

E

three who joined with him may also have come from the same factory. The claim he made to the invention of lustre is examined in Chapter IX, and there is no doubt of his eminence as a colour maker. Haslem wrote, 'many of his receipts for colours and fluxes are still [1876] in use by enamel colour makers, and the number 8 flux of the district is the number 8 in his book'.[189] Even today, nearly a hundred years later, there is scarcely a china painter in Staffordshire over the age of fifty who has not used more colour fluxed with 'number 8' than he cares to remember and few who cannot describe the excellent qualities of 'Hancock's Red'. Henry Daniel's colour books are filled with colours by John Hancock, or colours using ingredients by him, and he seems to have remained at the Spode Factory for eleven years. The last reference to him in these books, which suggests his presence there, is a detailed description of a process headed 'Mr John Hancock Senior new gold made out 1816'. In this year, Haslem records that he joined Wedgwood, where he remained for the rest of his life.[189] The next Daniel entry relating to him confirms this, as well as suggesting that Daniel and Spode continued to benefit from the old master's inventive ability after he had gone from the payroll: 'Hancock's enamel blue same as used at Wedgwood's 1819'.

John Hancock had a large and successful family, but the two who are of interest in the Spode story are John and George, the first because he joined Daniel and Brown with his father, and the second because his ability as a flower painter and the dates of his movements raise the possibility of his being the Hancock referred to in Stanza 14 of the Ode:

> John and George were the two eldest sons of John Hancock, sen. George, the second son, was first employed at Derby in 1819, and he brought with him a number of women who were engaged to paint slight flowers and patterns of a cheaper class than those which were usually done up to that time. Women had long been employed in painting china and earthenware in Staffordshire, but their introduction at Derby was distasteful to the old hands. For some years previously that part of the works known as the 'Old Factory', on the site of which the Nunnery was afterwards built, had been closed, and it was then re-opened for the accommodation of these women. In the following year John Hancock also removed to Derby with his family; one son and three daughters had been brought up to china and earthenware painting, and they were added to the new colony in the old works. John Hancock was engaged as a colour maker and ground layer, and he and eight or ten painters and gilders, together with the women, were superintended by his brother George.
>
> The early method of laying grounds, or covering borders and large surfaces with one colour, was to paint them with a flat brush, and it was difficult to put some colours on a smooth surface so as not to shew the brush marks. Yellow was less difficult to work than most others, which may account for its occurring so frequently among the old grounded patterns. Some few other colours, such as

peach-bloom, fawn, or pale red, were also much in use, as they could be laid evenly, being so thin as to be little more than stained oil. The present method of laying grounds by dusting finely ground dry colours on a surface previously oiled, was introduced about 1817, and the mode adopted was at first kept a profound secret, the men working at it being usually locked in a room by themselves. Where parts of a grounded pattern are required to be left white, or to be afterwards painted, they are first laid over with a colour, usually rose-pink, mixed in water, with a portion of treacle to hold it together—this is called stencilling. In oiling the piece, previous to dusting on the dry enamel colour, the parts which have been stencilled are washed over with the oil and receive the colour equally with the other parts. The pieces are then immersed in water, which, flowing under the oil, permeates and loosens the stencil colour, and this is then carefully removed with cotton wool, leaving those parts perfectly white, and the colour remaining on the parts where required. John Hancock was one of the first who practised the new method of ground laying. He was also a clever painter, particularly of birds, and his imitation of the latter in the old Sèvres style was perfect. He was celebrated as a maker of enamel colours, and for many years most of those which were used at the old Derby works were made by him. His knowledge of bodies and glazes was very practical, and the help he afforded when difficulties arose, as they often did, was considerable. He had a good knowledge of glass painting and staining, having practised those arts for some years at Messrs. Davenport's, of Longport, before he was employed at Derby. He continued to work at the Derby factory until his death in 1840, aged 63 years.[190]

Evidently, from the fact that he worked at Davenport's for a 'period of years', John Hancock was not continuously with Daniel from 1805 until he went to Derby in 1820. But two recipes were recorded by Daniel headed 'John Hancock junior' very shortly before an entry dated May 1817—so his stay at Davenport's may have been shorter than Haslem suggests, or may have been an intermission during his employment by Daniel. Haslem's description of his skill as a bird painter and his speciality of imitating the old Sèvres style of painting them calls to mind the multitude of Spode patterns decorated with birds which were introduced before 1820, some of which may have been his work. His original engagement of 1805 with Daniel and Brown did not describe him as a painter but as an enameller and ground layer; and when he joined Derby, it seems that it was his proficiency in the new method of laying ground colours which was his main asset to them. Almost certainly, he learnt this from Daniel at the Spode Factory.

A great deal of confusion surrounds the history of this technical innovation, caused partly by a failure to understand the terms employed and partly by a misunderstanding of statements by Simeon Shaw (see p. 181). The ground laying process has its origin in the very beginnings of enamelled decoration, but the oil-and-dust method of ground laying was an early nineteenth century innovation. In England, that is. Sèvres were employing it long before, and a Copeland and Garrett recipe book correctly describes the method as 'the French way'.[100] Haslem's explanation of the process is clear and correct. Ground colours are described as 'laid' whether applied with a brush or by the later oil-and-dust method, a subsequent additional refinement to which is the flattening of the oil with a silk pad to ensure a perfectly even surface for receiving the powdered colour. As Haslem points out, the oil-and-dust method was an important advance, enabling richer tones to be applied evenly. Since the new method was slower, and therefore more expensive, it never entirely superseded the old brush method, which was—and still is—perfectly adequate for pastel shades.

Haslem states that the new technique was introduced at Derby in 1817; but a study of many Spode pieces dating from well before this reveals that several ground colours, notably red, were being applied by this method at an earlier date. It is quite possible that Henry Daniel was responsible for its introduction in England. His recipe books contain six different oils for laying grounds, each one designed for a different colour.

There is no direct evidence that the Hancock who was a flower painter at Spode was John Hancock. It may have been his brother George. Haslem refers to George's skill with flowers as his 'chief excellence', although he was also rated highly for his technical knowledge of potting and decoration.

> He worked for Billingsley at Mansfield, and doubtless owed some of his skill as a flower painter to Billingsley's teaching. Although he had not that artist's delicacy of touch or gracefulness of grouping, yet his flowers were always well modelled and boldly painted.[191]

George Hancock's recorded movements after leaving Billingsley in no way preclude his being at the Spode Factory c. 1812, which is the date when there is the first evidence of the presence there of the Hancock who was the colleague of Sherwin and Burgess (see p. 53). After Billingsley left Mansfield, George Hancock returned home to the Potteries and in 1809 was working for Ridgway. 'He also worked for other firms in the Potteries, and for a time resided in London . . . He afterwards returned to the Potteries, whence he arrived in Derby, as already stated in 1819, continuing there until 1835, when he left, having entered into an engagement with Mr Edwards, a Solicitor, to superintend the making of china at Burton-on-Trent'.[191] Back in the Potteries by 1836, he turned up in France in 1839 but died in his home country in 1850. There is evidence that a George Hancock was known to Henry Daniel, among whose surviving papers is the end of a letter giving details of a gold treatment process, which concludes 'this is what the person sade that I had it of—your obedient servant, George Hancock, March 10th, 1836'. A detailed study is invited of known pieces of George Hancock's work and Spode products of the period 1812 to 1819.

Painting and Gilding China or Earthenware.

5 Growth, 1806–1833

'The first pottery of consequence in this place [Stoke] is Mr Spode's manufactory of china and earthenware, and is considered one of the most complete establishments of its kind in the kingdom. Some idea may be formed of its extent from the quantity of coal consumed, which is upwards of 200 tons per week, and from the number of ovens wherein the ware is baked, amounting to eighteen large furnaces, many of which are used three times each, weekly, the whole year round. There are about 800 people, of all ages, employed in this concern. The materials used in the manufactory are brought from a considerable distance; the clays from the counties of Dorset, Devon, and Cornwall, and the flint principally from Kent. There are two steam engines connected with the manufactory, the oldest of which has been erected nearly forty years; and the other, a most beautiful atmospheric engine of 36 horse power was put up by Boulton and Watt, about ten years ago. These engines grind all the flints, glazes, colours, etc; sift the liquid clay, or slip; compress the prepared clay into a more compact mass; and put in motion the throwing wheels and turning lathes, which, in other factories is effected by pedal and manual labour.

'Here almost an endless variety of earthenware is made of every colour and fabric, and of a quality which has obtained for it an extended and merited celebrity.

'China, too, has here been brought to the greatest perfection, both as regards its colour and transparency, and the taste displayed in its decoration. Here is also made the recently invented stone china, which is remarkably strong and durable, and in every respect much like the oriental; there is an immense quantity of it sold at present; and no doubt, but as it becomes better known, it will be introduced into very general use'.[194]

This eye-witness account of Spode II's factory in 1819 clearly shows the dominant position he had reached by that date and the vast scale of his activity. On his death, in 1827, one of his obituarists commented: 'Whatever the pressure of the times, he kept up his great Manufacturing Establishment, so as to give employment to the numerous persons, who were dependent upon it'.[138]

This is one of the most significant things ever written about Spode II. Its importance lies not in the saintly motive attributed to him but in the statement that he did keep this great business going all the time. There is no evidence that his factory ever closed, ever diminished in size or ever, like some, abandoned the manufacture of porcelain for a time. To anyone in the Potteries who had lived through the thirty years preceding his death this must have seemed an achievement worth particular mention, for there had been times when to survive alone could be accounted success.

For the first eighteen years following Spode II's return to Stoke, England was almost continuously at war. Napoleon's Berlin Decree of 1806 closed virtually every market in Europe—except Russia—to her commerce, and the counterstroke of a general blockade brought down on her merchants and manufacturers the retribution of an embargo by the Americans. The Staffordshire potters, with their traditionally large export business, were hit particularly hard. Even the British Government appeared in the guise of an enemy, proposing a tax on their products in 1811. This was a year when thirty of them filed through the bankruptcy courts and Josiah Wedgwood Junior wrote, 'the business is not worth carrying on'.[148] Spode II and Caldwell headed the successful opposition to the new tax and were voted a piece of inscribed plate each by their fellows, who fully realised what their failure to prevent this added imposition could have meant in times which were hard enough.[196]

Most of the bad times in the Potteries were common to the whole of the country. The recurring shortages of grain and high food prices were general. If William Adams, a lieutenant in Spode II's Yeomanry Troop, ever drew his sword in anger, it was not, as inscribed on its blade, 'England's soil from Gallic rage to save' but to use the flat of it on his own starving countrymen, rioting for bread in the streets of the Six Towns.[275]

The coming of peace in 1815 did not solve the country's economic problems. In 1820, the total exports of pottery to America, the largest overseas customer, were less than a quarter of the total for 1814[148]—a year when the two countries were actually at war. Nor was the more reliable home market immune from serious depressions: the newly formed Potters' Union was misguided enough to choose one for its first strike in 1825. Being positively welcomed by some of the masters, it failed, not surprisingly, to achieve its aims. The outcome was far different in the next strike of 1834-5, when a new union secured a 25 per cent increase in wages.[226] Bulging order books made the difference: 'the trade had been for sometime previously in a very prosperous state'.[277]

John Ward cast a retrospective glance over the first forty years of the century and was obliged to notice

> That, not withstanding the great increase of the [pottery] business, and the improvements, and trebled population to which it has given rise, the success of individuals who have embarked in it has been extremely hazardous, and their failure has been the result, in more than a majority of instances. We do not hesitate, indeed, to assert, that during the period we refer to, we have witnessed the ruin of a larger number of Potters than are now engaged in the trade.[274]

Spode II is not the only proof that, despite the frequently adverse times and the hazardous nature of the potting trade, the rewards for success could be great. Whatever the difficulties, the industry over all continued to expand— but success was hard won, and potting in the early nineteenth century was characterised by intense competition among the manufacturers. They competed in price, in variety, in designs and in ideas.

Spode II, Potter to the Prince of Wales and later the King, with his fine London premises and well-established connections among aristocratic and middle class buyers, would never have been forced to regard price as the main selling point of his goods. In the fight for business, the 'better end of the trade' no doubt escaped the most sordid of the excesses which smaller firms must have endured, but keen prices were vital in every sector of the market. Several complaints by Wedgwood on the competitiveness of Spode's have already been mentioned in Chapter 3. In 1810, their traveller wrote from Glasgow that Spode II had not only produced two new patterns in imitation of theirs but that they were cheaper:

> I could not learn the price exactly but was given to understand they were much cheaper than ours—Spode's Blue printed plates are 6/1d. a dozen, except one pattern which he sells at 6/6d.[109]

One of the patterns Spode II is alleged to have copied was an underglaze blue print. In this field, few would dispute his pre-eminence in quality—yet, even here, he was cheaper and apparently became more so, for in 1812 a report reached Etruria that 'Mr Spode's Rome plates are charged 5s.0d, per dozen wholesale',[114] a price 15 per cent lower than the one mentioned two years before for a pattern which must have cost the same to produce. In 1826, James Wordley, a dealer in Liverpool, purchased Blue Italian six-inch plates from Spode at 2s.0d. per dozen (see Appendix III).

It is an old and civilised tradition among pottery manufacturers that the utmost cordiality and ostensible co-operation should prevail between them as they employ every known device to get the better of one another. They have never been slow to band together for the good of the trade and

> Many of them united in the year 1813, under the appellation of a CHAMBER OF COMMERCE, to advance the prices of their goods, and adopted a Price List, commencing January 1, 1814; by which all the ordinary species of ware are yet [1843] regulated.[277]

The use of common price scales, in fact, goes back much farther than the date given by Ward in the passage above and is still (1970) employed by firms who are described, for this reason, as 'gross list houses'. The pact of 1814 solved nothing, for, as Ward added, 'large discounts have been conceded in many instances, and the nett prices have been thus materially reduced'. The use of discounts made it sometimes difficult to discover by exactly how much you were being undersold: in 1811 Josiah Bateman of Wedgwood was told, 'If you can get Spode's mode of dealing and prices, particularly a comparative statement of the Retail and Wholesale, it will be very useful'.[115]

Another way of competing with prices, even while apparently abiding by those generally agreed upon, was by giving extra measure. Here, again, Spode II was prepared to join battle, as the following report to Etruria in 1807 shows:

> To succeed in the Country trade we must not be niggardly in our sizes, the best makers act otherwise e.g. Spode's pint jug holds three half-pints . . . J. Ridgway makes larger ware than anyone.[116]

In order to comprehend this method of competition, it is necessary to understand something of the descriptions traditionally used in the pottery trade. Collectors may find it worth entering this maze since it explains certain impressed numbers they sometimes find on their pieces, particularly teapots and jugs. Only in Alice's Wonderland or Staffordshire could a pint jug which holds a pint and a half appear normal. To describe an article by its capacity in this fashion was, in fact, unusual. A pint jug, for instance, was more commonly a '12s', part of a system of sizes first explained in 1686 by Dr Plot[227] and, much later, anonymously in 1804:

> The rule of our forefathers presents itself to our view in the original standard of count, denominated by the size of a pint mug, by which we are to understand, that all articles that may be deemed *hollow* ware, of whatever shape, containing one pint, are counted 12 to the dozen. If they contain less, the quantity is increased; if more, the quantity is diminished. As when we reckon a vessel holding six pints, at 2 to the dozen, to a coffee-can containing only one third of a pint, at 36 to the dozen. These things are so well known, that they require no further explanation. Dishes, plates, etc., generally denominated *flat* ware have their value estimated according to the number of inches they measure, comprising the size of 8″ to 24″; and most kinds of table and dessert ware have their value fixed in the same way.[54]

These traditional sizes, 'wisely introduced for the good government of Potters, in regard to the many and various articles they have occasion to manufacture, for the convenience and pleasure of mankind', formed the basis of any agreed price scales which were drawn up. But nothing could prevent one potter from making his sizes larger than another's. This reached a stage where dealers were able to 'purchase jugs so as to double them'. In other words, they would pay the recognised price for a dozen jugs but buy them from a manufacturer whose 24s jug ('half pint') held a pint, 12s jug ('pint') held a quart, and so on. The anonymous writer protested that 'The monstrous size of goods is the bane

of all our profits' and warned darkly that, if left uncorrected by the potters themselves, 'it will then be indispensably necessary to adopt such measures, as may
in the event establish that power in the hands of those whose authority cannot
be slighted'. Legislation was actually proposed in 1826 to regulate sizes in
pottery and was determinedly opposed by William Taylor Copeland[55]—
apparently with success, since luckless assistants in china shops are still trying
to explain to disbelieving laymen such peculiarities as 'seven-inch plates' which
measure eight inches.

The enormous range of items produced by potters in these years is yet
another reflection of the intense competition for business. Foreign markets
made their own peculiar demands. These were not limited to outlandish productions, such as hookahs, but embraced normal tableware items—as they still
do. Only recently has it become possible to sell tall cups in the North American
market, where they are as traditionally unwanted as they are demanded in the
United Kingdom. To this day, the American preference is for a flat wide-
rimmed plate; Switzerland demands large milk jugs; and two sizes of soup
tureen are desired in Italy. The needs of export markets, however, only partially
explain the astounding diversity of sizes and shapes to be found in Spode's
productions. The real cause must be that the increasing refinement in living
standards among the middle classes and aristocracy resulted in a more and more
particularised demand for items in pottery, which the manufacturers not only
responded to but actively encouraged. For example, it was no longer possible,
as in the eighteenth century, for a factory to make a 'cup'. Tea cups and after-
dinner coffee cups, both handled and unhandled, had to be available together
with breakfast cups and odd-size cups—half way between breakfast cups and
tea cups in size—known as Norfolk or Irish cups. To these must be added a
wide choice of shapes in the special cups traditionally made for caudle and
chocolate. Teapots were available in up to six sizes, jugs sometimes in fourteen,
even candlesticks in eleven. A choice of three different sizes of bed-pan might
be justified as an anatomical accommodation; but to offer twelve sizes of chamber
pot is more like pandering to the flesh.[56]

With Spode II in the forefront, potters not only offered every kind and size
of normal and abnormal tableware item but also racked their brains to discover
any possible new application of their product. The Spode china oil lamp
illustrated in Plate 242, twenty-seven inches high and complete with a china
shade, all richly decorated, represents a typically bold foray into the luxury
market. But the King's Potter could also supply a fingerbowl, smoking pan,
tripe pot, churn, couped milk pail, tobacco cup, wine funnel, sick feeder, lemon
drainer, apothecaries' syrup pot, suckling pot, closet pan, set of dinner carriers,
trumpet-mouthed spitting pot[56] or a little mug, made and sold for pence,

decorated with a scene of your favourite seaside resort (Plate 125). To present-day production executives—devotees of 'variety reduction', the arid art of making more and more of less and less—this array is a nightmare world. But to the collector it is a delight, and to the customer of the time it was no more than he expected.

Diversity in the number and size of items was not alone sufficient to satisfy the demands of this clamouring market; shapes and decorations were equally varied. For the first fifteen years of the century, Spode managed comfortably with two basic teaware shapes; but by the end of the next fifteen years this had been multiplied at least threefold. The same striving after novelty is apparent in every area of the Factory's activity, and in none is it more conspicuous than the field of underglaze blue printed ware. As the century began, the lucrative turnover this represented was concentrated on a mere handful of patterns—versions of the ever-faithful Willow in the forefront. By the end of the Spode Period, an almost countless array had been introduced. Every trend and taste was pounced upon. If preference were shown for a pattern with a romantic Italian subject, it was not long before it was joined by four others in similar vein. Patterns used subjects ranging from simple English scenes to outlandish Levantine ruins, from Aesop's Fables to tiger-hunting in India; and as the very colour blue began to pall with certain sections of the public, jaded appetites were tempted with a pallet of new colours. Potting found itself a fashion trade.

One of the results of the scramble for novelty was an intensification of the potters' time-honoured pastime of copying each other. Spode II was never slow to accord the sincerest form of flattery to his competitors. The evidence is before our eyes—reinforced by some loud complaints in surviving Wedgwood correspondence, which have been quoted. Spode II may have been more philosophical when he found himself on the receiving end, as he often did; but we shall never know. If he made any complaints, they have not been preserved for us. He certainly took a calm and humane view when he suffered the worst form that copying could take: downright theft. When Thomas Appleton left Spode to work for William Mason in 1811, a 'parcel of moulds' left with him.[181] Spode settled for an abject confession from Appleton in the local newspaper and a payment by him of five guineas to the Pottery Dispensary.[136]

Appleton's new employer, smarting under the implication, rushed into print to deny 'soliciting or obtaining in a clandestine manner from the said Mr Spode, his patterns, moulds or shapes' and claimed that Appleton's moulds 'were not worth sixpence'.[181] Perhaps he protested too much.

A healthier field for competition was available in the very techniques of the Staffordshire potters' craft. Always ingenious, they engaged in a constant and thoroughly praiseworthy contest to improve their products. One major step

forward was taken by Spode II when he introduced felspar into the composition
of his china. Pieces marked Felspar Porcelain are familiar to all students of early
nineteenth-century china, whether their interest is exclusively Spode or not.
The story behind these marks is, therefore, of some general interest.

It is as well to understand clearly that Felspar Porcelain is bone china.
Felspar is an ingredient in porcelain which can fill the role usually taken in
English bone china by Cornish stone. Cornish stone, in fact, contains felspar;
but the spar itself has the advantage of being a purer material and much more
constant in its performance. It is the petunse of the Chinese. Had it been
available from the start, English potters would have used it; but the first native
deposits of felspar did not begin to be exploited until February 1819. These were
at Middletown Hill on the Wales–Shropshire border, and the man responsible
for their discovery was Thomas Ryan.

Middletown Hill was an old mining site. The Romans had mined there for
lead, and there had been various mining activities in the eighteenth century for
a variety of minerals.[57] Ryan examined it in 1818 and discovered

> Alumine combined with Silex in two families of Felspar, Barytes in two states of
> crystallisation, Magnesia, and Lime in a vein twenty two feet wide; Steatite, and
> Pitchstone; also Arsenic, Cobalt, Nickel, Zinc, Lead and Copper.[58]

It seems to have been a kind of chemical Aladdin's Cave, and Ryan lost no
time in obtaining a twenty-one-year lease on very favourable terms. He began
his operations in February 1819, having experienced no trouble in finding
partners, who doubtless found his proposals extremely attractive.

> The system of Mining I adopted, contemplates disposing of the Earths found as
> matrixes in the Veins, so as to cover the expense of working. . . Any vein of ore
> found, therefore, could be worked to a profit; and not only because of thus gaining
> something for materials which *must* come out of the mine, but also by removing
> those, which would else be obstructions to the operations. And, if I could only
> get for the Felspar the sum it cost raising, I should obtain the Lead, Cobalt etc.
> however small or great the quantity, as a surplus product.[58]

Ryan mentions no problems in disposing of the ores he mined, but this was
not the case with the felspar. Before starting, he had carefully assessed the
market for the various products of the mine. Having examined the felspar found
at Limoges—which was extensively used in potting—he had come to the
conclusion that English potters would provide a ready market for his, which was
similar. He had, however, grossly overestimated their chemical knowledge,
much inferior to his own, as his experience with Mr Rose of Coalport, the
nearest pottery to the mine, was to show:

> The only knowledge of Potting then possessed by me was merely that of properly

combining the Earths and Minerals by Metallurgical Chemistry. But persuaded that this felspar was most important to the English Potter, I forwarded samples to different persons for their trials; all of whom, by treating the substance similarly to the Cornish Granite, failed in their attempts, pronounced it of no value for Pottery; and on the Wharfs in Staffordshire I had many tons lying, wholly valueless. Mr. Rose of Coalport, having made this assertion also to the Rev. J. Murray, so alarmed that gentleman, that he disposed of half his number of shares to a lady. The statement caused a Panic among the Partners; and to vindicate the matter, I went to Coalport, and during a whole month engaged in experiment, by which I produced such Porcelain, that the Society of Arts awarded their gold medal to Mr. Rose for his Porcelain Glaze, altho' he had declared that its base, the felspar, was good for nothing.[58]

Mr Rose was as quick to exploit Ryan's success as he had been to spread premature alarm and despondency. Although he began the letter he wrote to the Society of Arts, 'Having for some time made use of a glaze for porcelain which gives me great satisfaction',[133] it could only have been in use for a matter of weeks or months, since on 30th May 1820, he received the award he had solicited. He incorporated mention of his gold medal into a large and elaborate backstamp which from then on he used for his felspar porcelain. The backstamp does not mention that the medal was awarded solely for the glaze, nor that it was 'the smaller, or Isis Gold Medal'. Two years later, J.Meigh of Shelton was awarded, for a leadless glaze for common red earthenware, the large Gold Medal which had been offered by the Society to anyone who could improve the lot of humanity in this respect.[59] Rose's claim to notice rested solely on the aesthetic merit of his glaze and its suitability for enamelled decorations and gilding. Mr Muss, and other artists to whom the Society submitted samples for experiment, pronounced it excellent in this respect.[133]

Ryan, who seems to have been a man of great enterprise and energy, having solved the problem on his doorstep, immediately turned his attention to Staffordshire and the idle tons of felspar lying there:

I engaged a small Pottery, at Stoke, prosecuted my experiments upon the Materials I had forwarded, exhibited a specimen to Mr. Spode, of the Mount, guaranteed a kiln full of similar Porcelain; but as his foreman refused to assist in the business, I was induced to employ as my assistant, a relative of Mr. Spode, who had been bred in a brewery, was then a warehouseman, and therefore had no more practical knowledge of potting than myself.[60] Mr. Spode gave an order for fifty tons at £15 per ton; the quantity on the wharfs was instantly removed to Stoke, and the order was completed in a short time. The cheaper sort of felspar was purchased in large quantity by E. Mayer & Son, T. Minton, Messrs. Ridgway, and others.[58]

The fact that Spode II was the first to be approached by Ryan may only indicate that he was the foremost china manufacturer in the district. But it could equally well show that by then his reputation in another respect was well established: 'Any improvement which was suggested found a ready patron in him; he never grudged risking a few hundreds for the chance of success and the encouragement of ingenuity'. [61]

The initial order he gave Ryan for his felspar reveals, in its quantity, the grandiose scale of his enterprise and, in the price he paid, a happy disregard for economy and a determination to have the best. [62] Although he does not mention the fact, Ryan would have doubtless found Rose's Gold Medal a valuable piece of ammunition in Staffordshire. Spode lost no time in producing, before the end of 1821, a backstamp equal in size and not unlike the Coalport one in general appearance for his own felspar porcelain. Other potters followed suit. The word 'felspar' became the vogue, and it kept its magic for more than twenty years. Strange that it was not until the beginning of the present century that the potency of the word 'bone' was realised and, after more than a century of unpublicised use, the true and lasting unique selling point of English china came into its own.

For a man who claimed only mining as his profession—which, in his own words, he had 'adopted, not from mercenary motives, but a desire to ameliorate the condition of the miners' [58]—Thomas Ryan performed more than adequately as a salesman. One suspects that he had prompted Rose into going after a gold medal and shown him how to use it. For his biggest and first customer in Staffordshire, he produced a publicity idea which was designed to be of equal benefit to his own company.

> At the commencement of 1823, Mr. Spode was engaged to manufacture a splendid Porcelain Vase, valued at £100, as a present from the Middleton Hill Mine Company to his Majesty. This was completed in April, and was exhibited several days in the large China Warehouse of the manufactory, to some thousands of visitors. Its chasing and enamelling are executed in the first style of the Art; and the whole is conspicuous for its unblemished beauty, the purity and delicacy of the material, the simplicity of the style, and the splendour of its ornaments. [63]

Ryan's efforts met with the success they deserved; his felspar was much more than a sales promotion idea, being responsible for a very marked improvement in the quality of both the body and glaze of the china made with it. It seems to have given renewed impetus to the entire industry. Simeon Shaw mentions how Ridgway introduced a new china body and range of shapes in 1821, and how, in about 1822, J.&W.Handley of Shelton 'introduced a porcelain from felspar chiefly'. [264] The same date saw Henry Daniel strike off on his own as a china manufacturer. [48] A real technical advance allied to a novel selling point is an effective combination in any trade and at any point in history. Shaw may not have overstated the case when he attributed to felspar the enjoyment by British porcelain of 'a new and important era, and excellence and superiority over any other, rapidly approximating to perfection'.[230]

The earliest, and largest, of Spode's felspar porcelain backstamps is dated 1821 and features the London address very prominently, as did the Factory's billheads (see Appendix II). The importance of the London business, the power and measure of control which it supplied, can never be overlooked in examining any of Spode II's moves as a manufacturer or any of his successes. Details of the various changes in the Spode London partnerships are given in Appendix II. From 1812 on, the practical management of the business there was entirely in the hands of William Copeland, who was joined by his son in 1824. The younger Copeland, William Taylor, stepped into his father's shoes when he died in 1826. Although he seems to have been a true Londoner in these early years, he found his bride in the Potteries—marrying, three months after his father's death, Sarah Yates, daughter of John Yates of Shelton, the china manufacturer. Shortly after, he began to achieve the series of distinctions in the City of London which, in 1836, culminated in his election as Lord Mayor.

The early exit from the business of William Spode, Spode II's eldest son— who, in 1812, seems to have retired to lead the life of a country gentleman on his estate in Surrey—would have seemed perfectly natural to his contemporaries at that date. His younger brother, Spode III, did exactly the same thing. It was the only life for a gentleman at a time when money and trade were normally regarded, even by those who made the one by engaging in the other, as strictly a means to an end. In a country where the possession of land had always been the basis of real power, and consequently all social ascendancy, an estate was every man's ambition. By 1819, William Copeland had acquired his and it had cost him £12,497, but it enabled him to be described in his grant of Arms that year as 'lord of the manor of Wyke, county Surrey, only son of William Copeland gentleman late of Longton in the parish of Stoke on Trent'.[100] Land could even win a posthumous promotion from yeoman for a long-dead father.

Even Spode II was buying an enormous estate in Staffordshire at the date of his death. This, at least, would have been the crown to a lifetime's hard work and achievement, much of it performed while his eldest son was living off its fruits in Surrey without even acknowledging his own name. Why William changed his name to Hammersley (see Appendix I) has not been discovered, but he may have felt unjustly victimised in possessing one which, in an age before branded goods, branded him—with commerce. The names of only a handful of manufacturers were then known to the public and his was one of them. Josiah Wedgwood's son had this trouble in Dorset.[222] Although never as fanatical on this subject as the old French aristocracy, English county society could only really forgive money if it was old, as every reader of Jane Austen knows.

One of the most valuable advantages of the Spode London business was that, in a way which would have been impossible from Stoke, it could harness for the Factory's benefit the snobbishness of English society and the devoted and wide-spread desire of the middle classes to emulate those they freely acknowledged to be their betters. The importance of a fashionable flavour is well brought out in a description of 1819:

> The London concern of this manufactory is conducted by Mr. William Copeland, in Portugal Street; the showrooms are a perfect exhibition, where numbers of nobility and gentry assemble daily, and have the gratification of selecting their own services. The numerous wares resemble a picture gallery, where the exuberance of genius meets the sight in every direction. The advantage to the public is incalculable, by a dependence on receiving a sound article, and at a moderate price. To witness the variety, beauty, and extent of the produce of the manufacture, we would recommend a visit to this fashionable resort, where the greatest attention is paid to the company while inspecting the collection.[194]

Nothing had changed since Josiah Wedgwood had written 'begin at the Head first, and then proceed to the inferior members'.[217] London set the pace, for it was there that the aristocracy did its shopping. Particularly well placed by reason of the royal appointment, Spode and Copeland in London could achieve quick acceptance and sales for new products, items or patterns in a way that potters fifty years before would never have believed possible—although not all their successes were as spectacular as that with Stone China on 3rd July 1817.

> Yesterday, at one o'clock, Her Majesty, accompanied by the Princess Elizabeth, went in a private manner, in the Countess Dowager of Cardigan's carriage, attended by her Ladyship, to visit Spode and Copeland's porcelain, Staffordshire, and extensive glass warehouses, in Portugal Street, Lincoln's-inn-fields where they were met by Sir Henry Campbell. The royal party were met by Mr. Copeland and Mr. Asbury[64] his nephew, strictly in private, and were conducted over the different departments. The newly invented china, called stone china, by Mr. Spode, was exhibited to the Queen; it so closely resembles India china, that it is with great difficulty that the difference can be discovered. Her Majesty bought a service for herself, and a variety of articles for presents. The Royal party remained upwards of an hour inspecting the spacious premises and expressed themselves highly gratified: as they had no Royal carriage, and as, at the Queen's express command, no preparation was made for her reception, they retired unobserved.[145]

Even by modern standards, this appears to be a remarkably effective piece of publicity; one can well imagine, therefore, the impact it must have made at the

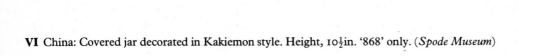

VI China: Covered jar decorated in Kakiemon style. Height, 10½in. '868' only. (*Spode Museum*)

time. It appeared in the Court Circular of *The Times*, which was probably the only feature read by women in the only national newspaper of the day, then a fraction of its present size. At a time when paid advertising for consumer goods was the almost exclusive preserve of quack medicines and similarly disreputable products, publicity of this kind was as valuable as it was infrequent.

In addition to direct sales to the public, Portugal Street acted as 'a depot for the supply for the London retail trade, as well as the extensive foreign connections of the firm'.[128] In London were the companies and merchants who controlled Britain's enormous overseas trade. It was to the greatest of these, the Honourable East India Company, that a Mr G.A.Prinsep applied, in 1821, for a licence to establish himself as a merchant in Bombay. Part of the evidence he produced to support his case was a letter from Spode and Copeland at Portugal Street, giving him permission to name himself as their agent and stating that they had put goods under his charge on consignment to a considerable amount. From this letter, it appears that they had previously consigned their goods to a 'native firm'.[65] Mr Prinsep was only partially successful, the Court of Directors resolving

> that the request of Mr. G.A.Prinsep to be granted free merchants indentures be not complied with, but that as he had produced proof that he is invited by several respectable persons to take charge of an Agency concern at Bombay, he is permitted to proceed thither for that purpose upon the usual terms and conditions.[104]

By an Act of 1813, Parliament had opened the trade to India, but the Honourable East India Company still held a position of power. It was not until 1858 that they relinquished the Government of India, and until then they continued to regard the sub-continent as their private empire. Outside merchants could not have found them among the easiest of the people with whom they had to deal. An extract from their Directors' Minutes of the 30th October 1822 indicates how summary, and no doubt inconvenient, their decisions could be: 'Messrs Spode and Copeland request freight for Calcutta for lustres for the use of the Mission Church there. The request was not granted'.[105]

Shaw records an order which should have given great satisfaction to Spode II and the Potteries generally—a service manufactured for the East India Company's station at Canton:

> In July, the same year [1823], Mr. Spode completed for the Hon. East India Company's Factory at Canton, a most splendid Table Service of Porcelain, of thirteen hundred pieces, valued at £400 to replace the Service destroyed by the Fire. The Porcelain was of the finest body made at the manufactory, alike distinguished for its beautiful Parian whiteness, and delicate transparency. The larger articles are perfect in the manufacture, and prove that perseverence has overcome the difficulties formerly regarded as insurmountable in producing large specimens

F

of the best Porcelain. The first style of embellishment has not been employed, but a second grade; yet the appearance is rich and splendid, and equal to any specimens of Dresden Porcelain.[257]

This must be the unlikeliest order in the whole history of ceramics. That the world's largest trafficker in Chinese porcelain should come to Staffordshire when it required ware for Canton is almost incredible. Shaw goes on to ask 'would it have been believed thirty years ago, that China would receive again specimens of her chief manufacture, from England?' and we may well ask if it would be believed one hundred and forty years later. Happily, Shaw's account is strictly accurate. The fire which destroyed the Company's premises in Canton took place in November 1822, and in April 1823 permission was given in London for them to be rebuilt and refurnished.[106] On the 18th September 1824, a payment of £476.15s.6d. was made to Messrs Spode and Copeland for porcelain under the heading of 'Factory Stores and Petty Merchandise'.[107]

Plate 164 illustrates a dinner plate, the centre of which is filled by the full coat of arms of the East India Company. It is likely that this plate is identical with those supplied for Canton. If by 'a second grade' of embellishment Shaw meant the absence of a ground colour, then this plate fits his description. It was not made for Canton, however, for on the back it has the printed device 'The London' in a scroll. The London was one of the East India Company's ships, and she made eight voyages to the East between 1819 and 1832. It is possible that she was the ship which took the Spode service to Canton since she left England in March 1824 for China, via St Helena and Bombay, returning in September 1825.[108] It is not unlikely that her captain, John Barnet Sotherby, took the opportunity to order an additional service for his ship while the main one was being produced. East India Company captains had an envied reputation for gracious living.

An indication of the scale of Spode II's trade with India is the fact that it is still possible to collect antique Spode there. It would be naive to imagine that the famous Indian Sporting Pattern (Plate 94) was produced specifically with this market in mind, since large quantities of it have survived in England, but it was certainly popular there. No doubt, Europeans in India displayed the same predilection for ware decorated with scenes of their favourite pastimes as did their relatives at home for the more familiar fox-hunting. I know of one collection of this pattern which has been formed by occasional purchases in various parts of India; and at least one Indian Regiment, the Madras Artillery, selected the border of the pattern for its mess service (Plate 300). No records have survived at the Factory of individual Spode services of this kind; but the records of the early Copeland Period reveal an enormous business in crested military services, a very large number of which were for regiments in the Indian Army.

It is likely that this class of business was enjoyed by Spode II as well as his successors.

A most interesting piece of evidence that Spode II's wares were not purchased solely by the British in India is provided by the supply of an extremely elegant china service to the King of Oudh. The decoration incorporates an interesting crest of a katar, a dagger of Mahratta origin, with fish supporters. Years later, in October 1842, the Factory manufactured a set of tiles for the king.[100] His kingdom was one of the main centres of the Indian Mutiny, in which the king himself played a prominent part—on the losing side. After the siege of Lucknow, his capital, his treasure and apparently even his tableware were seized. The 9th Lancers, who were present on the occasion,[66] still have one of his ice pails, illustrated in Plate 162; and four small pieces from this service are in the collection of R. Spencer Copeland, which also contains another remnant of what may have been a fine set produced for the East—a beautifully painted cup with the portrait and coat of arms of Futteh Ali Shah, King of Persia from 1798 to 1834 (Plates 159 and 160).

In 1846, the *Art-Union* magazine justified the detail and space devoted to the Copeland and Garrett factory as follows: 'not only because of the importance of the subject, but because the kingdom, our Colonial dependencies, and nearly all the Continental markets are extensively supplied from this establishment'.[127] By this date, Englishmen had learned not to refer to the United States of America as a colonial dependency, and its omission from this brief description of the Factory's export markets is significant. Since the eighteenth century, the American market had been of the greatest importance to Staffordshire. Some factories catered for it exclusively, devoting their entire production to satisfying its needs; but there is no evidence that Spode II ever had any particular involvement there. Collectors have searched in vain for antique Spode pieces decorated with specifically American subjects.

It is more likely that Spode II traded with Canada. Certainly this later became a very important market for the Factory. For at least twelve years following 1842, Copeland and Garrett enjoyed a monopoly as suppliers of tableware to the Hudson's Bay Company.[67] Excavations at Fort Vancouver produced shards of no less than thirty-three different patterns dating from the Copeland and Garrett and Copeland Periods but not a single piece which it was possible to identify as the manufacture of Spode II. This may, however, reflect only the fact that the Fort was not constructed until 1825.[68]

That the New World was not entirely neglected during the earlier period is shown by an entry in one of the Factory colour books for a colour for printing 'the Mexican Arms tableware', ordered via London in June 1830.[100] Plate 80 illustrates a piece of about this date which bears the arms of another South

American state or, rather, confederation of states: the Confederation of Colombia.[69] In 1831, this dissolved into the three sovereign states of Colombia, Ecuador and Venezuela. It would have been strange if private individuals, as well as governments, in this part of the world did not supply business. I have been informed by an Argentinian gentleman that large Spode services feature not uncommonly in country house sales in his country.

The mention in the 1846 *Art-Union* article of Europe as an important export market for the Factory is confirmed by Jewitt, who refers specifically to the sale of Spode's 'ironstone china' to 'France and other countries'.[207] This could not have been until after the end of the Napoleonic wars. Until then, Russia was the most important and practically the only European market open to English merchants. A Spode handbook of 1817 lists eight sizes, ranging from one pint to six quarts, of 'sauce pans for the Emperor of Russia'.[56] One remarkably fine Spode service, part of which is illustrated in Plate 271, fell prey to the fortunes of war on its journey to Russia in about 1814. Happily, it met with an honourable fate, becoming one of the most treasured possessions of a Norwegian lady, Henrietta Rosenkilde, whose family has lovingly preserved it ever since. Her daughter recorded its story, which she had often heard her mother tell:

> Of the [Russian] Consul General's gift of a tea service to my mother I think I will write a few words, as it may be of interest to future generations of her family, who may be interested to know about it.
>
> I know only too well that one should not pay too much attention to earthly goods but I cannot resist writing these few lines about this treasure which was in my parent's home and treated as a special family heirloom. It lived in a corner cabinet in the drawing room and was only brought out on very special occasions . . .
>
> My mother's story of this tea service goes as follows: It was ordered for the Court at St. Petersburg but the ship was captured during this time of war and brought into Christiansand where the contents were sold. Consul General Brunett bought the tea service and gave it to my mother as I have said above. My mother was then engaged and soon to be married to my father, Jens Edward Kraft.[70]

By 1827, when Spode II died, his business was a formidable size. Although the London partnership produced a greater total profit than the Factory at Stoke, their respective valuations at this date were not wide apart:

Stoke potworks:	£15,000	London Premises	£8,000
Stock & Utensils:	£29,874	Stock & Utensils	£25,300
	£44,874		£33,300

London stock was valued at the wholesale selling price less 20 per cent, but finished stock at the Factory was valued at selling price less 50 per cent. In comparing the two stock figures, it must be remembered that stocks of finished goods in London would have been much greater than those at Stoke, where the largest portion of the value was taken up by raw materials, moulds, equipment, etc.[100]

In 1829, William Taylor Copeland estimated that the half share of profits owing to the estate of Spode II from the London business for the sixteen and a half months from 1st March 1826, until his death on 16th July 1827, was about £6,000. This was the time when Wedgwood, after sixty-three years of direct representation in the capital, were closing down their London premises— presumably because they could no longer make the enterprise pay.[71] In 1831, the total London profits were £11,501 and, in the same year, the Spode interest made a profit estimated at £8,000 from the Factory and its rents. The rents can be assessed at about £1,500: so in this year, total profits from sales of ware appear as about £18,000, divided between London and the Factory in the ratio of two to one. The substantial profit made at Stoke came from the large home trade conducted from the Factory itself. Spode and Copeland, at Portugal Street, handled the export markets and outlets within the capital; but the rest of Britain dealt directly with the Factory, a geographically more convenient arrangement in most cases. The division does not seem to have been absolutely rigid. Portugal Street had some customers 'in the country', and at least two foreign agents—one in Osnabrück and another in Amsterdam—dealt directly with Stoke.[100] On 1st March 1833, a sum of £6,834.14s.7½d. was outstanding to the Factory for goods supplied to two hundred and one different retailers and private individuals throughout the length and breadth of Britain. For the day, the sums of money involved were huge; and some estimate can be made of the scale of the business implied by stock and profit figures of this size by the fact that in the year 1841 to 1842 the total value of all the goods sold by Mintons— at that time the Spode Factory's most formidable rival—was £45,654.5s.1d.[72]

When Spode II died in 1827, he was buried by the church which he had played such an active part in rebuilding. He had been senior church warden and donated £500 to it. Within the very cornerstones were commemorative slabs manufactured by him.[233] He was not neglected by the obituarists and his virtues did not go unrecorded. References to his generosity are not to be dismissed as the usual fulsome outpourings. Even the critical Ward noted that 'he was the liberal rewarder of their [his servants] integrity, merit and industry'.[284] In his will, he left £100 each to his housekeeper and six of his office staff, and £50 each to another four.[100] This was a modest sum in relation to his fortune, but it was probably equivalent to a year's salary for each of them and was a gesture no more typical then than it would be now. A contemporary account is given the ring of truth by being circumstantial:

> His gardens were splendid, and amongst several houses of the same kind was one
> grapery, the produce of which was devoted to the sick poor, and not a bunch would
> he allow to be gathered from thence for any other purpose. A cart loaded with
> vegetables went round twice a week amongst his dependants, from which they
> who were most in need were supplied.[61]

Although he may not have been the greatest public benefactor the Potteries
had seen and could hardly have accumulated his vast fortune solely through
charity and kindness there is no reason to think of him as the heartless proprietor of a dark, satanic mill. In the first years of the century, the conditions of
pottery workers and their relationship with their employers were probably
better than they were later to become. In making princely provision for the
members of his own family, it is to his credit that he did not overlook others
altogether.

Josiah Spode III and his elder brother, William, were the main beneficiaries
from the will of their father and were also its executors. After the estate had
provided more than £112,000 for various other legacies, the value which
remained for equal division between the two of them was in excess of £210,000.
The Factory, the partnership with W.T.Copeland, and the Mount—his father's
great house—all fell to the lot of Spode III, who was no stranger to the business:

> At an early period of his existence, he was removed to the residence of his paternal
> grandfather, at Stoke Upon Trent, Staffordshire; and he was educated at the Free
> Grammar School,[73] Newcastle-Under-Lyme, in the same county. As soon as his
> youth permitted, he was initiated in the business of a potter, under his grandfather,
> and he continued engaged in it till about the year 1810, when he retired to the more
> quiet pursuit of agriculture, on his estate at Fenton, near Stoke.... In consequence
> of the sickness which ultimately proved fatal to his father, Mr. Spode returned to
> the business, and remained in it till his demise.[141]

The date given for his retirement from the Factory is a few years too early,
since he did not acquire his estate at Great Fenton, a gift from his father, until
shortly before his marriage to Mary Williamson in April 1815 (see Appendix I).
His period of control of the family business was to last a mere two years. In
October 1829, Simeon Shaw rushed to the printers to insert in his *History of the
Staffordshire Potteries*, then being type-set, the sad news that the man to whom
it was dedicated was dead.[258] He had died suddenly, at the Mount, on the sixth
of the month. Two days before, he had returned from a trip to London in his
usual good health; but he was seized with apoplexy and died within three
hours.[139]

The Spode dynasty was not yet extinct. There was a Josiah Spode IV, only
child of his father; but in 1829 he was only five years old. Had Spode III, like

his father and grandfather, married young, instead of at the age of thirty-eight, the subsequent history of the firm might have been entirely different. Spode IV was never to come into the business. He was, indeed, taken out of the district by his mother before he even reached manhood. For three and a half years following the death of Spode III, the responsibility for the Factory fell on his two trustees, Hugh Henshall Williamson and Thomas Fenton.

Hugh Henshall Williamson was brother-in-law to Spode III and described by him as his 'good friend'. A man of wealth, in 1834 he became High Sheriff of Staffordshire. His income derived from his extensive lands and interests as a coal master in Tunstall, three miles north-east of which lay his mansion and country seat, Greenway Bank.[278]

Thomas Fenton, a lawyer, had married Spode III's aunt, Ann. Their home was Stoke Lodge, a building of some historic interest, less than a mile from the Factory and the Mount. A member of one of the most ancient families in the district, Thomas Fenton could claim descent from William de Fenton, Constable of Newcastle in 1255. In 1837, he was appointed Steward of the Manor to this ancient borough, 'a post of great professional importance and emolument', and by 1843 he was also Town Clerk of Newcastle.[280] His interest in local history proved useful to Simeon Shaw.[236]

On Monday 18th October 1829, the Factory, which had been closed on account of Spode III's death, was re-opened 'to the great joy of the work people'. They, more than anyone, must have been glad to hear that the executors proposed 'carrying on the concern with spirit'.[140] Forty years later, however, one of W.T.Copeland's obituarists referred to the next phase in the Factory's history as one in which it 'languished in the hands of trustees'.[142] Although the profit figures quoted earlier make the comment seem unfair, it is likely that it was justified. The number of employees given for 1819 was eight hundred (see p. 60), but for 1833 it was seven hundred.[74] It would certainly seem unfortunate that neither of the trustees had any direct experience of pottery manufacture. In such circumstances, the presence of W.T.Copeland must have been frequently required in Stoke and increased reliance placed on the senior staff at the Factory.

Foremost among those whom Spode III had employed in a senior capacity was William Outrim who, perhaps more than any other man, was responsible for the actual running of the business from 1829 until the end of the Spode Period. He was at the Factory before 1813 and became the right-hand-man of Spode II, then Spode III, and finally the new partners, Copeland and Garrett, who entrusted him with the most confidential matters and treated him with the greatest respect—more as a colleague than a servant. Since both of them spent most of their time in London, they were fortunate in having a man of such experience and integrity permanently on the spot at Stoke. We should probably call him a company secretary today, but a contemporary description was 'man of affairs'. He drew no distinction between his service to the Factory and to the Spode family. With equal efficiency, he called in debts from tardy retailers and the tenants of Mary Spode, Spode III's widow. He ordered the Factory's supplies and her footmen's buttons; settled disputes with workers and her differences with local tradesmen. For such personal services above and beyond the call of duty, he was rewarded on at least one occasion with a pair of pig puddings sent down to him at the Factory from the Mount.[100]

On 1st March 1833, W.T.Copeland purchased the London premises and the half share of the business there still belonging to the executors of Spode III. At the same time, he acquired the whole of the manufacturing establishment at Stoke. The cost was heavy: £13,491 for the Factory and its adjacent land and £30,387.19s.5d. for its stocks of materials, finished and part-finished goods, utensils and implements. This total of nearly £44,000 compares with the value of £5,000 which, in his will,[100] thirty-six years before, Spode I had placed on his works, their contents, the adjoining Meadow with its mill, and his house. His son's house, the Mount, was not included in the sale—which may have been just as well for Copeland since it had been valued at £10,258 in 1827, excluding its contents. As it was, other large sums of money needed to be found. In addition to the Factory, there was £8,000 for the London premises and £13,500 for the Spode half of the stock-in-trade there. He also paid £8,950 for the Spode share of Fenton Park Colliery—which had grown to one half of the whole—and £11,000 for one hundred and eighty-nine houses in Stoke which had been built by Spode II and were largely inhabited by the Factory's workers. An enormous accumulated debt of £50,228.19s.10d. for goods supplied from Stoke to London remained, and it was arranged that this would be cleared over a period of five years with interest at 4 per cent.[100]

With Thomas Garrett, his new partner but old colleague, William Taylor Copeland, son of Spode II's former 'confidential servant', launched the Factory on the next phase in its career.

First procefs of potting is "Throwing," forming round pieces of ware with the Hands and Machine.

The Turner turning in a lathe and regulating the clay ware which the "thrower" has formed.

6 Pattern books and numbers

With mathematic marks each piece is grac'd
But speak the number soon they find your taste.

The factory poet thus sums up well the benefit of a pattern numbering system. For speedy reference and the avoidance of mistakes in ordering and manufacture, such a system is essential for potter and retailer alike. The one adopted at the Spode Factory was the simplest: it started at No.1 and just continued. In about 1822, the need was felt to introduce a secondary system, for underglaze decorations, and this also started at No.1 but 'B' was used as a prefix. In 1852, Spode II's successors reached No.10,000 in the main pattern series and recommenced with No.1, using the prefix 'D'. It was not until 1874, when another 10,000 numbers had been consumed, that separate prefixes for china (1/) and earthenware (2/) were introduced. It is regrettable that in the Spode Period it was never thought worthwhile to make such a differentiation, especially since the Spode pattern books never contain an entry indicating the type of body used. A very large number of patterns, however, were used for more than one body and the regret is a minor one compared with the fact that the books, well preserved, have survived.

To the manufacturer, the number of the pattern is the essential mark of identification on a piece—more important than his own name. For this reason, many Spode pieces, particularly early ones, are found with the number as the only mark of provenance. On the whole, Spode II was a 'good marker'. A majority of Spode pieces are marked either with the name or the pattern number, very many with both. But one distinct category of wares will never be found with pattern numbers, since none were ever allocated. With underglaze blue-printed patterns, the existence of the copper engravings themselves acted as pattern records at the Factory and they were, relative to the thousands of enamelled patterns, too few in number to lead to errors in ordering by retailers. Prints in colours other than blue were frequently given pattern numbers; and pattern numbers were nearly always allocated to printed patterns of any kind if they had additional enamel or gold decoration, no matter how slight.

Another class of wares for which pattern numbers were naturally not allocated were those produced as matching pieces for services made by other potters—Chinese, Continental or English. Many examples of these are known, and they can be extremely confusing. I have never discovered a Spode piece marked with another manufacturer's number; but it is possible to discover, for instance, a cup just marked 'Spode' made to match a saucer from another manufacturer which is only marked with *his* pattern number and no name. This would lead to the obvious but incorrect inference that the pattern number is Spode's and both pieces were manufactured by him.

The category of wares where the absence of pattern numbers, and a consequent lack of a surviving record at the Spode Factory, is most to be regretted is that of special orders—often extremely fine, and for well known people. It is a sad fact that the more important and interesting the order completed by Spode II the less chance there is of finding it in his pattern books. They were there to fulfil a mundane need, and if they recorded triumphs it was only incidental. The recording of patterns which were going to be re-ordered by a number of people over a period of time was of prime importance; but expensive special commissions which tended to be, to use the Factory expression, 'one offs' could safely be neglected. If matchings were later required, samples of the original could be obtained.

Many orders of this type were, in any event, virtually impossible to record. Some of the water colour entries in the pattern books are fine works of art in themselves, obviously done by the artist responsible for the actual decoration; but many are of pedestrian quality, varying according to the skill of the man who had the job of keeping the records at a particular time. It could well have been beyond the powers of such a man to attempt a useful record of a service like the one illustrated in Plate 281, made for the Lubbock family and consisting of several hundred pieces, every item decorated with an original floral composition using two botanical studies, each of which was never repeated. The cost of letting him attempt such a task would certainly have been prohibitive; and since it was pointless to record the simple gold line which finished each piece, this service—one of the Factory's most remarkable achievements—is quite unnoted in its records. If the special order consisted of one or two elaborate pieces only, there was even less chance of it being recorded, since the manufacturer being called on to provide a matching piece at a later date was virtually out of the question. Examples of this are the extremely rich loving-cup illustrated in Plate 174, and the punch bowl, illustrated in Plate 171, made for the Dumfries Burns Society.[75]

It is puzzling to find a service as expensive as the one illustrated in Plate 271 without a single piece bearing its pattern number, 2352. It could have been one of the first services produced in the pattern, completed before the allocation of a number; but the obvious explanation for the absence of pattern numbers on many pieces is carelessness on the part of the enameller or gilder whose duty it was to apply them. If a piece had a gilt decoration, then the gilder, as the last operative to handle it, would probably have had the task of applying the number —a duty for which he may not have been paid extra. Both pattern numbers and the Spode name can, rarely, be found in gold, but this has no significance. The marks were normally applied in red enamel, or some other colour, and the gilders would have had a separate palette for this. Gold was not normally used, not only because it was a waste of precious metal but also because enamel could be applied more quickly.

When important pieces of Spode are discovered completely unmarked, the reason must be sought in the realm of policy. As late as 1845, Herbert Minton was afraid to put his name on his own wares for sale in London, fearing that the London retailers would object.₁₇₅ Spode II's possession of his own extensive premises in Portugal Street, and the fact that the Royal and aristocratic patronage he received made his name well known to the public and was a positive aid in selling his goods, explain why he never had a similar problem. He did, however, produce fine sets for Blades of London (Plate 185) and marked them only with their name and not his own.[16] It is feasible that some other valuable customers, although not wanting their own name on their purchases, preferred not to have Spode's, either. Completely unmarked pieces are frequently similar to Sèvres in shape and style of decoration and may have been sold as such. But not by Spode II. He appears to have been prepared to sell his wares unmarked or marked with his own or his customer's name, but not with that of another manufacturer. Some of his competitors did not share such scruples.

Nearly five and a half thousand patterns were introduced during a period of not much more than thirty years. It is a formidable total, but the number of original designs is very much smaller than it suggests. Some patterns, in one form or another, occur again and again, often over a long period of time. A certain gilt border might prove popular, in which case it would spring to mind for use with a ground colour background if such a pattern were required. If this proved successful, other colours would be tried. Once given a theme, permutations were endless: any combination of centres and borders could be tried. If one proved too expensive, it could be 'slighted'—that is, made simpler and quicker to execute; if the market went the other way, it could be 'made fuller' or more 'highly finished'. The practice was even more prevalent in the field of print and enamel decoration. A design which proved successful was usually the subject of continuous experiment, extending over the full range of bodies made at the Factory. It could be adapted and altered to increase or reduce the price, or just to provide something new. By using engravings already in existence, considerable expense was spared; and it might always be hoped that the existing popularity of one version would pave the way for that of another. Potters played with loaded dice, if they could.

Some of the patterns which continued to sell over a long period became old friends to retailers and factory hands alike—and friends should be known by a name, not a number. Almost none of these names appears in the Spode pattern books, but many have survived in the Factory by word of mouth, the patterns having continued in some form or other to within living memory or even to the present. Almost invariably, these names are truly descriptive. Some, like Tower and Peacock, are obviously so, relating to the most conspicuous features in the patterns themselves. Others, like Tumbledown Dick, Frog, and Cabbage, seem at first sight obscure in their origin. But in the first, the bird *does* look as though it is tumbling off its twig (Plate 117); in the second, part of the border *does* resemble a spreadeagled frog (Colour Plate IX); and in the last, if you have never seen whatever outlandish Oriental leaf is meant to be depicted, then a cabbage is a good enough guess (Plate 285).

Until quite recently, patterns were regarded by their makers as roses which would smell as sweet with any name and their christenings were casual, unpremeditated affairs. Today, they are studied occasions, as like as not with representatives of the advertising and marketing worlds present to act as godparents. Not so many years ago, a very expensive modern Spode china service with a classic Greek key border decoration was prominently displayed in an exclusive London shop with its name—'Jam Tart'. This was the name sadly chosen as the lesser of two evils by the shop's buyer. When he had enquired for one, feeling that to use a pattern number in his display was too impersonal, he had been given the alternative of 'Stop and Go' or the one he finally selected. The origin of the first name is self-evident—a Greek key border does stop and go. But that of the second is to be found in the Potteries expression 'a piece of jam tart', meaning easy work: 'a piece of cake'. So it was, for the gold printers who produced it. The pattern has since had no less than two rather pretentious titles bestowed upon it, both of which are, to this day, doggedly ignored by the older generation of Spode craftsmen.

More than one copy of the pattern books was needed. From the excellence of their condition, the surviving ones must have been master copies kept as a company record, possibly by the master himself. At least one other copy was necessary, for use in the decorating department. This would have been in the charge of the head of enamelling—Henry Daniel before 1822. Three times in the books the instruction occurs to 'refer to Mr Daniel's book' for details. His copy would have been much more detailed, with added information on colours and, possibly, particulars of painters and gilders. A few tattered remnants of one of these early working copies survives, almost thumbed out of existence. Virtually the only decipherable sheet left is the one with a Sherwin centre, referred to in Chapter IV. A working copy of patterns between Numbers 4530

and 5374 remains which is in good condition, but it gives no names for decorators. Other copies would no doubt have been useful to the London sales staff
and the company's commercial travellers, but the only survival which might
have been designed for this purpose is a small pocket book containing a handful
of inexpensive 'B' patterns annotated with prices.

It is only to be expected that the need for a pattern numbering system and
record should make itself felt before being introduced. The solution would
naturally follow the problem, and the first entries in the pattern books have all
the signs of an uncertain start. The books begin with Number 133, and it is
tempting to suppose that the sheets are missing for the previous one hundred
and thirty-two. But one wonders if this is really so on later discovering four
entries, all on the same page, numbered in sequence 147, 159, 218, 241 (Plate
106). Seven similar but lesser sins of omission occur before Number 307. The
likeliest explanation is that the pattern numbering system was introduced
before the pattern book itself. This would mean that the very early Spode
numbers could have been introduced well before the date 1799 indicated by
their watermarks. The first custodian of the book would have had the initial
task of wandering round the decorating department collecting recollections,
scraps of paper and private records. The departure from the Factory of a
decorator before he yielded the information on his patterns would account for
all the gaps among the numbers. A certain interval would naturally occur
between a pattern seeing life for the first time and being recorded. Even much
later, Patterns 3200 and 3201 have no illustration, just the note 'our people have
lost all knowledge of this No.'. These are isolated instances, however, for by
Pattern 307 the system was working well. Missing entries continue—but only
twenty in the following three hundred numbers, and twenty in the five hundred
following those.

The question of the date of a particular Spode piece must always be of the
greatest interest. A date sequence for Spode pattern numbers can only reveal
the time of their introduction, but the span of life following this was frequently
very short. Some patterns, like 967 and 1166, lived on for decades; but these
were the exception and, with an average birth-rate of more than three new
patterns a week during the Spode Period, the infant mortality rate must have
been high. The fact that watermarked dates appear on many of the pages in the
Spode pattern books is a piece of good fortune: but too much can be made of it,
since watermarks can only date one way. But this they do without question: a
piece of paper can be used at any time after its manufacture, but certainly not
before. Any examination of the dating of Spode's patterns must begin with
these watermarks. All that it is safe to conclude from them can be summarised
as follows:[76]

Pattern 564 and before—earliest possible entry 1799
      565 to 1056   1804
     1057 to 3692   1806
     3693 to 4167   1822
     4168 to 4517   1825
     4518 to 5057   1827
     5058 to 5446   1831
     5447 to 5766   1833
     5767 and after   1836

Fortunately, there are some scattered pieces of evidence which enable this rather scant information to be supplemented.

It is strange that the newspaper report of the Prince of Wales' visit in 1806, given in Chapter III, makes no mention of any purchases from the man he had just appointed as his potter—particularly as he 'ordered several articles to be made for him' when he visited Wedgwood on the same day; and when he was at Davenport, the day following, ordered 'Services of the finest and most valuable kinds' as well as ornamental wares for which he 'gave orders for a collection of the most beautiful and high finished Specimens'.[35] Probably because it was a special commission—and therefore, as remarked earlier, had little chance of being recorded—it has proved impossible to trace the Sherwin pattern 'from which the Prince of Wales' order rose'. The visit did leave its mark in the pattern books, however, in the form of the extremely rich and expensive pattern, 1112, which is illustrated in Plate 156. This could well have been made just for the Prince, and no pieces have yet been discovered. Very close by are Patterns 1168 and 1185. These are rare, and the only pieces I have seen are the sandwich set in Number 1168 illustrated in Plate 155 and a square tray and plate in Number 1185, the former illustrated in Plate 157. Together, these pieces provide the only examples known to me of the Spode Prince of Wales mark (Mark 17: Appendix IV). This mark is so seldom encountered that it must either have been a five-minute wonder, started in the enthusiasm of the moment and soon abandoned, or, less likely, reserved for ware produced for the Prince. It seems safe to place the introduction of these three patterns as immediately after his visit in September 1806. This dating is a particularly satisfying one since, fortuitously, it embraces the famous 1166 (Colour Plate VIII and Plate 221).

Nine of the patterns between Numbers 1691 and 1703 are of the same type: gold prints from coppers engraved for bat printing. They were manufactured by a process which was patented by Peter Warburton. The patterns themselves and Spode's use of the process are discussed on page 184, and it is reasonable to date their introduction to after the patent was taken out in February 1810.

In one of Henry Daniel's colour books is a recipe for a colour 'for printing convolvulus border in Number 2111'. This is the seventh entry following one dated the 16th August 1812, so the introduction of this pattern can be taken as after this date. In another book, he entered a 'French blue used to pattern 2809'. Since this entry occurs after one dated May 1817 and before another dated 1819, its introduction is neatly bracketed between the two dates.

A Spode price scale book$_{100}$ contains a list of pattern numbers in two groups. The first group is headed 30th April 1822. Beginning with Pattern 3759, it continues up to 3793, when the date October 1822 appears. This is followed by the numbers from 3794 to 3828. These lists virtually pinpoint the introduction of the patterns and are of particular interest in view of the departure of Henry Daniel in August 1822.

These pieces of evidence make a useful supplement to the watermarks in giving dates after which certain patterns must have been introduced. But evidence of the existence of a particular pattern before a certain date is equally valuable. One of Henry Daniel's colour books$_{101}$ provides it for Pattern 648, with a recipe for a yellow-green colour to be used for it. Since the entry precedes one dated November 1805, the pattern will have been introduced before that date.

On 22nd August 1810, a report was sent to Wedgwood at Etruria:

> Mr. Spode has got up a pattern which is meant to have an effect similar to the Chrysanthemum No. 5 or 6 the colours and ground are exactly the same, but instead of the Chrysanthemum he has introduced a sort of fleur de lis and opposite it on the other side of the plate is something, like a tulip, also two Oak branches crossed, and placed opposite each other the leaves of which are broad, in deep blue under the glaze and traced in gold, in the same way as the branch in the Chrysanthemum, and in the centre of the plate is a scalloped shell circular about the size of a shilling; the next set I meet with I will be more particular, and if I can I will either send you a pattern or a sketch.$_{109}$

The description, despite a small error, is so detailed that there is no mistaking the pattern. It was an extremely popular one which appeared in at least thirteen versions over a period of time. The first version which can be traced in Spode's pattern book is Number 1690, and this also fits the description in the report of the decorative treatment. The pattern is illustrated in Plate 116.

Excellent evidence that a pattern has been introduced before a certain time is its presence in a dated invoice. Among the Spode archives is a transcript, made by some blessed but anonymous soul, of a bill to Stephen Tempest, Esq, for a good quantity of teaware in Pattern 1922. This is dated July 1813 and is given in full in Appendix III.

VII China: Footed beaker. Height, 6¼in. Mark 10. (*R.S.Copeland Esq.*)

One of Henry Daniel's colour books gives a recipe for a 'green for 2540, 2541, 2538, 2546 and dark side of 2544'. The compilation of this particular book can be dated at before 5th September 1816, since this date appears among annotations made in it, in a different hand and ink, after its completion.

Details given on Page 196 demonstrate that Pattern 3248 was in existence by July 1821; and two dated entries in one of the Spode Factory colour books show that Pattern 4003 was in existence before 26th October 1824, and Pattern 4699 before June 1830.

It would be good to know the very last pattern introduced before Copeland and Garrett took over from Spode III's executors in March 1833, but an approximation will have to suffice. The highest pattern number I have seen on a Spode piece is Number 5109. The very highest will probably be two hundred more, since a Copeland and Garrett record of crested tableware orders has an entry which shows that Number 5349 had been introduced before July 1833.

If this varied evidence is assembled, it is possible to get a clear picture of the sequence of the pattern introductions by date. This is provided overleaf in what is hoped will prove a convenient dating chart. It is remarkable that there was so much constancy in the tempo of the introduction of new patterns during the period. The absence of any marked variation makes it possible to provide an easy formula for arriving at the approximate date for the introduction of any pattern, except perhaps the first few hundred. For those who like such things (and which collector does not?) it is as follows:

$$\frac{\text{pattern number}}{150} + 1800 = \frac{\text{approximate date of}}{\text{introduction of pattern}}$$

The second series of pattern numbers, the 'B' patterns, are of much less importance than the main body since they cover only a short, later period and there are fewer of them. They number nine hundred and forty-five in all, but less than half of these concern the Spode Period. All appear to share the common characteristic of being executed under the glaze, either by the print and enamel process or freehand. Most of the latter are painted in an extremely bold, quick fashion—aptly dubbed 'peasant style' by Reginald Haggar (Plates 127–129). The first thirteen entries in the 'B' pattern book are for patterns of this type, and they are prefixed 'C'. They present no problem. It is obvious that they have been fortuitously bound into the book at a later date. Not only is the paper, which is watermarked 1829, quite different from that which follows but also they are headed 'duplicate sheets'. They are of interest because they explain why, in 1852, the Factory went to 'D' for its next prefix. All of these 'C' numbers are in the same peasant style and all are illustrated by London Shape teacups.

Watermarks are more liberally scattered among the 'B' pattern numbers

Date of introduction of Spode patterns

Top continuous line indicates date before which and bottom
continuous line date after which the patterns specified must
have been introduced.
Dotted line indicates probable approximate date of introduction
of all patterns.

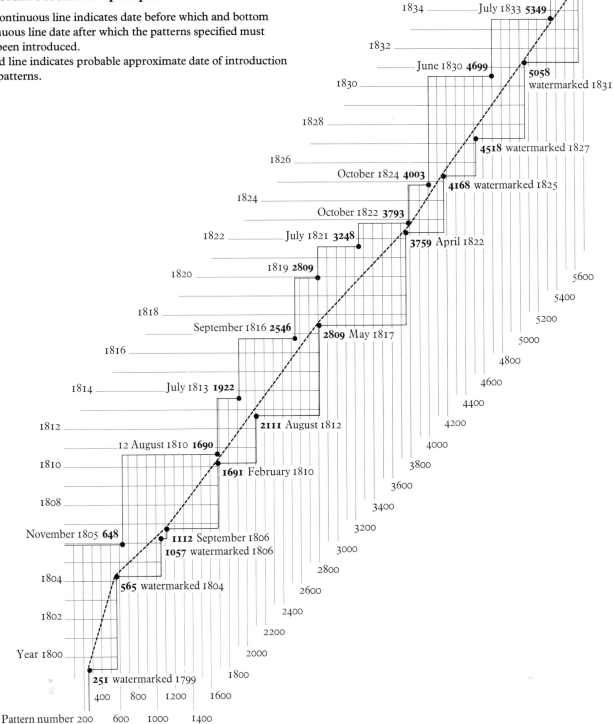

than in the other books, and they change more frequently. They appear, on average, at every tenth pattern and reveal the following:

Pattern B111 and before, earliest possible entry 1822
  B112–B160   1825
  B160–B285   1827
  B286–B387   1831
  B388–B458   1833
  B459–B597   1836
  B598–B768   1837
  B769–B945   1839

It would be excusable to guess that the 'B' series was started in late 1822 and was an example of a new broom—Henry Daniel having just left—sweeping clean.

An opportunity of improving on the estimated date sequence suggested by the watermarks is provided by relating patterns in the main books, the dates of which can be estimated, to 'B' Patterns which made use of the same copper engravings. Many 'B' number patterns are plain prints in colours other than blue, or are underglaze printed and enamelled. Certain of the patterns produced in blue prints were also widely used for enamelled versions, which were entered in both the normal pattern books and, when entirely underglaze, the 'B' pattern book. These variants could, of course, have been produced at any time subsequent to the Factory obtaining the necessary copper engravings; but a number of them appear in clusters, suggesting that as soon as a pattern achieved success as a blue print it was quickly tried out in various other ways. A good example is Camilla pattern (Plate 53). Of the ninety patterns between Numbers 5419 and 5508, no fewer than thirteen are different versions of Camilla or its border; and so are seven of the fifty patterns between B406 and B455. Any conclusion based on evidence of this kind cannot be beyond suspicion, but a close examination of seven such groupings common to the 'B' Pattern book and the main ones suggests the following:

    B100 was introduced in 1824
    B150   1828
    B250   1830
    B350   1832
    B400   1834.

7   Shapes

THE SPODE 1820 SHAPE BOOK

The bewildering diversity of shapes and sizes produced by potters in the early nineteenth century has been mentioned earlier. They are to be found at their most abundant in Spode II's china range. This could be anticipated, both as a corollary of the widespread popularity and large scale production of the ware and from its very nature—a luxury product, catering for the whims and fancies of the prosperous classes rather than their necessities. Faced with such profusion, the prospect of producing an illustrated catalogue could well have dismayed the strongest, and no such publication has ever been discovered for any class of Spode's products. Spode collectors have therefore never been as fortunate in this respect as some others. As early as 1774, Wedgwood produced a quite detailed and beautifully illustrated catalogue of useful wares. A subsequent one, in 1817, contained illustrations drawn and engraved by no less an artist than William Blake.[214] Leeds produced their first catalogue in 1783, following it in later years with three enlarged editions.[270] Even a relatively small firm like Whitehead, now utterly obscure, managed an ambitious production in 1798 with a text in four languages.[77]

Although Spode II apparently managed his sales promotion remarkably well without a printer's aid, some kind of comprehensive collection of shape illustrations was obviously desirable for internal use by the Factory and the firm's sales staff. Such a record remained unknown until 1967, when Geoffrey Godden identified an illustrated transcript of a throwers' and turners' handbook in the Joseph Downes Manuscript Collection at the Henry Francis du Pont Winterhur Museum in America. Similar handbooks have been in the Spode archives for years, but they are very incomplete in their detail and sparsely illustrated compared with this one. By a remarkable coincidence, the original of the book was found a few months later in an old, locked safe at the Spode Factory. Written boldly on the first page is 'Josiah Spode 1820', although some of the entries it contains bear the date 1821. Both the American and the Factory copy are written and sketched by the same hand: every item follows in the same sequence in one as the other. Even blank pages and mistakes correspond. That one is such an exact copy of the other indicates both were designed as reference books, keyed together for use in different places. It is a reasonable assumption that the copy now in America was formerly in use at Spode's London warehouse, notwithstanding the technical details it contains which would have been superfluous

to the sales staff there. A sample entry from the book, showing these, is reproduced here:

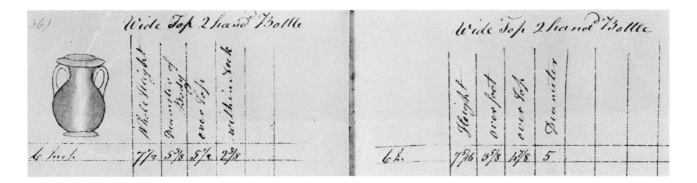

The measurements on the left are the dimensions to which the thrower
needed to work; those on the right, naturally less, are the turner's. Contraction
in the biscuit fire would reduce the piece to the 'trade size', given in the far
left-hand column. This is the only size of interest to the collector of today—or
the consumer of the time. Unfortunately, it is not always given in the book. It
was always an approximation. The item shown above, for example, which is
illustrated in Plate 278, measures six and a quarter inches, not six. It is puzzling
to find in the book variations in the dimensions for the clay size and finished size
of up to one quarter, indicating an excessive contraction in the fire. China
contractions today are roughly estimated as a sixth in height and a seventh in
breadth.

Contemporary illustrations[53] of the two trades involved are reproduced on
page 79. In 1846, William Evans wrote an excellent description:

'At a strong bench or table, near the throwing wheel, is a baller, (usually a young
woman) with a large lump of the clay before her. This manipulation of balling is
performed thus:—with a brass wire a piece of clay is cut off the lump, and with
all possible force by the person slapped down again on the mass; this laborious
work she repeats, by cutting in different directions, until the intersected part
presents a smooth homogeneous surface, without any appearance of air bubbles;
because, were one of these left therein, its expansion, during baking, would spoil
the article. She then cuts off a small lump, with thin brass wire, and weighs it,
when the body is valuable and the vessels must be of a definite size; next she
squeezes it well together, and forms it into a ball, which she hands to the thrower
as he requires a supply. The thrower sits on a low seat in the corner of the box
frame, with his feet on the sides of the disc or wheel head, and his arms resting on
his knees, keeping steady his hands while they modify the clay into any required
form. On the side of the frame he fixes in a lump of clay a peg, or stick, at that

distance from the centre which indicates the height and expansion of the vessels he must throw. Taking a ball of clay, on the wheel being in motion, he casts it very forcibly on the disc or head, and to expel any air bubbles, forms it into a conical pillar twice or thrice; then inserting his hand, or finger and thumb, with the other hand on the outside, he gives it the rude figure of the vessel; and with a wage or pattern (formed of earthenware, and well glazed) he smoothly finishes the inside, and then, with a brass wire, cuts it loose from the head. The baller then hands him another ball, and dexterously lifts the vessel off the disc, and places it on a board, on which it remains, (occasionally turned upside down) until it is sufficiently dry to bear, without injury, the manipulations of turning and handling.

The turner's lathe resembles that employed by mechanics, only the spindle is longer, and some of them have a collar, moveable by a catch, for the particular manipulation called engine turning. On the end of the spindle, outside the head-stock, is a screw, for the several chucks required by vessels of different sizes. A pulley with three grooves of varied sizes is also on the spindle, on which is the cord passed round the wheel, which is fixed on a crank shaft. Connected with this crank is a treadle; and beside the frame which holds the spindle, stands the treader, usually a young woman, who, by a motion of one foot, keeps up the velocity required, and can perform some manipulations requisite, without the attention of the turner being distracted from the vessel before him. Near the treader is a board, on which are vessels to be turned, which she severally hands to the turner, as he requires a supply. Standing in front of his chuck, he fixes his vessel on it by a slight pressure with his tool, as the spindle has retrograde motion; then the proper motion being communicated, with a tool of soft iron, properly sharpened by filing, he takes off the superfluous quantity, and then the treader catches hold of the cord, and gives the spindle retrograde motion, during which the turner lays a broad tool on the vessel, and gives a certain polish to the outside; after which he applies a sharp tool to cut it loose, and then he places it on the board before him, for the handler if requisite, or to dry for being baked biscuit.[165]

Throughout the Spode period, and for long after, virtually all holloware pieces, including cups, were 'thrown and turned'. The thrower's craft is the best known and amongst the most elemental of all methods of forming clay. The multitude of items, even in the largest factories, which began life on a thrower's wheel is one reason why it is impossible to regard them as purely industrial products.

Both trades were recognised as very skilled and were well paid, the throwers being the more highly rated of the two. On 30th September 1820, Spode II informed Josiah Wedgwood Junior that 'the best hands, our Turners have 4s. per day and the throwers 5s. per day and if we are busy are allowed to work over hours'.[120] In 1825, Henry Daniel hired Jesse Hill as a turner at a wage of 27s. a week.[101] Wages improved only slightly as the century wore on, and in 1891 throwers stated their wages at 40s. a week, turners at 33s. By this date, the two trades were already under heavy pressure—particularly throwing and it was claimed that 75 per cent of the articles formerly made by throwers were being either pressed or jiggered, leaving them only the larger pieces.[78] Throwing is now all but extinct in commercial potting. Even the large articles, which throwers retained for themselves until thirty or forty years ago, are now usually made by the slip cast process. The turners have survived better, since no process has ever been devised which can impart to an article the crispness of finish that theirs can.

The 1820 shape book deals exclusively with china; but since far more items were made in this than any other body, and Spode's earthenware and stone china largely followed the same models as those in china, a fairly wide picture of the Factory's shapes appear. This is, of course, limited to those which were made by the thrown-and-turned process. For this reason, plates, dishes, comports, and many fancy shapes which are not round are notable omissions. Many pieces in the last category did, however, contain some part in their make-up which was indebted to the two trades. This explains the surprising presence in the book of items like the Dolphin Tripod, Shape 99. But there are a number of other items whose appearance is a mystery, since they contain no feature which relates to the process. Notable among them is the Old Oval Teapot and Sugar, Shape 241.

The sketches have been arranged in groups, by type of item—a convenience which the original book lacks. Devoid of their accompanying technical dimensions but, in the index provided with the illustrations, given their names as used in the Factory at the time, they are now published for the first time. But with a word of warning: they cannot be regarded as providing a completely comprehensive assembly of Spode thrown and turned china shapes. Obviously, many appeared in the thirteen years of the Spode Period which elapsed after 1820. Some earlier shapes would have been abandoned by that date. It is also evident that not every variant of an existing shape and all the many specially commissioned pieces were included.

In examining them with a critical eye, it must be remembered that these sketches were never meant for publication, being designed solely for domestic reference and identification. But they will be found surprisingly accurate in detail of line, if not proportion, as could be anticipated from their purpose. They are not to scale, and the numbers have been supplied to them purely for convenience and do not indicate the sequence of their appearance in the book or provide any guide to date.

The Spode 1820 shape book

Icepails, wine coolers, punch bowls

Shape number 1   Porous Shape, Antique Double Icepail. *One size*

2   New Shape, Beaded, Antique Double Icepail. *Two sizes. 'made for London Feb. 1820'*

3   Flanged Top, Antique Double Icepail. *One size (Colour Plate I and Plate 193)*

4   Derby Shape Icepail. *One size*

5   Jar Shape Icepail. *One size*

6   Single Icepail. *4in. within top. 'made for London Jan. 1819'*

7   Dresden Shape Icepail. *One size*

8   Upright Double Icepail. *Two sizes*

9   Lady Stafford's Shape Icepail. *One size (Plates 162 and 202)*

10   Basket Rim Icepail. *One size*

11   Flower Embossed Icepail. *One size*

12   Embossed, Antique Wine Cooler. *One size. 'made for Wordley & Co.'*

13   Gadroon Wine Cooler. *9in.*

14   Flanged Top Punch Bowl. *One size, three gallons or 18in. diam. 'made for Wordley & Co. Nov. 15th 1819' (Plate 171)*

15   Punch Bowl. *10 sizes, the largest eight quarts (Plate 284)*

Gardenpots and stands

16   French Shape. *3 sizes (Plates 186 and 187)*

17   New Shape. *3 sizes (Plate 186)*

18   Cottage Shape. *3 sizes*

19   Gardenpot on Three Claws. *3in. and 4in. high*

Jars and Vases

20   Two-Handled Jar

21   Pierced, Covered, Pedestal Antique Jar. *6in. and 7in. (Colour Plate VIII)*

22   Beaker Top, Grecian Shape, Pierced Covered Jar. *5, 6 and 7in. (Colour Plate VIII)*

23   Beaded, Pierced Covered, Rams Head Handled, Antique Jar. *4, 5 and 6in.*

24   Beaded, Dresden Shape Jar. *9 sizes, 4in. to 16in. (Plate 222)*

25   Beaded, Two-Handled, Covered Vase on Pedestal. *6 sizes, 4in. to 9in.*

26   Beaded, Parisian Shape Jar. *5, 6, 7 and 8 in. (Plate 222)*

27   Bell Top, Beaded, Square-Foot Jar. *6, 8 and 10in.*

1 2 3 4 5

6 7 8 9 10 11

12 13 14 15

16 17 18 19 20 21

22 23 24 25 26 27

Jars and vases, continued

Shape number 28   Grecian Shape, Two-Handled Jar. *5, 7 and 8in. (Plate 175)*

29   Beaded, Antique Jar. *8 sizes, 4 to 11in.*

30   Two Handled, Antique Jar. *8 sizes, 4 to 11in. (Plates 146 and 215)*

31   Narrow Top, Antique Jar. *9 sizes, 4 to 12in.*

32   Beaded, Flanged Top Jar with Snake Handles. *4in. and 6in.*

33   Two-Handled, Cabinet Jar. *4, 5 and 6in.*

34   French Shape Jar. *3 sizes*

35   New Shape French Jar. *9 sizes, 4 to 14in. (Plate 189)*

36   Two-Handled, Athenian Jar. *7 sizes, 4 to 10in.*

37   New Shape Jar. *9 sizes, 4 to 14in. (Plate 180)*

38   Beaded, New Shape Jar. *9 sizes, 4 to 14in. (Plate 221)*

39   Egg Shape, Two-Handled Jar. *4in.*

40   Glass Shape Jar. *8 sizes, 3 to 10in.*

41   Vase Shape Jar. *4, 5 and 6in.*

42   Dutch Shape Jar. *3, 4, 5 and 6in. 'plain and for embossed figures'*

43   Beaded, Vase Shape Jar. *4, 5, 6 and 10in. (Plate 220)*

44   Beaded, Acorn Shape Jar. *6 and 8in.*

45   Sèvres Shape Jar. *6, 8 and 10in.*

46   Upright Jar. *36in. 'this jar is thrown in four parts'*

47   Antique, Covered Jar with Turned Down Stand. *One size*

48   Two-Handled, Covered, Coronation Jar. *4, 5, 6 and 7in.*

49   Canister Jar. *7in.*

50   Taper Jar with Broad Rim Cover. *5 sizes, 6 to 17½in. (Plate 293)*

51   Unhandled, India Shape, Covered Jar. *15½in. 'made in earthenware Nov. 1819 for London'*

52   Two-Handled, India Shape, Covered Jar. *15 and 18in.*

53   Capt, Covered, Egg Shape Jar. *3, 4 and 5in.*

54   Covered Vase. *6, 8 and 10in. By this someone has at a later date written, 'Mr Goss's New Medalion Vase of 1857'*

55   Warwick Vase. *One size*

56   Beaded, Ball Shape Jar with Pierced Cover. *6 sizes, 4 to 12in. (Plate 210)*

57   Two-Handled, Pierced, Covered Etruscan Jar. *6 and 8in.*

58   Round Top, Pierced, Covered Jar with Crocodile Handles. *11 sizes (Colour Plate II)*

28   29   30   31   32   33

34   35   36   37   38

39   40   41   42   43   44   45

46   47   48   49   50   51   52

53   54   55   56   57   58

Scent jars, bowpots

Shape number 59 Wide Top, Bottle Shape, 3 part Scent Jar. *5, 6 and 7in.*

60 Dutch Shape, 3 part Scent. *6, 7 and 8in.*

61 Low Scent Jar. *7 and 8½in.*

62 3 Part, Jug Shape, Scent Jar. *6in.*

63 3 Part, Barrel Scent Jar. *5 sizes, 5 to 10in.* (*Plates 108 and 256*)

64 Herculaneum Scent Jar. *One size*

65 Low Antique, 3 part, Covered Scent Jar. *9in.*

66 Covered Scent Jar with Satyr Head Handles. *3 sizes*

67 Pierced, Covered, Antique Pedestal, Bowpot Centre. *Height 6 and 8in. 'no lining to the 6in.'*

68 Beaded, Scolloped Top, Pierced, Covered Bowpot on Claws. *3¼in. high*

69 3 Part, Eel-Handled, Square-Foot Bowpot. *8in.*

70 Twist Handled Bowpot. *7 and 9in. 'made to a blue delf pattern'*

71 Patera, Pot-Pourri Bowpot on Square Plinth. *7, 8 and 9in.* (*Plate 181*)

72 Taper Shape, Pierced, Covered Bowpot. *4in.*

73 Barrel Covered Bowpot. *7 sizes. 'plain or for dipping and figures'*

74 Antique Bowpot. *3½, 4 and 4½in.*

Bottles

75 Lizard Bottle and Stopper. *2 sizes* (*Plate 220*)

76 Covered Bottle Jar to a Metal Pattern *2in.*

77 One-Handled, Short Neck Bottle. *6in.*

78 Wide Top, Two-Handled Bottle *6in.* (*Plate 278*)

79 One-Handled, Long Neck Bottle. *6in.* (*Plate 278*)

80 Beaker Top Bottle. *3½in.*

81 Dutch Covered Bottle. *2, 2½ and 4in.*

82 Two-Handled, Covered Bottle. *3in.*

83 New Shape, Lizard Bottle. *3½, 4½ and 6in.*

84 Ball Shape Bottle. *5 and 15in.*

Incense burners and phosphorous pots

85 Beaded, Upright, Scolloped Incense Burner. *2½in.*

86 Bow-Handled, Incense Burner. *3¾in.* (*Plate 219*)

87 Pyramid Incense Burner. *One size*

59   60   61   62   63

64   65   66   67   68

69   70   71   72   73   74

75   76   77   78   79   80   81

82   83   84   85   86   87

Incense burners and phosphorous pots, continued

Shape number 88 Antique Incense Burner. *One size*

89 Three-Legged, Imaged Handled, Beaded, Incense Burner. *One size*

90 Beaded, Low Incense Burner. *One size*

91 Beaded Incense Burner with Dolphin Handles. *2½, 4 and 5in.*

92 Antique Phosphorous Pot. *One size*

93 Egg Shape Phosphorous Pot. *One size*

94 Fly-Handled Phosphorous Pot. *One size*

95 Beaded, Fly-Handled, Phosphorous Pot with Bottle and Cover. *One size*

96 Fly-Handled, Low Round, Phosphorous Pot. *One size*

Various pieces

97 Beaded Pyramid Stand. *approx. 15in.*

98 Pillar *used in above*

99 Dolphin Tripod. *3 sizes (Plate 221)*

100 Lamp Pedestal and Shade. *(Plate 242)*

101 Pyramid *with a Sexagon Pedestal pressed to suit*

102 *Undescribed*

103 Pierced Basket and Triangle Frame and Lining. *10in.*

104 Cream Stean. *One size*

Matchpots and beakers

105 Matchpot. *3 sizes*

106 Beaded Matchpot. *3 sizes*

107 Matchpot Dipped for Embossed Figures. *2 sizes*

108 Oval Pedestal Matchpot. *One size (Colour Plate 11)*

109 Pedestal Matchpot. *4 and 4½in.*

110 Beaded, Beaker Matchpot. *4½ and 5in. (Plates 182 and 194)*

111 Beaker Matchpot. *2, 3, 4½ and 5in.*

88   89   90   91   92

93   94   95   96

97   98   99   100   101

102   103   104

105   106   107   108   109   110   111

Matchpots and beakers, continued

Shape number 112   Beaded Beaker on a Foot. *6, 7 and 8in. (Plate 181)*

113   Beaker on a Foot. *6 and 7in. (Plates 203 and 227)*

114   Beaker, Imaged Matchpot. *One size*

115   New Shape, Fish Handled Beaker. *3½, 4½, 6 and 7in. (Plate 244)*

116   Antique, Beaded Beaker. *8 sizes, 1¾ to 8in.*

117   Beaded, Wide Beaker. *6 and 7½in.*

118   Scolloped Edge, Flanged Top Beaker. *4, 5, 6 and 7in.*

119   Bodied Beaker with Snake Handles. *10 and 12in. (Plate 294)*

120   Flat Top, Covered Beaker. *6in.*

121   Beaker on Three Claws. *5, 6 and 7in.*

122   Beaded Beaker Matchpot on Claws, Pierced Cover. *4½, 5, 6, 8in. (Plate 179)*

123   Four Claw Feet Beaker on Square Pedestal. *4 and 5in.*

124   Beaded Matchpot with Bulge Bottom on 3 Claws. *2 sizes*

125   Beaded Beaker on Claw Feet with Pierced Cover. *3¾ and 5in.*

Violet pots and baskets

126   Flanged Top, Pierced, Covered Violet Pot and Stand. *One size*

127   Antique Violet Pot. *One size*

128   Two-Handled, Covered Violet Vase and Stand. *One size*

129   Pierced, Round, Violet Basket and Lining. *3¼in.*

130   Low, Two-Handled, Turned Down Basket. *3, 5 and 7in.*

131   Union Bucket. *One size*

132   Flanged Top, Pierced, Covered, Bow-Handled Bucket with Embossed Handle. *5in. (Colour Plate* VIII)

133   Pierced, Round Basket with Pierced Cover and Turned Down Stand. *4in.*

134   Beaded, Bow-Handled Bucket with or without Pierced Cover. *4 sizes*

Centres, cream bowls and salads

135   Round, Scolloped Centre on a Foot. *6, 8½ and 9in.*

136   Round, Scolloped Centre Bowl. *8in. 'made for U.S.C.'*

137   Round, Pierced Basket on a Foot for a Centre. *9½in.*

138   Round, Scolloped Centre on Foot. *10in.*

139   Two-Handled, Covered Centre Bowl. *2 sizes*

140   Round, French Cream Bowl on 3 Claws. *One size. 'three heads on each'*

141   Round, Fly-Handled, Cream Bowl and Stand. *One size (Plates 198 and 296)*

142   Vase Shape, Cream Bowl. *One size. 'same stand to this as to above'*

143   Two-Handled, Low, Antique Salad. *10 and 11in.*

144   Two-Handled, Scolloped, Round Salad on Foot. *10in.*

112   113   114   115   116   117   118

119   120   121   122   123   124   125

126   127   128   129

130   131   132   133   134

135   136   137   138   139

140   141   142   143   144

H

Broth bowls and ornate cups and stands

Shape number 145   Old Shape Broth Bowl and Stand. *3 sizes*

146   New Shape Broth Bowl and Stand. *4 sizes (Plate 283)*

147   French Shape Broth Bowl with Round Stand. *One size*

148   London Shape Broth Bowl and Stand, Flower Embossed. *One size. 'all moulded'*

149   Broth Bowl and Stand. *3 sizes. 'made for U.S.C.'*

150   Swag Embossed Broth Bowl and Stand. *One size. 'these are moulded'*

151   Fly-Handled, Cabinet Cup. *One size*

152   Bell Shape, One-Handled, Uncovered Cabinet Cup. *One size*

153   Small, One-Handled, Cabinet Cup and Stand. *One size*

154   Bell Shape, One-Handled, Cabinet Cup with Turned Down Stand. *1¾in. (Plate 222)*

155   Eel-Handled, Cabinet Cup and Stand. *Small and ½ pint*

156   French Cabinet Cup and Stand. *2 sizes*

157   Two-Handled, Taper Shape, Cabinet Cup and Stand.

158   Silver Shape, Two-Handled, Covered Cabinet Cup and Stand. *(Plate 188)*

159   Etruscan Shape, Two-Handled, Covered Cabinet Cup and Stand. *4½in.*

160   Beaded, French Chocolate Cup and Stand for Déjeuner.

161   One-Handled, Flanged, Chocolate and Stand on Claws. *3½in. 'made for London'*

162   Two-Handled, Bell Shape Chocolate and Stand with Cross Knob. *2 sizes (Colour Plate v)*

163   Imaged Handled, Covered Chocolate with Turned Down Stand *(Plate 229)*

164   Antique, Covered Chocolate and Stand with Griffin Handles.

165   Covered Bucket Chocolate and Stand. *2 sizes (Plate 217)*

166   Bell Shape, One-Handled, Caudle Cup and Stand on 3 Claws.

167   One-Handled, Antique Cocoa Cup and Stand. *2 sizes*

168   Dresden Shape, One-Handled, Uncovered Caudle Cup and Stand.

169   Grecian Shape, Two-Handled, Covered Caudle Cup and Stand.

Candlesticks

170   Reading Candlestick, Beaded and Embossed. *4½ and 7in.*

171   Round Foot, New Shape Candlestick. *5½, 7½, 10in. 'for London Dec. 1819'*

172   Beaded, Round Foot Candlestick. *1¾ and 2in.*

173   Round Foot Candlestick. *7 sizes, 4 to 10in.*

174   Round Foot Candlestick. *2 in. 'made for London June 1820'*

145   146   147   148   149   150

151   152   153   154   155

156   157   158   159

160   161   162   163   164

165   166   167   168   169

170   171   172   173   174

Candlesticks, continued

Shape number 175 Globe Bodied Candlestick. *2½in.*
176 New Hand Candlestick. *4in.*
177 Hand Candlestick. *2, 3, 4 and 5in. (Plate 194)*
178 Hand Candlestick, Dipped for Embossed Figures. *2in.*
179 Beaded Flat Candlestick. *4in.*
180 Flat Candlestick. *4 and 6in.*
181 French Flat Candlestick. *4 and 5in.*
182 Flat Candlestick. *2¾in.*
183 Flat Candlestick with Mushroom Nozzle. *4in.*
184 Pierced Cylinder, Flat Candlestick. *5in.*
185 Small, French Candlestick and Extinguisher.
186 Flat Candlestick and Extinguisher. *4, 5 and 6in.*
187 Griffin Candlestick. *(Colour Plate* 11)
188 Gadroon, Flat Candlestick. *2¾in.*
189 Large, Pressed Candlestick and Extinguisher.
190 Upright, Van Dyke Candlestick.
191 Flat, Van Dyke Candlestick.
192 Elephant Candlestick. *2 sizes*

Inkstands

193 Beaded Tripod Inkstand. *One size*
194 Beaded Globe Inkstand. *One size*
195 Upright Inkstand. *3in.*
196 Shell Handled Inkstand. *One size*
197 Three-Part Round Inkstand. *One size*
198 Round Fixed Inkstand. *One size*
199 Saucer Shape Inkstand. *One size*
200 Antique Inkstand. *One size*
201 Vase Shape Inkstand. *One size*
202 Gothic Inkstand. *One size*
203 Tumbler Inkstand. *'plain in stone, beaded in china'*
204 Griffin-Handled, Fixed Inkstand. *One size*

175   176   177   178

179   180   181   182   183   184

185   186   187   188   189

190   191   192   193   194

195   196   197   198   199

200   201   202   203   204

Inkstands, continued

Shape number 205   Materials for Slab Inkstands. *Note: these are thrown and turned items – inkpot and liner (or tube) and sealing wax candlestick – for an inkstand made by a different process*

206   Beaded, Round, Cylinder Inkstand.

207   Beaded, Coronation Inkstand.

208   Turned Down Inkstand.

209   Churn Shape Inkstand.

210   Bulb Inkstand. *$1\frac{5}{8}$ and $2\frac{3}{8}$in. high*

211   Materials for Tray Inkstands. *Inkpot, liner or 'tube', Sand box and Wafer Box. See note on shape 205*

212   Materials for Cupid Inkstands. *See shape 211*

213   Materials for Half-Round Inkstands. *See shape 211*

214   Materials for Triangular Inkstands. *See shape 211*

215   Materials for Basket Inkstands. *See shape 211*

Toilet sets

216   Water Ewer and Hand Bowl. *8 sizes*

217   Antique Ewer and Bowl. *6 sizes*

218   New Shape, Covered, Slop Bowl. *9in.*

219   Flat Rim Chamber. *9 sizes*

220   Dresden Shape Chamber, Bowl and Ewer. *9 sizes*

Coffee pots

221   Egg Shape Coffeepot. *2 sizes (Plates 145 and 271)*

222   Flower Embossed, Vase Shape Coffeepot. *One size*

223   Vase Shape Coffeepot. *5 sizes. Supplied with stand (Plates 272 and 285)*

224   New Capt Coffeepot. *One size*

225   Beehive Shape Coffeepot. *4 sizes*

226   Cane Shape Coffeepot. *One size (Plate 145)*

227   French Coffeepot. *One size*

228   Churn Shape Coffeepot. *4 sizes*

229   Upright Coffeepot. *3 sizes. 'made for London March 1820'*

230   Coffee Biggan. *One size*

205

206

207

208

209

210

211

212

215

213

214

216

217

218

219

220

220

221

222

223

224

225

226

227

228

229

230

Teaware

Shape number 231   Globe Shape. *4 sizes of teapot and sugar and 5 of milk jug*

232   Low Round Egyptian Shape. *5 sizes of teapot and 4 of milk jug and sugar (Plates 261 and 285)*

233   Upright Capt Shape. *One size throughout*

234   Round Paris Shape. *3 sizes of teapot, one size of milk jug, sugar and bowl*

235   Beaded Déjeuner Shape. *One size throughout (Plate 264)*

236   Ball Shape. *4 sizes throughout (Plates 98 and 99)*

237   Flower Embossed, Low Round Shape. *One size throughout*

238   Etruscan Shape. *2 sizes of teapot, one of sugar, 4 of milk and 3 of bowl. Teacup has either a saucer or a stand (Plate 265)*

239   French Shape Teapot. *4 sizes*

240   Barrel Shape Teapot. *4 sizes and toy size*

241   Old Oval Teapot and Sugar. *4 sizes of teapot, one of sugar (Plate 257)*

242   Round, Sweep Neck Teapot. *5 sizes, largest 'to hold 18 cups' (Plate 272)*

243   Tea Canister. *5 sizes*

231

232

233 234 235 236 237

238

239 240 241 242 243

Jugs and sugars

Shape number 244   Low Dutch Jug. *11 sizes up to 4 quart*

245   Flat Bottom Jug. *7 sizes*

246   Low Dutch Jug Dipped for Embossed Figures. *10 sizes up to 4 quart (Plate 253)*

247   Dutch Jug. *9 sizes up to 2 quart (Plate 98)*

248   Dresden Shape Jug. *8 sizes*

249   Barrel Jug, Hooped and Plain. *9 sizes*

250   Antique Jug. *7 sizes. 'necks are moulded' (Plates 134 and 139)*

251   Flemish Jug. *6 sizes up to 3 quart*

252   Bottle Milk and Stand. *One size*

253   Covered Bottle Milk with Turned Down Stand. *Small size and ½ pint (Plate 221 and Colour Plate VIII)*

254   Round Milk on 3 Feet. *One size*

255   Rio Milk, Covered. *One size*

256   Low Round Milk and Sugar.

257   Two-Handled, Sugar Bowl on a foot. *5in. diam.*

258   Flanged Top, Round Sugar on a foot. *One size*

259   French Sugar. *4 sizes*

Custards and buttertubs

260   Pail Custard with Pierced Cover. *One size (Plate 255)*

261   Embossed Pail, Pierced, Covered Custard. *One size*

262   Beaded Pail, Pierced, Covered Custard. *One size*

263   Barrel, Covered Custard. *2 sizes*

264   French, Covered Custard. *One size*

265   Antique, Two-Handled, Covered Custard. *One size*

266   Old Shape Buttertub. *One size*

267   Buttertub with Fixed Stand. *3 sizes, one deep and the others shallow*

268   Buttertub and Stand to Glass Pattern. *One size*

269   New Shape Buttertub. *3 sizes*

270   Round, Fixed Buttertub with Ears. *One size*

Muffiners and egg-cups

271   Vase Shape Muffiner. *One size*

272   Common Shape Muffiner. *One size*

273   Globe Shape Muffiner. *One size*

274   Egg-cup for Round or Triangle Egg Stands.

275   Lip or Bell Shape Egg-cup.

276   Antique Egg-cup.

277   Pedestal Egg-cup.

278   Egg-cup Fixed on Stand.

279   Common Shape Egg-cup.

280   New Shape Egg Hoop.

281   Old Shape Egg Hoop.

244   245   246   247   248   249

250   251   252   253   254   255

256   257   258   259

260   261   262   263   264   265

266   267   268   269   270   271   272   273

274   275   276   277   278   279   280   281

Pipes

Shape number 282   Tobacco Pipe. *'made for London March 1816'*

283   Chillum. *'made for London June 1820'*

284   Hookah Bottle. *8 and 9in.*

285   Hookah. *'made for London June 1820'*

Various pieces

286   Flat, Covered Centre and Partitioned Cover. *3 sizes (Plate 107)*

287   Soup, Sauce and Cream Bowl Ladles.

288   Round Turtle Pan. *7 sizes from 7 to 14in.*

289   Covered Casserole Pan and Stand. *8½in. diam.* '*2 Embossed sprigs on each side and 3 on cover. Pine Knob*'

290   Round Coverdish. *8, 8½, 9 and 10in.* *'made for London March 1821'*

291   Rose Shape, Deep Supper and Cover with Twig Handle.

292   Round Patty. *5 sizes*

293   Round, Scolloped Pan with Twist Handles. *8, 9, 10 and 11in.*

294   Tulip Stand. *One size*

295   Flanged, Covered Cup. *'made for London July 1819'*

296   Upright, Pierced, Covered Pail. *One size*

297   Round, Covered Wafer or Snuff Box. *3 sizes* '*Plain or Beaded*'

298   Rose Spout Tea Taster. *'usual and small toy size'*

299   Watering Can. *One toy size*

300   Conjuring Sprinkling Cup. *One size*

301   Bowl with a Leafage Cover. *One size*

302   Stand with Basket in Centre and Two-Handled ¼ pint Bowl to Fit. *7½in. diam.*

303   Bow-Handled, Cream Bucket. *4 and 5in.*

304   Beehive. *3 sizes (Plate 285)*

305   Orleans Light Bowl and Foot for the King. *'the Bowl is made of a mould and the foot and neck thrown'* *(See Note 89)*

306   Font Bowl on a Foot. *8in. diam.*

307   Turned Down Butterpan and Stand. *One size*

308   Turned Down, Pierced, Covered, Violet Pan. *5in. diam.*

309   Beaded Hoop. *½ pint*

310   Pineapple Stand. *9 and 10in. diam. (Plate 218)*

311   Pine Pedestal. *2 sizes.* *'made for London Jan. 1820'*

312   Tumbler. *3 sizes*

313   Low Mug, Dipped for Embossed Figures. *9 sizes*

314   Porter Mug. *8 sizes (Plate 238)*

315   Upright Mug. *One size*

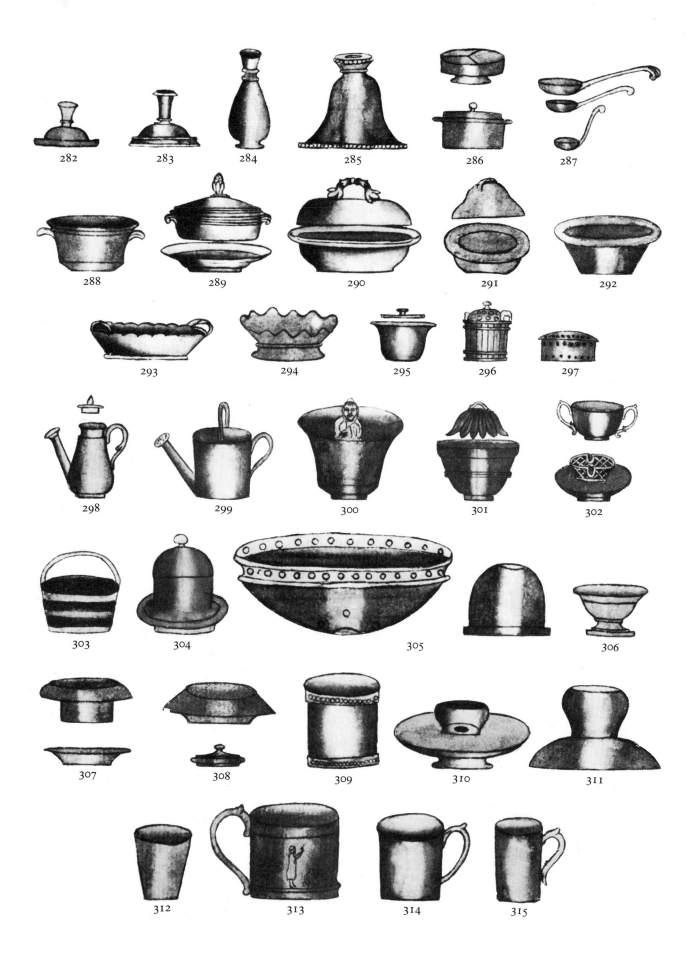

282   283   284   285   286   287

288   289   290   291   292

293   294   295   296   297

298   299   300   301   302

303   304   305   306

307   308   309   310   311

312   313   314   315

Toys

Shape number 316 Dutch Toy Jug.
317 London Shape, Toy, Handled Cup, Saucer and Can.
318 Ball Shape, Toy Teapot, Sugar and Milk.
319 Low, Toy, Teapot, Sugar and Milk. *2 sizes*
320 Toy Jug on a foot.
321 Bute, Toy, Handled Teacup and Saucer. *2 sizes*
322 Toy Can. *2 sizes*
323 Common Shape, Toy Cup. *larger size. 'made for London May 18th 1815'*
324 Fly-Handled, Covered Toy Can with Turned Down Stand.
325 Vase Shape, Toy Coffeepot.
326 Common Shape, Toy Cup and Saucer. *2 sizes*
327 Dutch, Toy Ewer.
328 Déjeuner Paris Toys.
329 Toy Slop Bowl.
330 Toy Cup made for T. Richards. *4 sizes*
331 Toy Chamber. *2 sizes*
332 Bow-Handled, Toy Bucket. *2in.*
333 Antique, Toy Jug and Stand.

Dressing table items

334 Rouge Pot.
335 Covered Pot 1½in. high. *'made for London April 1821'*
336 Thick Grooved Pomatum Pot. *2¼ and 3¼in. high*
337 Pomatum Pot. *2 sizes. 'made for Cook'*
338 Upright Toilet Pot with Flat Cover. *4 sizes*
339 French, Covered Pomatum Pot. *3 sizes*
340 Covered Scent Bottle. *2 sizes*
341 New Shape, Round Soap Drainer.
342 Three-part, Upright Soap Drainer.
343 Ring Stand with Knob Pillar. *3½in. diam.*
344 New Shape Round Soap Drainer and Toilet Pot. *2 sizes, the larger also called 'sponge box'*

316

318   319

317

320

322

324

325

321

327

323

330

331

332

326

333

328   329

334   335   336   337   338   339   340   341

342   343   344

ORNAMENTAL WARE

Spode II produced very little that was not ornamental but almost nothing that was designed purely for ornament. The most lavishly decorated cup was still, in essence, an article of utility; however infrequently called upon to do so, the richest vase could always contain flowers; a spill pot might be a masterpiece of painting and gilding, but its place was still on the mantelpiece where it could do its job; and an egg-cup, even when modelled with three goats' legs (Shape 277), still remained an egg-cup. For figures, the greatest class of objects in ceramics which are designed purely for ornament, we search almost in vain. And some would even deprive him of the one field where he sought only to please the eye and amuse, explaining away his 'toys'—quite erroneously—as pieces produced for commercial travellers to use as samples. Even these delightful miniatures, which he sold in large quantities, not all richly decorated, may often have found their first home in the nursery with the doll's house before being rescued for the collector's cabinet. That some pieces were designed for the cabinet from the start is indicated by the use of the term 'cabinet cup', and it is hard to think of any other destination for pieces like the Watering Can, Shape 299—although the Rose Spout Tea Taster, Shape 298, evidently had a use. The Conjuring Sprinkling Cup, Shape 300, could only be fully appreciated when it was used. When half full, it could be used normally; but if filled beyond this, the entire contents siphoned out through a hole in the bottom: no doubt the cause of much hilarity at the expense of the heavy-handed in the late stages of parties to celebrate the Immersion of Buddha and, with no religious or historical justification, an equal source of amusement when transplanted to England.

Since the word 'ornamental' is really inappropriate except for a tiny minority of Spode's ware, it will be further abused and made a convenient heading for items which do not fit neatly into the category of tableware.

The names used in the 1820 shape book reveal no rigid ideas on classification. The description 'pot pourri', certainly used at other factories, hardly appears, 'scent jar' and 'bow pot' being preferred. The original use of an article was often commemorated in its name after it had been adapted for something quite different, which accounts for custards and matchpots with pierced lids. Sometimes, the shape of the article rather than its use decided the name. Bottles, for example, are of two kinds: scent bottles and jars shaped like bottles. The term spill pot was never used, presumably only being necessary to avoid confusion after the invention of the lucifer match later in the century. No clear-cut distinction appears between jars and vases; and a glance at the caudle, cabinet and chocolate cups does nothing to reveal a way of distinguishing between them. We may take encouragement from the fact that the same confusion was present at the time: the chocolate cup, Shape 161, is described in another contemporary Spode

VIII China: Left to right and top to bottom: (1) Antique Shape pedestal jar. Height, 7¼in. Mark '967' only. (2) Bottle Shape milk jug and stand. Mark 10 and '2610'. (3) Bow-handled bucket. Width, 5in. Marks 10 and '3975' (see Wordley invoices Appendix IV). (4) Tulip cup. Mark 10. (5) Fly-handled cabinet cup and saucer. Mark 11. (6) Grecian Shape jar. Mark 10 and '1166'. (7) Beaded matchpot. Mark 10 and '2078'. (8) Chocolate cup and stand. Mark 10. (Pieces 3, 5 and 7: *N.Bernard Esq.* Other pieces: *Spode Museum*)

shape book as a cabinet cup, and the custard, Shape 265, as a posset cup.

The names of some items are revealing. We learn that Shapes 140 to 142, usually termed sucriers (the English word, by the way, was good enough for Spode), were not intended for sugar at all but for cream. We can confirm from Shapes 266 to 270 that these elegant and often well-decorated pieces really were used for butter, and from Shape 283 we are able to add a new word—chillum— to our vocabulary. It is doubtful if one of these will ever be found nearer home than the Levant, but it is interesting to find that Spode enjoyed a share in the specialist business of supplying hookahs to the East, first recorded at Wedgwood in about 1782.[221] The pineapple stands, Shapes 310 and 311, remind us of how the luxuries of the past have become commonplace. Even at the beginning of this century, the pineapple was a most expensive fruit in uncertain supply;[79] and at the beginning of the last century it was a costly rarity with which the avocado of today cannot compare. It was a delicacy which moved Charles Lamb to ecstacy: 'too ravishing for mortal taste, she woundeth and excoriateth the lips that approach her—like lovers' kisses, she biteth—she is a pleasure bordering on pain from the fierceness and insanity of her relish'.[212] Imported from the West Indies, and not to be compared in size with those of today, a pineapple merited pride of place on the table of any hostess fortunate enough to have one; and the decoration of its stand was often, as with the one illustrated in Plate 218, as luscious as its intended contents. Now, these stands have been suspected of being incomplete pieces with missing parts which, if present, would reveal their function. The same inevitable difficulty in understanding their contemporary culinary context consigns all the pestles and mortars made by Spode and other potters to the use of apothecaries, when they were to be found in our grandmothers' kitchens as desirable articles of equipment in an age before packaged food and instant everything.

The Spode pattern books are of assistance in dating some of the shapes, since several are used by way of illustration. The first jar to appear in them is Shape 20, at Pattern 886, a magnificent decoration in gold and lustre, *c.* 1805. Shape 37, probably the most popular of all Spode's jars, first appears at Pattern 1669, *c.* 1810, but may have been in production well before then. 'Beaded' ornament—a line of modelled pearl-shaped relief, usually reserved in white against a solid gilt ground and well exemplified by the matchpots in Plate 182—is a very noticeable feature on many Spode ornamental pieces. It appears first in the pattern books with Shapes 43 and 110, at Patterns 1617 and 1618. Following these, items incorporating this form of ornament appear very frequently, suggesting *c.* 1810 as the date for the introduction of the style.

A particularly ambitious group of jars is the seven from Shape 21 to 27. These are all of similar style and feature heavily as a group in the pattern books between Patterns 2553 and 2730, all lavishly decorated. They were probably all introduced together, *c.* 1817. A notable but, since it is a cast piece, understandable omission from the shape book is the popular covered jar illustrated in Colour Plate VI and Plate 243. The Tuscan jar illustrated in Plate 214 was introduced *c.* 1821 and, like several earlier shapes, subsequently appeared deformed by an excrescence of Coalbrookdale-type flowers and birds. A group of such pieces is shown in Plate 254. This style of embellishment, currently enjoying a great vogue among collectors, seems to have been a late introduction at Spode and was at the height of its popularity in about 1825.

Matchpots were humble enough items in their origin, but some of the most expensive Spode decorations were used for them. Their popularity is reflected by the large number which have survived and the diversity of their styles and sizes. Those given in the 1820 shape book are interesting in their variety. The first one to feature in the pattern books, at Pattern 337, is even simpler than Shape 105, being perfectly cylindrical with no rib near the bottom. Shape 105 itself appears at Pattern 895, *c.* 1805, and the ornate Shape 114 shortly after at Pattern 975. Several matchpots were made in sizes so large that they cannot legitimately be classed as such.

Scent jars and bow pots are troublesome pieces for collectors, who cannot always be sure that they have the article complete. Several of those in the 1820 shape book are shown with three pieces: the jar itself; a perforated cover; and a presser for resting on the sweet-smelling mixture of dried flowers and herbs. But most have no presser illustrated. I have certainly never seen a presser with a violet pot, an article seen frequently and presumably being a small specialist pot pourri for dried violets. If only the jar is found, devoid even of its perforated cover, it should not be assumed that it is incomplete as some would certainly have been sold like this. Shape 56 is illustrated five times in the pattern books, twice with a cover but three times without.

Georgian society, to its credit and the general benefit of potters, gave close attention to disguising its smells. Reinforcement for the traditional pot pourri in its unequal contest with smouldering candlewicks and worse arrived from France at the very beginning of the nineteenth century in the form of the incense or pastille burner. The pastilles they burnt must have been effective since their use spread rapidly. In 1811, Wedgwood received a report from the field that 'the burning of pastilles is no longer confined to the higher ranks of people but is extending everywhere'.[111] In addition to the wide range contained in the shape book, cottage pastille burners—as popular in their day as they are now among collectors—were also made by Spode in both china and earthenware (see Plates 109 and 252). Whether or not phosphorous burners are refinements in this field is unknown to the author.

Cabinet, chocolate and caudle cups, so difficult to distinguish, all have one thing in common: in the main they were decorated with the Factory's most lavish and expensive patterns. Cabinet cups, being for show, could be expected to be showy; and chocolate cups were luxury items for a luxury beverage, the price of which was kept artificially high by import duty until 1853.[199] The reason for the decorative nature of caudle cups is not so evident. Caudle is spiced, sweetened oatmeal gruel with wine, brandy or ale added and sometimes the yolk of eggs. Dr Brewer, in his *Dictionary of Phrase and Fable*, described it disparagingly as 'any sloppy mess'—but it is doubtful if he ever tasted it since it was valued as the ideal invalid food for women in childbed. Custard, which did not come out of packets in Spode's day and could be made in versions as nourishing as one pint of cream to every twelve egg yolks, was another recommended food for 'invalids'. Costly decoration for caudle cups may have been favoured for reasons of sick-room psychology, but it could equally have been because of their suitability as gifts. Their use by people in bed explains the preponderance of saucers with sunken wells, to which the descriptive name 'trembleuse' was given long after the idea had been devised at Meissen.[198] Saucers of this kind are also often found for broth bowls, used for another favoured food for the sick. These, too, are frequently richly decorated and they appear early in the pattern books: one similar to Shape 145 but with different handles as early as Pattern 309, and Shape 147 at Pattern 530.

Many more candlesticks were produced than appear in the 1820 shape book. The first tall candlestick found in the pattern book, at Pattern 403, is similar to Shape 173 and had two variations: one with a hexagonal base, and the other with a tulip shape top. This shape was apparently obsolete by 1820; but Shape 177, which appears as early as Pattern 449, was never superseded. Another early appearance is Shape 187 at Pattern 958, *c.* 1806. The very small candlesticks were designed for use in melting sealing wax and sold as adjuncts to the many different desk sets made. Among the larger items included in such a set were an inkstand, a letter-rack and a pen-tray.[205]

The two gardenpots, Shapes 16 and 17, were favourite items for illustrating patterns. Shape 16 was the earlier and appeared first for Pattern 317. Although this shape continued virtually throughout the Spode Period, it made few appearances after the introduction of Shape 17, first used as an illustration for Pattern 671.

USEFUL WARE

The most remarkable feature of the earliest Spode tableware is the large number of sandwich sets, made in earthenware. They were all to the same basic design: a number of semi-circular covered dishes grouped around a centre. A rare example, in china, is illustrated in Plate 155. The centres varied considerably and, in addition to the kind illustrated in this china version, there was Shape 286. An example is illustrated in Plate 107, decorated with Pattern 254. These useful articles were still being manufactured—on a much reduced scale —in this century, but had become known as 'supper sets'. Their earlier popularity is understandable since they were ideal for almost any meal—particularly the gargantuan breakfasts of the time—and the possession of one, complete with the wooden tray in which it fitted, some plates, a few meat dishes and a soup tureen made a complete equipage.

Dinnerware was really the preserve of earthenware and, later, stone china. The production of plates, dishes and their attendant serving pieces was the main function of these two bodies. Teawares in them are rare by comparison. The position was reversed in china, and early china dinnerware is virtually non-existent. Dinnerware in china seems not to have become popular until the 1820s. Indeed, before then, when experience had not yet produced satisfactory techniques for making the larger items required, it must have been prohibitively expensive due to losses in manufacture.

All three bodies—earthenware, china and stone china—were extensively used for dessert wares, the main Spode shapes incorporating Twig Handled Comports of the kind illustrated in Colour Plate IV and Plate 212. In china, the range of shapes was very extensive and embossed decorations were extremely popular. Rich decorations were often lavished on such ware, and the sale of very expensive dessert sets remained a feature of the fine china trade right up until the 1930s.

Although the 1820 shape book contains sketches of cup shapes, those of normal tea, coffee and breakfast cups have not been included with the others. They have been reserved to receive more particular attention here and, where possible, illustration by precise scale drawings from specimens. Cups deserve such detailed treatment for several reasons. One writer has even seen a near mystical significance in them:

> The great—and, we rejoice to add, the successful—rival of the 'pewter pot'. It has wiled many an artisan from the public-house to his 'home'; it is the uncompromising enemy of selfishness and vices even more detrimental to comfort and prosperity: it is, in fact and in truth, the object to which the wife should ever look as the best coadjutor in the cheerful and honest management of a household. The tea cup is the surest and safest solace; it can never sadden, or endanger, or betray.[130]

If further justification is necessary after this, it can be added that no one item is as important to a factory as a cup. None is produced in such large quantities. Because of this, and the likely major effect it will have on sales, the general introduction of a new shape in cups is never undertaken lightly. Spode cups, in their considerable variety, are highly collectable articles in themselves, affording an opportunity to compose a neat miniature picture of evolution in design throughout the period. They have the added advantage of being relatively easily found and, particularly when unmarked—as they frequently are— inexpensive.

Spode tea services usually have adequate marks on the main serving pieces; but often the cups and saucers, even in late wares, bear only the pattern number with no name. Frequently they are devoid of marks altogether. These are happy omissions for the experienced collector. Innumerable factories made cups very similar in shape to Spode's—but, as with all items, they are never exactly the same. Some slight variation in proportion and size is inevitable, even between Spode cups of the same shape, but these are never sufficient to confuse an eye trained to detect the Spode shape from the 'same' made by another factory. This is best illustrated by the London shape cup, universally popular and frequently encountered:

The centre cup is Spode, that to the left is Minton, and the one to the right is unmarked: 'All cases are unique and very similar to others'. The pronounced flange of the Minton cup and that of some other manufacturers is never encountered in Spode specimens and provides a sure method of differentiation. The cup on the right has been deliberately selected because of its very close similarity to the Spode one: but distinct differences are apparent, particularly in the turning of the base and the line of the handle. A cup bearing an equally close similarity to Spode's was produced by Charles Bourne. The handle and general proportions of his are almost identical to Spode's, the only obvious difference being in the foot: the line of Bourne's is more angular and the inside of it much more steeply turned. Charles Bourne, who took over the factory of Samuel Spode in about 1818, modelled many of his products on those of Spode II. But although his potting could be of equal quality and, much more rarely, his decoration also, his paste never was.

A cup is more vulnerable to breakage than a saucer, but more of the former have survived than the latter. This is hardly surprising in view of the numerical advantage they enjoyed to start with. In the early nineteenth century, the standard composition of a tea-set included twelve tea cups, twelve coffee cans and only twelve saucers which were common to both (see Appendix III). Saucers without wells to hold the cup seem to have been standard throughout the first two decades of the century: it was this feature which made their use with different sizes of cups possible. Any objection to the practice would have needed to be on aesthetic rather than practical grounds. The saucer without a well was not conceived as an economy measure, having survived from the previous century when tea cups—but not chocolate cups—were without handles and the saucers, which often had feet high enough for them to be held by, were used to drink from.

> The saucer seems to have perplexed our ancestors at the time of its first introduction; its first use was believed to be merely to cool the tea, and then it was unfashionable to drink from the cup; at a later time the use of the saucer was understood to be confined to saving slop, and thence forward the cup alone was to have the honour of being raised to the lips.[129]

Apparently, a 'dish of tea' then meant precisely that: but I possess a cream ware loving mug, dated 1780, which depicts a lady taking tea, demurely holding the cup by its foot while the saucer rests on a nearby table. Perhaps the fashion was already changing by then. Cups without handles continued to be made well into the nineteenth century. Certain export markets would have demanded them, but their frequent discovery nearer home shows that some English people preferred them that way—either from conservatism or because, being determined to drink out of their saucers, they saw no point in paying extra for useless handles on their cups.

The sketches opposite, with approximate dates of introduction, give an idea of the evolution in cup design. Towards the end of the second decade of the century, the tendency to more ornate styles and greater diversity in shapes became marked, although the earlier shapes ran through the entire Spode Period, particularly in the fine stone and earthenware bodies. Even in china, earlier cup shapes continued in production long after the appearance of new ones. When a new shape was put on the market, it was usual for it to be launched with a number of new patterns. For this reason, the pattern books (which used cups for illustration more than any other item) provide a good guide to their date of introduction as well as their subsequent popularity. Most cups were produced in at least four sizes: the tea cup; a breakfast cup, considerably greater in capacity than the tea cup; a Norfolk cup, midway in size between the two; and a coffee cup. The first three were identical except in size, but the coffee cup was always tall and of a quite different profile. With the solitary exception of the

Bute *c.* 1800   Royal Flute *c.* 1800

Porringer *c.*1810   London *c.*1813   New Dresden *c.*1817

Etruscan *c.*1817   Bell *c.*1819

Gadroon *c.*1822   Pembroke *c.*1827   '4643' *c.*1829

Octagon *c.*1829   '5146' *c.*1833

can shape, however, all coffee cups followed through the design of the tea cup, any adaptation being limited to what was necessary for their increased height. They were by no means of demi-tasse size, as the sketches below indicate: it was usual for the coffee cup to hold as much as the tea cup and sometimes more. They are illustrated with the tea cups in seven of the shapes dealt with below, but all shapes had them.

Bute or Common Shape tea cups and cans were the first produced by Spode II and were made in stone china and earthenware as well as china. The can was never completely ousted by other shapes and is frequently found with London Shape tea cups. The Bute tea cup waned in popularity after the introduction of the London Shape and by 1820 was being produced in only very limited quantities in china, although it remained the main shape in the other bodies. The early and rather rare Old Oval Shape, illustrated in Plate 257, will always be found to accompany Bute Shape cups. The reverse is not true because the New Oval Shape, illustrated in Plate 260, was introduced before 1810. The handles, taken from Sèvres, are good identifying features: most manufacturers produced similar shaped cups but very few with a handle which has the characteristic Spode 'kick in' at the bottom, also found on the Old Oval cream jug (Plate 258). When the same handle is encountered from other factories, it will usually be found too small in proportion to the cup when compared with Spode's. Swansea, who used this handle, are an exception—but their cup is distinctly different in its proportions.

Both tea cup and can were manufactured by Spode with the normal plain handles, universally employed elsewhere. But although these were production lines and not special matching pieces, they are extremely rare and were probably an unsuccessful experiment over a very short period, *c.* 1815. If a Spode Bute can is encountered with a handle identical to that of a London Shape coffee cup, its lack of balance—not being modelled to fit a vertical-sided cup—is immediately apparent. It will almost certainly be a matching piece for a service by another manufacturer whose cans had handles of this kind. Foremost among these was Derby. The same quick and easy method of solving a small problem of this kind was later used with far greater success with a New Dresden Shape handle on a Bute can. Spode Bute cans are sometimes found with tapering sides, making a beaker-like shape; but these are rare.

Royal Flute Shape Three fluted shapes were among the earliest cups pro-duced. In addition to Royal Flute was *Flat Flute*, in which shallow vertical flutes ran the full depth of the cup, and *Shank Flute* which was similar but with the flutes in spiral. The tea cup of the latter closely resembles Royal Flute; but that of Flat Flute and the coffee cans in all three shapes are Bute with a slight flange out at the top and, of course, the addition of scalloped edges and the necessary fluting. All handles are of normal Bute Shape but the tea cups may also be found unhandled, as in the sketch. Royal Flute was the most popular of the three and was certainly in production before 1804: its main if not sole use was for blue printed decorations. The three shapes are not known to have been manufactured in any body except china.

Porringer Shape, almost invariably in china, is rarely encountered and is 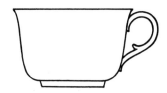one of the rarest entries in the pattern books. It was used as the cup shape for the service for the King of Oudh mentioned in Chapter V and was supplied in Pattern 1922 in July 1813 (see Appendix III). Pattern 1922 is a bat print and the shape is known decorated with another pattern of this kind, a floral one, Number 500.

London Shape is the most commonly found Spode cup shape in china and was also manufactured in earthenware. Bute cans are frequently found with London tea cups, and New Oval Shape serving pieces—or those illustrated in Plate 263—normally accompany them. Introduced *c.* 1813, London Shape achieved parity with Bute *c.* 1815 and had become the dominant shape by 1820. It enjoyed some degree of popularity throughout the Spode Period, despite the many subsequent new shapes. In a modified form, it is still produced in large quantities at the Factory.

New Dresden Shape was so called to distinguish it from Dresden Shape, which is illustrated later. A china shape, it is normally found with the emboss-ment here illustrated on the tall cup and was usually decorated with patterns consisting of small, painted floral sprays—the only type of pattern for which it was really suited. Introduced *c.* 1817.

Etruscan Shape was in production before 1820 but probably not before 1816. It seems to have been at the height of its popularity *c.* 1825. Coalport produced the same shape and the angular handle sketched, which they favoured, can also be found on Spode cups—but only rarely, since it was early ousted by the serpent handle. A late and very rare variation is a ring handle. Only found in china, the shape had a full range of accompanying teaware items which are illustrated in Plate 265 and in the 1820 shape book, Shape 238. Etruscan cups were also used with other shaped serving pieces as in the service illustrated in Plate 270.

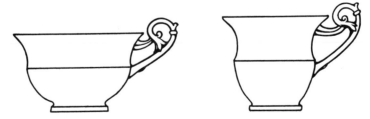

Bell Shape, only used in china, was introduced before 1820 but achieved real popularity some years later. The cups are normally found with the Octagon Shape items illustrated in Plate 266.

Gadroon Shape was—and remains—a very important shape for most Staffordshire potteries and for none more than Spode, where it was produced in tea, dinner and dessert wares, in china and earthenware, in very large quantities. One of the dominant shapes in the pottery trade, it is variously known as 'pie crust', 'dog tooth', and 'scrat edge' as well as by its proper name. Although popular in silver throughout most of the seventeenth century, its use for china seems to have been delayed. Shaw credits it to Ridgway:

> In 1821, Messrs. Ridgway of Cauldon Place, Shelton, introduced a Porcelain of Bone Body, with a new glaze, that surpassed every other kind then produced. And to its excellent quality was added entirely original models of the several articles of Dinner and Desert Services; (also subsequently used for Blue Printed Pottery) much resembling the beautiful ornamental Pieces used for Silver Plate, with gadroon edge, and tasteful appendages.[265]

Shaw's date is supported by evidence from the Spode pattern books. The first illustration of an item with a gadroon edge is a tetragon plate at Pattern 3402, which is *c.* 1822. Several entries for this shaped plate occur, indicating an active production of dessert wares, and by the late 1820s gadroon teaware was accounting for a large proportion of all new patterns introduced. Teaware shapes are illustrated in Plate 268.

Pembroke Shape was introduced, for china only, *c.* 1827. The embossed version shown here seems to have been more popular than the plain one. Each version had its own accompanying shapes and these are illustrated in Plates 269 and 262. It became a dominant shape in the 1830s.

'4643' *Shape*, since its real name is unknown, is called after the pattern with which it makes its first appearance in the pattern books, indicating a date *c.* 1829. Found in china only, its accompanying teawares are in a distinctly Victorian style: some are shown in Plate 267. In the early 1830s, it enjoyed a popularity equal to that of Pembroke Shape but did not prove as long lived.

Octagon Shape, in china, is perhaps the best proportioned of the later shapes. It was introduced *c.* 1829, at virtually the same time as '4643' Shape, and it frequently shared this shape's teapot, sugar and cream jug.

'5146' *Shape* is another china shape the real name of which is unknown, although an early Copeland cup of virtually the same shape was known as Melon Shape. Its introduction *c.* 1833 makes it the last shape introduced in the Spode Period. The only examples of this shape I have seen to date are marked Copeland and Garrett. It is an excellent example of the proliferation of models which characterises this late period and was produced both plain and embossed. In another version, it has an identical handle but a slightly narrower base to the cup. There was even a variation of this last variation: a modified form of the cup with full depth spiral fluting.

Although the most important shapes have been dealt with in detail, the list is by no means exhausted. In particular, a very large number of unhandled tea bowls were produced. All of these were of basically Chinese shape, but variations in outline were endless and would be confusing to attempt to list. New tea bowl shapes were still being introduced in the 1820s.

It is difficult, when examining some of the shapes remaining, to decide whether to attribute their rarity to commercial failure or the fact that they may have been produced for one particular customer or as matching pieces. Cups given in the 1820 shape book and not dealt with above are given opposite, but these sketches are from those given in the book and are not accurate drawings of actual pieces, all to scale, like those given so far. They must therefore be taken only as a guide.

EMBOSSED DECORATION

Embossments, extensively used on china dessert wares and less frequently on dinnerwares, abound in the teawares. Virtually every shaped cup and most of the accompanying teaware items appeared at one time or another in one or more of the several embossed designs employed by Spode II.

The technique employed for producing these low relief ornaments is not to be confused with that of sprigging, used for the high relief decorations found

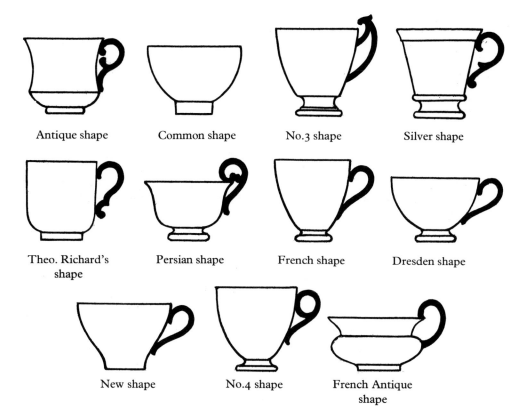

| Antique shape | Common shape | No.3 shape | Silver shape |

| Theo. Richard's shape | Persian shape | French shape | Dresden shape |

| New shape | No.4 shape | French Antique shape |

on jasper, basalts, stoneware and, later, china jugs and other items. With the latter, the ornamental motifs are made in separate moulds and 'sprigged on' to the piece. In the former, these motifs are built into the mould used to make the whole piece. A less expensive method, it was capable of producing an excellent crisp effect when combined, as it was by Spode, with good potting, careful glazing and a readiness to replace moulds frequently at the first sign of wear.

Wicker Weave Embossed was probably the earliest decoration of this type. It first appeared as an illustration in the pattern books for Numbers 1181 and 1182, *c.* 1806, and was employed for a full range of dinner and dessert items. Pattern 1182, illustrated in Plate 206, seems to have been popular.

Dolphin Embossed appeared for several patterns following on Number 1655, *c.* 1810. The illustrations in the pattern book all employ the swan-lidded sauce boat illustrated in Plate 277. I have never found it on teaware. A dessert plate is illustrated in Plate 201. It is one of the rarest embossed decorations employed by Spode and, though still in use *c.* 1815, seems never to have become popular.

Flower Embossed was enormously successful. It has been identified on virtually every shape of cup produced by Spode and was much favoured for dessert ware and for many other items besides. The design itself seems to have originated at Chelsea, but there four sprays were used instead of three and a heavy accompanying floral embossment circled the plates below the rim. Extremely popular in Staffordshire, versions of this design were used by many potters on china, and it can even be found as a sprigged motif on pieces by Wilson and others. The Spode version consists of three distinct and different sprays, although on some pieces—notably, cups—only two were used. Examples are illustrated in Plates 196 and 301 and several others. C.Bourne produced the closest design to Spode's, but most versions reveal distinct differences in drawing. A version with separate small sprays between the main three, which is frequently found on unmarked wares, is often incorrectly attributed to Spode. Another very common and incorrect attribution, more insulting since the ware is invariably crudely made, is that of a compact and repetitive floral embossed border running continuously round the rims of plates and below the shoulder on hollow-ware pieces. I do not know of Spode ever producing a border of this type.

From the moment of its introduction, in about 1813, Flower Embossed was established in favour in both tea and dessert ware, dinnerware being added to its list of conquests later. From the start, a peculiarly large number of 'envelope plates' were produced, of the kind illustrated in Plate 208. Appropriately, floral painted decorations preponderate and Pattern 1943, amongst the earliest, remained perhaps the most popular. Rim depth coloured grounds with the embossments reserved in white were obvious and often used decorations. A light blue coloured ground was the one most favoured for this.

Swag Embossed, which was also introduced in about 1813, was so crowded and heavy that, in contrast to the much more successful Flower Embossed, it precluded any attempt at a tasteful and complementary arrangement of its patterns. Comparatively short-lived, it had virtually ceased in production by 1822 and seems to have been only rarely used for anything except teaware. The dinner plate in Plate 228 is a rare example.

Dresden Embossed is usually only encountered on the cups from which it takes its name (see New Dresden cups above), but it was also used on Bute tea cups. Introduced in about 1816, it was popular. Its decorations tend to be of an inexpensive kind with slight, painted sprays and a minimal gilt finish.

'*Spear Leaf Embossed*', the correct name of which is unknown, is illustrated in Plate 204 and is of great interest. The design runs right round the rim of the plates and is completely non-repetitive in its excellent drawing. Introduced about 1820, its use never became common and examples are rare.

'*Butterfly Embossed*', which first appeared in the pattern books in about 1824, was popular for dessert services. Several other embossed designs, with edges similar to this one but without designs on the rim, were introduced for dessert ware at about the same time. Colour Plate 1 illustrates an icepail with this embossed decoration.

'*Wreath Embossed*', a design very similar in shape to the favourite gilt wreath motif illustrated in Plate 265, was introduced in about 1820 for teawares. A similar design was widely employed by the Swansea Factory. Another version, which had the addition of crowded floral clusters, was introduced at about the same time. This 'Floral Wreath Embossed' was the more popular of the two.

Other embossed decorations which are found in the pattern books seem to have been very short-lived and produced in only one or two patterns. In this category, all introduced in about 1815, are '*Honeycomb*', a rim depth emboss-ment on china; '*Acanthus*', a narrow repetitive border of leaves a short way in from the edge of the plates and '*Acanthus and Scroll*', which was similar but with the addition of a repetitive inner border of acanthus scrolls. The inner border of the last made an appearance again, in about 1822, in '*Floral and Scroll*', accompanied by an embossment of forget-me-nots at the edge. The highly ornate '*Urn and Flowers*', a motif repeated four times on the rim of the plate, is also from about 1822. The last embossed decoration introduced in the Spode Period was '*Fishscale*', on cups of '5146' Shape.

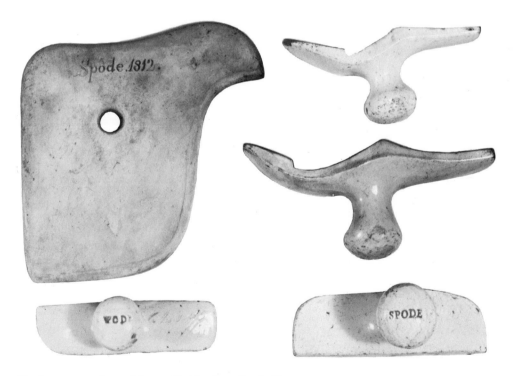

Earthenware tools used for profile shaping. *Spode Museum.*

8 Traditional wares

STONEWARE, 'JASPER' AND SPRIGGED DECORATION

The description 'stoneware' has to be accepted as a necessary evil. Possibly the most overworked word in ceramics, it is pressed into service to describe wares as dissimilar as eighteenth-century salt glaze, Rhenish beer mugs and the fine peacock marl productions of the Turners. When used to describe a class of products made by just one manufacturer its meaning can naturally be curtailed, but with Spode it still has to embrace a family too large for semantic comfort. The best that can be said by way of definition is that Spode's stonewares, although usually translucent to some degree, are obviously not china; their colour ranges from buff to off-white, and most articles are finished with a smear glaze except, for reasons of utility, the interior of hollow-ware pieces. Jugs and mugs preponderate and so do decorations of sprigged motifs.

Some pieces—like the one in Plate 152, which is completely unglazed—are so close-textured and white that it is hard to differentiate them from Parian. Indeed, collectors may be forgiven for wondering if this early Victorian 'invention' was not born at all but, like Topsy, just grew. Alternatively, a piece of this kind could easily be classified as jasper—at least, what passes as such in many collectors' cabinets and some museums.

The term 'jasper' is correctly applied to a ceramic body, not to any particular colour. First made by Josiah Wedgwood and John Turner in about 1775, early jasper is unmistakably a fine porcelainous production with a characteristic wax-like appearance. I have not yet encountered Spode pieces of this kind. In the early nineteenth century, the composition of jasper bodies moved a long way from Josiah Wedgwood's original formula and the word became associated with the familiar blue colour. That this was so, even in professional potting circles, is demonstrated by some of Lakin's formulae published in 1824.[211] Three of these are given opposite, with an early original Wedgwood jasper formula[158] alongside for comparison.

All three of Lakin's bodies were fired at earthenware temperature. What he called 'Jasper Body' would have been blue in colour; the 'White Body', exactly the same in formulation but without blue calx, he describes as 'perfectly adapted also for the purpose of figures in baso-relievo and other ornamental work'. Neither could be recognised as producing what Wedgwood would have designated jasper. The quite dissimilar stone body was described as 'properly adapted for the manufacturing of Jugs, Mugs, etc'. From observation, it is

IX Stone China: Left to right and top to bottom: Landscape Pattern, Number 2857 (see also Plate 282); Pattern 2886 (see also Plate 289); Peacock Pattern, Number 2118; Willis Pattern, Number 2147; Frog Pattern, Number 3248; Ship Pattern, Number 3067. All six dinner plates have Mark 19a and their pattern numbers. The plate in Frog Pattern also has, in script, 'Used at the Coronation of His Majesty George the 4th — 19th July 1821'. This is reproduced on page 196.

	Jasper body	Superior white body	Stone body	Wedgwood jasper
Cawk	35·4%	37·0%	—	57·1%
Blue clay[80]	35·4%	37·0%	25·49%	28·6%
Bone	17·7%	18·6%	—	—
Calx	4·4%	—	0·01%	—
Cornish stone	—	—	49·00%	—
Cornish clay	—	—	24·50%	—
Glass	—	—	1·00%	—
Flint	7·1%	7·4%	—	9·5%
Witherite	—	—	—	4·8%

likely that Spode employed a body mix similar to these for his stonewares, and the pieces of jasper blue ware illustrated in Colour Plate 11 and Plates 151, 153 and 154 are also of this type. All are of the 'jasper dip' variety. Pieces of Spode in 'solid jasper', although they have been encountered, are extremely rare. The shade of blue employed is variable, as it was with most manufacturers.

Among the Spode slabs deposited in the cornerstones of Stoke's new parish church, in 1826, was one which Shaw described as jasper. Since the purpose of the slabs was 'to transmit to generations far remote, invaluable memorials of the perfection to which the Potter's Art in this neighbourhood had arrived in the early nineteenth century', this jasper one must be a perfect documentary piece of what passed for excellence in this respect at that date. Its study must be left to generations far remote, since it will only be available to ours in the unhappy event of Stoke needing a new parish church in our lifetime.[233]

The earliest-looking piece of Spode stoneware I have encountered is illustrated in Plate 140. It is light grey in colour and quite unglazed. It has a particularly interesting relief ornament, but this is uncharacteristic since it has not been produced from a sprig mould. Sprigging—the technique of applying decorative motifs made in separate moulds to the main article in the clay state— is a form of ornament associated with the stonewares, jaspers and basalts of all manufacturers. Its use also extended to china. This was a later development made by several firms,[174] and Spode pieces of this kind are illustrated in Plates 253 and 256.

The appeal of sprigged wares is largely due to their fine detail. By filling a sprig mould with clay, firing the impression, making another mould from the contracted result and repeating the process, there was almost no limit to the diminution possible—all without the slightest loss of detail, and irrespective of the welcome scope in size given to the original modeller/artist. The same trick also gave the potter who was prepared to take pains a simple and inexpensive method of producing, from a minimum of original material, a range of decorative borders, bands and terminals limitless in size. Deft application, neat finishing and skilful undercutting were then needed for a first-class result. To smother such work with an obscuring blanket of thick glaze was a sin avoided until the later, china, sprigged wares—which have, for this reason, a debasement from which their elegant shapes and tasteful gilding cannot save them. Simple undetailed sprig motifs, designed solely and especially to provide a relief for painting upon (Plate 255), were deservedly more successful.

In the stonewares, a rich dark brown colour was favoured as a background for the ornaments in the same way as the more familiar blue in jasper pieces. Brown was a good complement to the various stoneware shades of buff or cream and was the colour mainly used for the necks and handles of jugs (Colour Plate 11 and Plate 138). A rich blue was also popular.

The subjects used in Staffordshire for sprigged decorations could be classified as: (1) Classical subjects copied from Wedgwood; (2) Subjects common to several potters; and (3) Subjects apparently peculiar to one potter. Like those of everyone else, including John Turner, many of Spode 11's products belong in the first and least desirable category. Hackwood's bacchanalian boys and playful infants disport themselves on the pieces illustrated in Plates 139 and 141; his models of Lady Templetown's preoccupied families troop solemnly round the sides of the china jugs in Plate 253.

In the second category, the most popular subject was the Huntsmen, typical examples of which are illustrated in Plate 137. This must have been everybody's favourite, used by a whole host of potters. Pieces are more often unmarked than not. When they are unmarked they are usually attributed to Spode but they rarely are.

In the third category (at least, to my knowledge) is the very interesting Indian Sporting subject on the centre jug in Plate 253. Although examples are rare in the extreme, several sprig moulds survive at the Spode Factory from this series, which was designed from the same source as the famous blue printed pattern (see Plate 94).

The Spode Factory still possesses a very large number of Turner sprig moulds. They are so numerous and varied that it is hard to believe that they do not represent the Lane End factory's entire stock; but a few known Turner subjects are missing, and at least one other manufacturer is recorded as having acquired some.[272] Exactly when this valuable collection was obtained is a subject for debate: perhaps in 1807, when the Turner brothers went bankrupt; or in 1829, when William Turner sold up his own subsequent business. They could,

of course, have been bought privately before the first bankruptcy in 1807 or
at any time after it. The notices of sale help little. In 1807, no moulds at all
featured in the list of items for sale; and the description 'an excellent assortment
of Block and Working Moulds, all of excellent Shape and Modern Patterns'$_{204}$
which appeared for the 1829 sale is an inaccurate and most unlikely way of
describing Turner sprig moulds. Bevis Hillier's view$_{202}$ that the Spode Factory
acquired them late rather than early gets strong support from the wares themselves. Of the many completely original Turner subjects, none seems to have
found its way on to Spode pieces. The basalt sugar box and cream illustrated in
Plate 144, decorated with embossed—not sprigged—Chinese figures, are
almost identical with those produced by Turner; but a comparison reveals
distinct differences and demonstrates that Spode did not use Turner moulds
for these articles.

BASALTS AND RED WARE

Among the earliest of the productions of the Spode Factory, basalts (black
Egyptian) continued to be made throughout the Spode Period and well beyond.
Captain Grant regarded them as distinguished by their imitative nature, their
excellent quality and their excessive rarity.$_{178}$ The first point is good, but a
glance at some of the items illustrated in Plates 142 to 145 may reveal more
originality than the Captain allowed. The quality of the wares is, indeed, usually
extremely high. The engine-turning found on pieces like the two coffee pots in
Plate 145 is always of a good standard, although it never reached the perfection
of Turner's. The teapot illustrated in Plate 142 would distinguish itself in any
company as a small masterpiece of hand-tooled decoration.

The rarity of Spode basalts is difficult to explain. Even sixty years ago the
discovery of a piece was, according to Grant, a red-letter-day for a collector. It
has been suggested that Spode rarely marked his basalts. Although no doubt
true of Spode I, it can hardly be believed of Spode II. There is no conceivable
reason why basalts—certainly not the least expensive of his products—should
have been victimised in this way, and unmarked pieces which can be safely
attributed to him are much rarer than marked pieces. Spode ornamental wares
in this body are unheard of. The bust of Wellington, which was illustrated by
T.G.Cannon in his book, *Old Spode*, and described by him as basalt is now
in the Spode Museum. It is, in fact, red ware with a metallic glaze simulating
bronze.$_{156}$

The first productions in red ware (red Egyptian) would no doubt have been
of the Elers type, made generally throughout the Potteries in the eighteenth
century. No marked specimens of this kind have come to light. The pieces
illustrated in Plates 146 to 149 date from the beginning of the nineteenth century,

when the ware enjoyed considerable renewed popularity. Often produced with enamel decorations, the one most frequently encountered on Spode pieces is Pattern 3339, which is illustrated in Plate 149. Another popular method of decoration for this ware was sprigged ornament in basalts, used on the vase in Plate 146 and the scent jar in Plate 148. The last of these is typical of the Egyptian subject matter which became popular after Nelson's victory at the Nile in 1798.

EARTHENWARE

Shaw mentions cream coloured and white ware as among the first products of the Spode Factory (see Chapter 1). To the best of my knowledge, he is talking about the same earthenware body. This statement is based on visual evidence provided by comparing the colours of fresh breaks in a very large number of Spode cream ware, blue printed and other pieces of all types and periods. Lest it be thought that the author is either a destructive maniac or the victim of some unimaginable catastrophy, it must be added that these fresh breaks were made in a careful selection from the several hundredweights of small, worthless shards excavated at the Spode Factory over the years. The colour of the body is off-white or very light cream—the natural, unstained colour of good English earthenware.

Glaze decided the finished colour of the ware. If a yellow glaze were used, then cream colour resulted—it could be any shade desired, according to the amount of stain used. Among other colours were dark green, rich brown (Colour Plate 11 and Plates 122 and 123) and white, which was the preferred colour for blue decorations. Spode blue printed wares have a white glaze, heavily stained with cobalt. Like the yellow of cream ware glaze, the blue of the white is easily detected where it lies thick in the crevices of footed pieces. Today, white earthenware is white in truth, stain being added to the body rather than the glaze. This is only partially the result of an improved technique, for although potters in earlier times tended to rely on their glaze for giving whiteness to their ware (a method which, incidentally, helped to conceal blemishes in the articles themselves) they were very familiar with the use of stains in bodies and produced a greater variety of these than is seen today. Colour Plate 11 and Plates 133 to 136 illustrate pieces of various coloured wares made by Spode.

Although a superior product for the day, both the glaze and the glazing of pieces in the normal Spode white-glazed body tend to lack uniformity. Patches of unglazed area abound, particularly on the bases of articles, and the glaze itself is often characterised by cloudy patches of blue. In the 1820s, an improved, finer and whiter earthenware body resulted in a higher grade of product which was called, and marked, Spode's Imperial. The glaze used still contained a cobalt stain but in considerably reduced quantity, and the glazing of the articles was more uniform. A further improvement came at the very end of the Spode Period with the introduction of Spode's New Fayence. Pieces of this are usually creamier in appearance than those in Imperial, the glaze being almost clear and the natural colour of the body therefore being more apparent. In many instances, however, it is almost impossible to tell the difference between the two improved earthenwares (see Marks 20 and 21: Appendix IV).

The stand illustrated in Plate 226, decorated with a hand-painted Chantilly Sprig pattern, is a very rare example of an improved earthenware body, made well before the two discussed above. Of a beautiful whiteness and texture, the article has a glaze which is virtually clear. Another piece of this kind, but heavily crazed, is in the Spode Museum. Although it is not marked Spode, its origin is not in doubt. Decorated with Pattern 282, it is the same shape as the dish illustrated in Plate 130 and is marked with the pattern number and Stoke China impressed (see Appendix IV). Only close examination reveals that these two pieces are earthenware and not china. Although quite opaque, their colour and glaze are superior to most examples of early Spode china. They must represent a rare class of Spode wares, possibly produced shortly before the introduction of bone china. One wonders if ware of this type and quality is not better described by the term 'pearl ware' than the coarser and quite unpearl-like ware, with its blue stained glaze, which is usually graced with the name.

ENAMELLED DECORATION

Freehand painting always remained an important method of decoration for Spode earthenware; but in the first decade of the century, and before, it was used exclusively for all polychrome patterns. The earliest entries in the Spode pattern books are for simple borders in typical eighteenth-century cream ware style. They are free from ostentation, well executed and perfectly adapted to the graceful shapes and narrow-rimmed plates for which they were designed.

Of the first fifty-four recorded Spode patterns, thirty-five are of this kind. The first eight pages of the earliest pattern book, showing thirty-two of them, are illustrated in Plate 106. Plate 107 shows three of these early patterns on pieces. Of the thirty-five, only twenty-six are original designs, the other nine being colour variants. Most contain more than one colour, but the early Spode preference for yellow and red is very marked: eleven are predominantly yellow, twelve predominantly red, and five predominantly a combination of the two colours. Another strong early characteristic was the way the designs were made into distinct, neat bands, by the addition of an inner line if necessary.

Patterns of this type were never completely superseded. An interesting but quite late example is illustrated in Plate 112 with Pattern 2577, introduced *c.* 1816. In the later period, as the pattern books became crowded with very heavy decorations of the print and enamel type, the legacy of the eighteenth-century style of borders was preserved by the underglaze paintresses, whose inexpensive work was recorded in the 'B' Pattern book. Pattern B24, illustrated in Plate 129, is a typical example of this. Although it was introduced *c.* 1822, it is, in fact, just an underglaze version of Pattern 1448, *c.* 1809. This, in its turn, is a variation of a pattern common to several other potters thirty or more years before, including Neale and Wedgwood.[215]

Pattern B1, illustrated in Plate 127, is a border pattern which has more of the character of the peasant-style painting typified by several of the patterns illustrated on the same page. Pieces decorated with patterns of this kind, a considerable number of which were produced during the Spode and Copeland and Garrett Periods, are strangely hard to find. They may have found their way mainly to export markets. Usually very simple in both their structure and execution, a few patterns of this type have some sophistication: but they all posesss an unselfconscious charm, which is common to all examples of this timeless and universal method of ceramic decoration, the building up of patterns from simple brushwork. Almost anyone, let alone the nimble-fingered girls of Staffordshire, could be trained to perform such homespun work, which owes nothing to artistic canons. Nearly all Staffordshire potters produced wares of this kind, many well into this century, and potteries in many parts of the world continue to do so today.

Most polychrome Spode earthenware patterns are not freehand painted. They are first outline-printed under the glaze and then coloured in by a paintress. The advantage of this method is obvious: it produced full, highly decorative patterns which looked a lot for the money. The printed outlines provided the necessary draughtsmanship, leaving the enameller only with the job of colouring. Skill was required in shading the colours, and deftness was necessary in filling in the outlines; but the technique was quick and inexpensive for the weight of decoration it supplied, and it is not surprising that it was extremely popular for Spode earthenware and stone china patterns. Many of the engravings produced for the process were used for a multitude of versions, each with a different colouring. One of the best examples of this is the very popular Tumbledown Dick pattern (Plates 117 and 170), produced in at least twelve versions on earthenware alone.

Patterns which had been engraved for an all-printed decoration were also produced in enamelled versions. These can always be recognised by the full shading and detail of the print. Outline engravings, intended for subsequent enamelling, were really quite unsuitable for use as plain prints, but Chinese Flowers (Plate 45) is an example of this being done.

BLUE PRINTED WARES

If the Spodes had produced nothing except their plain blue printed earthen-wares, their reputation would still be assured. The scope of Spode II's ambi-tions and the vast resources at his hand urged him to manufacture virtually everything available to the pottery industry of his day and, in a field so large, it was inevitable that there should be much that was imitative and some that was inferior to the best of his competitors. Such criticism is silenced by his blue printed wares, the general high quality of which has been a byword for a century and a half. Amid all his other enterprises, the blue printing decorating process inherited from his father was never for one moment neglected, and this tradi-tional feature of the Spode Factory's activity expanded with the business. On Spode II's death, it struck at least one contemporary that 'the invention which principally made Mr Spode's fortune was of the blue-white ware'.[61] A general work of the nature of this book cannot hope to deal adequately with the subject: nearly thirty years ago Sydney B. Williams, an avid collector, produced a volume devoted exclusively to it[289] and much more recently it has received the equally enthusiastic attention of J. K. des Fontaines.[88] But no history of Spode could be taken seriously which did not have something to say on the subject, and a few things are yet unsaid.

The reputation of Spode blue and white rests on the potting of the wares themselves, a mastery of the printing technique, the quality of the engravings employed, and the nature of the blue itself. A contemporary illustration of the process appears on page 11 and in 1846, William Evans wrote a concise and ac-curate description of it which could be an eye-witness account of today (1970), so little has the original method and equipment changed:[81]

> Blue printing is the name for the manipulations of taking impressions (in colours, blue, green, pink and brown,) from copper-plates engraved in a style peculiar to the artists of the pottery districts. . . .
>
> The press is placed within four feet of a stove-plate, kept constantly heated, that when the copper-plate is laid thereon, its engravings may more easily admit the colour as it is rubbed over it. . . The colour is well mixed on a very hot iron plate, into a fluid, called technically an oil. . . The printer places his plate on the stove, rubs in the colour, with a broad pallet knife scrapes off the excess, and then with his boss cleans the plain sides, and places it on the bed of his press; he next brushes the sheet of tissue paper over with a solution of soft soap and water, puts it on the plate, rolls it between the rollers, and the instant the return of the press leaves it dry by the hot plate, he carefully takes it off. . . A cutter (a little girl, training up for the next manipulation) takes the impression, cuts away all the white paper, then separates the impression into its parts. . .
>
> A transferer, with considerable tact and judgment, places on a biscuit vessel the several parts in their proper arrangement; and then, with a rubber of flannel . . .

she rubs the paper upon the article, with much force. . . The dry and absorbent porosity of the ware aids the adhesion of the colour in the oil, and when the task is completed, each vessel is . . . immersed in water and with soft water and a sponge the paper is washed off. . . The ware is kept in a heated room to evaporate much of the water imbibed in washing off the paper, which is requisite to prepare it for the fluid glaze; and also, is heated to red heat, to harden on the colour, and volatalise the oil particles, else the glaze would not adhere.[166]

Teamwork is the essence of the process. Indeed, solo performance is the very antithesis of all pottery decoration. Even the work of the most talented painter can be ruined by the humbler kiln man if, in his own field, he is not as expert as the artist. In printing, the first vital member of the team is the engraver, even though unknown to those who use his work. Bad printing can spoil the work contained in the finest engraving, but no amount of manipulative skill can make a bad engraving look good.

The art of engraving was highly evolved before the introduction of blue printing to pottery. But the refinements of the book engraver, and those whose work resulted in the earlier on-glaze black printing, was not possible for under-glaze blue printing on absorbent biscuit ware until several technical advances had been made. Most important of these were the introduction of 'wet' printing —using the paper soft-soaped instead of dry—and improvements in the quality and nature of the paper itself. Before the second decade of the nineteenth century, engravings were being produced which compare with any later ones. Full use was made of stippled effects and different depths of cut to produce effects of light and shade. Early engravings were coarse. They relied entirely upon lines for their effect, sometimes cut across each other (cross-hatched) for crude shading effects. These lines were cut to a uniform and considerable depth, producing printed ware with virtually no tonal values.

In a brief account of the beginning of blue printing at Spode I's factory, Shaw supplies the name of the first engraver and the first printer employed by him:

About 1784, he introduced the manufacture of Blue Printed into Stoke; on the improved methods successfully adopted by Mr. Ralph Baddeley, of Shelton. The Patterns were—for Table Services what is now called the Old Willow, with a border of a willow and a dagger; and for Tea Services the Broseley, from the Pattern used at Caughley. The engraver was named Lucas, and his first printer was named Richards, from Caughley. Specimens of this ware, shew the great strength of the engravings, and consequent deep blue of the ware. The first transferrer Mrs. Mary Broad, of Penkhull, (recently buried at Stoke), informed us that she remembered the first dish printed in Blue at Stoke, being long carefully preserved as a specimen.[253]

Elsewhere, Shaw names Thomas Turner of Caughley as the previous employer of both Lucas and Richards, and he shares the credit for some important innovations in technique between the latter and a former workmate of his named Ainsworth: 'These two printers first introduced the Composition called Oils, and the method of washing the paper off the bisquet pottery, and hardening on the colours previous to the immersion in the fluid glaze'.[252]

Unfortunately, Shaw's account of the Spode Factory's first engraver is almost flatly contradicted by Jewitt, whose story only corresponds in that Shropshire is given as the original fount of knowledge:

> On the expiration of his apprenticeship, Thomas Minton continued to be employed for a time at the Caughley China Works under Mr. Turner, and then removed to London, where he engraved some patterns for Josiah Spode. From London, having married, he removed into Staffordshire, in 1788 or 1789, where the rapidly increasing demand for blue printed earthenware gave promise of a good opening for so skilful a draughtsman and engraver as he had become... Here he became very successful, one of his chief employers being Josiah Spode, for whom he engraved a tea-ware pattern called the 'Buffalo', which continued in demand for many years; the 'Broseley', so called from being produced at the Caughley Works, the 'Willow Pattern', and many others. In the latter he was assisted by Henry Doncaster of Penkhull. . . . . Mr. Minton had two apprentices, one of whom Greatbatch (father of the eminent artist William Greatbatch, engraver of the 'Waterloo Banquet') became chief engraver and manager of that department at Spode and Copelands.[209]

We are left in some doubt concerning the man responsible for Spode's first engravings. Jewitt's mention of the Greatbatches, father and son, is particularly interesting since William Greatbatch engraved the portrait of Spode II, painted by Keeling in 1806, which is illustrated in Plate 83. Although the Factory's engraving department in Spode II's time must have been extremely large, use was still made of outside engravers. In 1815, one of these, Thomas Sparks—then in Stoke, although shortly to move to London—wrote to Josiah Wedgwood Junior refusing to reduce his charges by 10 per cent and explaining that he was charging no more than had been paid by Mr Spode and others over a long period.[149] The existence of 'engraving factories', in some cases very substantial ones, largely explains why so many patterns were common to several manufacturers.

The accounts of Shaw and Jewitt provide the names of three patterns produced by Spode I: Buffalo, Broseley and Willow or Old Willow. The problem of identifying pieces decorated with these as definite products of Spode I is, like all questions concerning his blue printed wares, complicated by the longevity of the patterns themselves and the almost everlasting nature of copper engravings.

But there is a distinct class of Spode blue printed wares which in every way bespeak their early date and these can, with fair safety, be attributed to Spode I. Not only are they decorated with engravings in which only the earliest techniques are apparent but also the transferring is without finesse, the joining of the prints at the borders and the positioning of the decoration on the pieces often being careless in comparison with the later wares. The potting of the articles also stands no comparison with later examples. In particular, plates and dishes have 'squared off', almost sharp, edges. Such pieces are invariably marked with one of the variants of the primitive Mark 1 or with Mark 2 (Appendix IV). This last mark seems also to have been used by Spode II for a while and can be found on his very early china pieces—but it is only to be expected that on returning to the factory in 1797 he would have continued the marks then existing.

The excellence of Spode blue and white owes not a little to the colour of the blue itself. Some patterns, notably Lucano and Indian Sporting, make the nearest approach ever achieved in blue printed ware to the luminosity of the finest Chinese blue, K'ang Hsi. The varying depths of blue within a piece are achieved by the different strengths in the engraving, but this does not explain why some patterns are always found in a distinct shade of blue which is not typical of others. Castle Pattern, for instance, is invariably light in colour (Colour Plate III). The reason for this is that an altogether different blue was used and the effect was quite deliberate. The lead glaze of the period was an important factor in the appearance of the blue, softening the printed outlines. Mercifully, the full 'flow blue' effect was never sought during the Spode Period. In the years which followed it, commercial pressure resulted in the general introduction in Staffordshire of this calculated insult to the engraver's art, with its deliberate effect of smudge and blur.

Illustrations of some seventy-four Spode blue printed patterns are provided in Plates 1 to 81 which follow. Where a pattern is illustrated more than once, it is because it was produced in more than one version with distinctly different engravings. Where possible, a dinner plate has been chosen to provide the illustration since this gives the best representation of the pattern—usually being the first piece executed by any ceramic designer. The patterns have been arranged according to subject, not date, in roughly the following order: Chinese landscapes; other Orientally-inspired designs; floral patterns; English subjects; Italian subjects; multi-scene patterns in which a different subject decorates each piece in the service; examples of badged or armorial work. The patterns illustrated represent all the Spode blue printed patterns known to me, with one exception: a floral pattern illustrated by S.B.Williams in Figure 154 of his book.[289]

Each pattern has been provided with a name. Where this or part of it appears in inverted commas, it is invented; otherwise, it is authentic—based upon either a list of patterns and names, *c*. 1875, which still survives at the Spode Factory or some earlier source. This question is an important one since, in 1877, Jewitt published a list of named Spode patterns with a date of introduction for each.[208] Quite obviously, this list must have been supplied to him by someone at the Factory at the time, and it has been possible to verify several of his dates by identifying their enamelled versions in the ordinary Spode pattern books, to the numbers of which it is now possible to assign fairly accurate dates (see Chapter VI). The appearance of an enamelled version proves, at the very least, that by the date of their use in this fashion the coppers were at the Factory. Where these are full engravings, quite obviously not designed for producing outlines, their first use would have been for plain prints.

The name and date supplied by Jewitt is given in the notes on individual patterns which accompany the illustrations, but a number of those in his list cannot be assigned and remain to puzzle us. It is important to remember that he headed his list 'printed patterns' and this does not mean plain prints exclusively. Three of the names he gives almost certainly refer to some never produced in any way other than by the print and enamel process: Bamboo, 1825; Ship, 1819 and Peacock, 1814 (Colour Plate IX). Quite possibly, all the others might be similarly explained; but since every collector of Spode blue printed wares hopes he will one day discover a hitherto unknown pattern, they are given to aid speculation: New Nankin, 1815; Blossom, 1817; Arcade, 1818; Oriental, 1820; Bud and Flower, 1822; Sun, 1822; Blue Border, 1823; Image, 1824; Persian, 1824; Blue Imperial, 1826.

Blue printed patterns

1 HAND-PAINTED *Stone China Dish, 14⅝in. long. Mark 19a*
This is not a printed specimen at all but a hand-painted matching piece for an existing
Chinese service. Such pieces are hard to find but are of the greatest interest—
especially when, like this one, they are of superior quality.

2 'TEMPLE-LANDSCAPE, FIRST' *Earthenware Soup Plate, 8¾in. Mark 2a*
The only marked specimen of this pattern known to me is the one illustrated, in the
possession of W.O.Sims Esq, of Richmond, Surrey, to whom I am indebted for this
photograph. Several engravings for the pattern survive at the Spode Factory. The
border is a slight variant of the popular Temple border, given its name by the pattern
illustrated in Plate 16. The primitive method of giving prominence to a figure by
placing it in a white cartouche should be noted and compared with Plate 3. The
plate has all the appearances of early manufacture and can be attributed to Spode I.
A remarkable feature is that on the reverse of the plate the name B.Leach appears
as a printed mark. Almost certainly this refers to a china dealer and customer of the
Factory. The mark is very large, measuring two and a half inches across, and has also
been found on a shard decorated with this pattern, excavated at the Spode Factory.

B⋅Leach

3 'TWO FIGURES' *Earthenware Dish, 16in. long. Mark 1a*
See also Colour Plate III. A very early specimen in harsh indigo blue. Examples of
this pattern produced by other manufacturers have been noted.

4 'DAGGER-LANDSCAPE, FIRST' *Earthenware Soup Plate, 9in. Mark 2a*
Shaw describes Spode I's first tableware pattern as 'old willow with a border of
willow and a dagger'. I have never seen a pattern which fits this description. Shaw
may be confusing us here by describing a pattern as 'willow' when he simply means
a Chinese landscape. This pattern, which is a very early one, does at least have a
dagger border. Possibly it is the one meant by Shaw; but this could equally be the
one illustrated in Plate 6.

5 'PARASOL FIGURE' *Earthenware Dish, 19in. long. Mark 3*
This pattern was also produced on Stone China.

6 'DAGGER-LANDSCAPE, SECOND' *Reproduction Plate, 9in. From an original copper engraving at the Spode Factory*
It is to be hoped that an authentic Spode piece of this pattern will one day come to
light. It is among the earliest patterns produced by the Factory. See note on Plate 4.

N.B. References to Marks: see Appendix IV.

1

2

3

4

5

6

7 'FOREST-LANDSCAPE, FIRST' *Earthenware Soup Plate, 9in. Mark 2a*
See also Colour Plate III and, for border, Plate 9. This is an early production. The
same pattern was produced later in the Spode Period, an example of which is
illustrated in Plate 8.

8 'FOREST-LANDSCAPE, SECOND' *Earthenware Plate, 9⅞in. Mark 3*
A later version of the pattern illustrated in Plate 7, showing a much superior
engraving technique and a higher standard of printing.

9 ROCK *Earthenware Plate, 8in. Mark 2a*
An early pattern which has the same border as 'Forest-Landscape', above.

10 WILLOW, 'FIRST' *Earthenware Tray, 9in. Mark 2a*
A very early example of the Willow pattern, in harsh indigo blue. According to
Jewitt, Thomas Minton engraved a Willow pattern for Spode I.

11 WILLOW, 'SECOND' *Earthenware Plate, 9¼in. Mark 2a*
    Another early example of the Willow pattern, in a much lighter blue than that in
Plate 10 but from a copper executed at about the same time.

12 WILLOW, 'THIRD' *Earthenware Soup Plate, 9½in. Marks 4 and 16a*
A later version of the Willow pattern, produced with quite different engravings from
the first two.

7

8

9

10

11

12

13 'FLYING PENNANT' *Earthenware Plate, 9¾in. Mark 2a*
An early production with a very distinctive border.

14 'TEMPLE-LANDSCAPE, SECOND' *Stone China Plate, 9½in. Mark 19b*
A later example of the Temple border used with a landscape centre.

15 'DAGGER-LANDSCAPE, THIRD' *China Saucer, 6¼in. Mark 16a*
This pattern has subsequently become known as 'Mandarin'. Examples are quite
common, always in bone china teaware. This may well be the 'Dagger Border' which
Jewitt gives as having been introduced in 1814. The other two patterns which use
this border, Plates 4 and 6, are of earlier date.

16 TEMPLE *China Soup Plate, 8¼in. Mark 16a*
This famous pattern, made by innumerable potters, is usually found in china
teawares when of Spode manufacture. This example has a gold edge. It is probably
the pattern meant by 'New Temple' in Jewitt's list, which he says was introduced
in 1814.

17 'QUEEN CHARLOTTE' *China Plate, 9⅝in. Mark 16a*
The name is an old factory one. Its possible origin is referred to on page 193.
Examples are uncommon, and those I have seen have always been in china. Pieces are
frequently unmarked. The pattern was also made in the Copeland and Garrett
Period.

18 BROSELEY *China Dish, 8in. Mark 16a*
This piece has a gold edge. Although Broseley is mentioned by both Shaw and
Jewitt as among the Factory's first patterns, this version, which is quite common, is
late. Jewitt gives 'Pale Broseley' as having been introduced in 1817. Twelve versions
of the pattern, with different gilt finishes, were entered between pattern numbers
2896 and 2920, *c.* 1818.

13

14

15

16

17

18

19 'TALL DOOR' *Earthenware Plate, 10in. Mark 16a*
See also Colour Plate III. This pattern is not of early manufacture but examples are
very rare.

20 BUFFALO *Earthenware Plate, 8in. Mark 16b*
Buffalo is given by Jewitt as the Spode Factory's first teaware pattern, engraved by
Thomas Minton. Although the engraving used for this piece is very early, the mark
is not recognisable as an early one. Jewitt does mention that the pattern 'continued
in demand for many years'. The pattern was produced by many potters and unmarked
pieces can rarely be attributed with safety to Spode.

21 NET *Earthenware Plate, 9⅝in. Marks 4 and 16c*
This is a late example of the pattern, but pieces of earlier date are known. Spode
examples are fairly common, as are those of other potters.

22 GRASSHOPPER *Stone China Plate, 9½in. Mark 19a*
I am not aware of examples of this pattern in any body except Stone China or New
Stone. Its border was used for enamelled patterns *c.* 1812, Numbers 2084, 2085 and
2086.

23 'LANJE LIJSEN' *Earthenware Plate, 9¾in. Marks 4 and 16a*
S.B.Williams traces the origin of the name, often anglicised as 'Long Eliza'.[295]
Pieces are fairly uncommon, but the pattern is not of very early manufacture.

24 INDIA *Earthenware Plate, 9¾in. Mark 16a*
The name of this pattern has been confused with Indian Sporting, but it is an
authentic Spode name. In the early nineteenth century, India was used as a synonym
for the Orient. Jewitt dates the introduction of the pattern to 1815 and this receives
confirmation from its first enamelled version, Number 2489. Specimens are
sometimes encountered with an inscription on the reverse which reads: 'This blue-
ware is printed from the calx of British cobalt produced from the Wheal Sparnon
Mine in the county of Cornwall, Aug. 1816'. The mine was near Redruth. The vein
of cobalt there was discovered in about 1807 and was later widely used by
Staffordshire potters.[287]

19

20

21

22

23

24

25 'OLD PEACOCK' *Earthenware Plate, 10in. Marks 4 and 16a*
This pattern was named by S.B.Williams. It is rare and of late production.

26 JAPAN *Earthenware Dish, 13in. Mark 4*
Jewitt lists 'New Japan', 1815, and 'Panel Japan', 1820.

27 DRAGONS *China Tea Saucer, 5⅝in. Mark 15a*
Pattern 2414, introduced *c.* 1815, was a version of this pattern enamelled in green.

28 'TROPHIES-NANKIN' *Earthenware Sandwich Set Section, 12⅝in. Mark 2a*
The full authentic name for this rare pattern was 'Nankin Border and Trophy Centre'. The piece illustrated is of early date but I have seen a later example produced from the same copper engravings.

29 'TROPHIES-ETRUSCAN' *Earthenware Plate, 9¾in. Marks 4 and 16a*
The full authentic name for this pattern is 'Etruscan Border and Trophy Centre'. The first enamelled version was Number 4155, and this corroborates Jewitt's dating of 'Etruscan', 1825.

30 'TROPHIES-DAGGER' *Earthenware Stand, 13½in. long. Copeland and Garrett mark*
The authentic name for this pattern is 'Dagger Border and Trophy Centre'. It was produced during the Spode Period and is still manufactured at the Spode Factory, with the name 'Fitzhugh'.

25   26

27   28

29   30

31 LILY *China Dish, 7in. Mark 16a*
This printed china piece is blue banded, and the centre and bands are traced in gold. The pattern was first produced by the Spode Factory at an early date, and I have seen an earthenware sandwich set section with Mark 2a. The pattern was common to several manufacturers, including Worcester and Minton.

32 LYRE *Earthenware Plate, 8in. Marks 4 and 16a*
This example has a brown enamelled edge and delicate red line tracery at the centre, but it was almost certainly produced without these additional refinements. Examples are extremely rare.

33 'LATTICE SCROLL' *Earthenware Plate, 9⅞in. Mark 16b*
See also Plate 79. Five enamelled versions of this pattern, Numbers 1680 to 1684, were produced *c.* 1810.

34 'FLOWER CROSS' *Earthenware Plate, 9¾in. Mark 15a*
Examples of this unusual pattern are very rare.

35 DAISY *Unhandled Earthenware Cup, 2in. high. No marks*
Several copper engravings for this pattern survive at the Spode Factory and this cup has been accepted as of Spode manufacture. It is an example of a 'sheet pattern' — i.e., the design is 'all over', so the engravings could be produced without considering a particular fit for various articles.

36 'LEAF' *Earthenware Soup Plate, 10in. No marks*
Coppers for this pattern survive at the Spode Factory, and Spode pieces are known with Mark 16c. This is another example of a 'sheet pattern'.

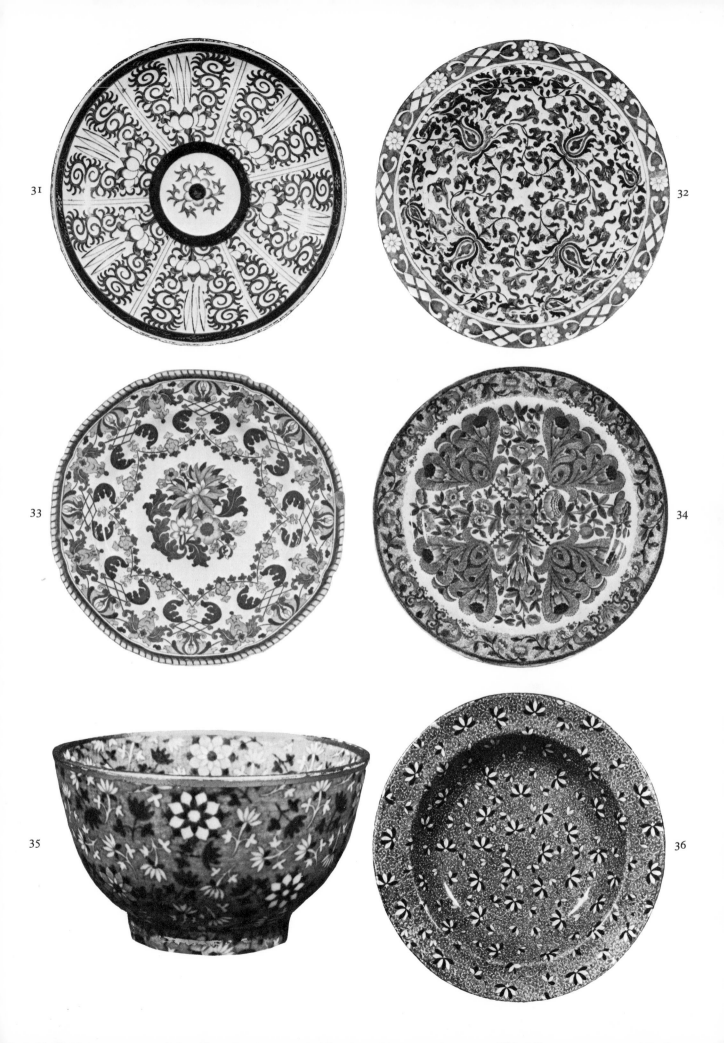

31

32

33

34

35

36

37 MARBLE *Earthenware Plate, 8½in. Marks 4 and 16a*
The pattern is also found on New Stone. Several enamelled versions were produced,
most of them completed by cutting a border and a small centre piece from the full
pattern. The first version I have traced is Pattern 3667, introduced *c.* 1821, which
confirms Jewitt's date for this pattern. Another early authentic name for this pattern
is 'Mosaic'. It has also been called 'Cracked Ice and Prunus'.

38 'FENCE' *Earthenware Sandwich Set Section, 12½in. Mark 2a*
This is an early production. A later variant was produced with the same centre but
with the border from Group Pattern, Plate 43. An example of this version is
illustrated in Figure 132 of S.B.Williams' book.

39 CHANTILLY SPRIG *China Plate, 9⅞in. Mark 16a*
An earlier hand-painted version of this pattern is illustrated in Plate 226.

40 'GLOUCESTER' *Earthenware Comport, 12in. long. Mark 2a*
This is the only Spode piece I know of the pattern, and it has all the marks of early
manufacture. An enamelled version with gilt sprays alternating with the printed ones
was Pattern 1866, *c.* 1811. The design is still produced at the Spode Factory and has
been given its current name.

41 'PEPLOW' *Earthenware Plate, 7¾in. Mark 16a*
The pattern name used dates from this century. The centre of this pattern, within
an entirely different border, was used in an enamelled version, Number 3060, *c.* 1819.

42 BOWPOT *Unfooted China Comport, 11½in long. Mark 16a*
Jewitt lists 'Bonpot' and 'Double Bonpot' as being introduced in 1822 and 1823
respectively. It is doubtful if the pattern illustrated is meant since three enamelled
versions of this, Numbers 1867 to 1869, were introduced *c.* 1812.

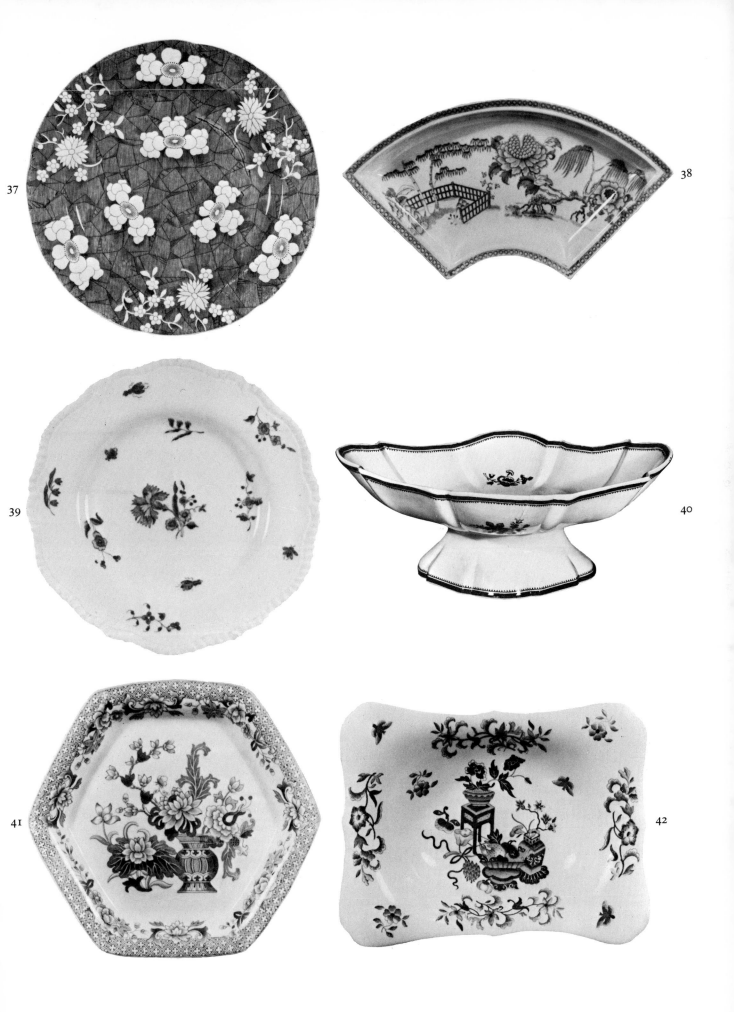

37

38

39

40

41

42

43 GROUP *Earthenware Soup Plate, 10in. Mark 4*
See also Plate 100 and the note above on Plate 38. The first enamelled version of
this pattern was Number 1437, *c.* 1809.

44 'ENGLISH SPRAYS' *Tea Saucer.*
Two enamelled versions of this pattern, Numbers 4760 and 4761, were introduced
c. 1829.

45 CHINESE FLOWERS *Earthenware Saucer, 6in. Mark 16a*
An enamelled version of this pattern, Number 2486, was introduced *c.* 1815. The
engraving was obviously designed for producing an outline print for subsequent
filling in with enamel.

46 FRUIT AND FLOWERS *Earthenware Plate, 7½in. Marks 4 and 16a*
The name of this pattern refers to the border. It was also produced printed in brown
in Pattern B139, *c.* 1826, and later in green, Pattern B184.

47 FILIGREE *Earthenware Soup Plate, 9½in. Marks 4 and 16a*
Jewitt dates the introduction of this pattern to 1823. This is confirmed by the first
enamelled version, Number 3914.

48 FLORAL *Earthenware Plate, 10in. Mark 23*
See also Plate 95. This multi-scene pattern was one of the last produced in the Spode
Period. The first enamelled versions, Numbers 4977 and 4978, which made use of
the border only, were introduced *c.* 1830. Examples are hard to find.

43

44

45

46

47

48

49 'CONVOLVULUS' *Earthenware Plate, 9⅞in. Mark 16b*
The first enamelled version of this pattern, with the background to the flowers entirely gilt, was Number 1864, introduced *c.* 1812.

50 JASMINE *Earthenware Plate, 9¼in. Marks 4 and 16a*
The name refers to the border. The first enamelled version introduced was Number B118, *c.* 1825. Later versions were Numbers 4540 and 4541, *c.* 1827. A green print version of this border—with a Geranium centre, as in Plate 51—was Pattern B142. This variant may also have appeared as a blue print, although an example has not yet been discovered.

51 GERANIUM *Earthenware Plate, 9¾in. Marks 4 and 16a*
The border only was used in an enamelled version, Pattern 3037, introduced *c.* 1818. Jewitt dates the introduction of Geranium to 1820. The border was a favourite for use with armorial centres (see Plates 78, 80 and 81). The centre was used with a different border in at least one pattern: see the note above on Plate 50.

52 BRITISH FLOWERS *Earthenware Soup Plate, 10in. Marks 4 and 16a*
Compare the centre with Botanical, illustrated in Plate 54. The two patterns are of similar date.

53 CAMILLA *Earthenware Plate, 10in. Copeland and Garrett mark*
The pattern is rare and I have not yet seen a piece marked Spode. It may have been introduced immediately after the Spode Period. A very large number of enamelled versions were produced, always with the pattern in full, and the first of these was Number 5419, *c.* 1833.

54 BOTANICAL *Earthenware Plate, 9⅞in. Marks 4 and 16a*
See also Plate 96. The pattern is a multi-scene one. The first enamelled version was Number 4565, *c.* 1828.

49

50

51

52

53

54

55 BLUE ROSE *Earthenware Plate, 9⅞in. Mark 20*
Three enamelled versions were introduced, Numbers 4162, 4163 and 4167, *c.* 1825.

56 UNION WREATH, 'FIRST' *China Saucer, 6½in. Mark 16a*
The pattern is rarely found, and examples are always china tewares of Gadroon Shape. The first enamelled version was Number 4158, *c.* 1825. Jewitt lists two patterns, of which the first probably refers to this: 'Union Wreath', 1826, and 'Union', 1822. Plate 168 illustrates the border used as an underglaze brown print on china with a badge centre.

57 UNION WREATH, 'SECOND' *Earthenware Dish, 20in. Mark 20*
The pattern is made up of the centre of Blue Rose and the border of Union Wreath, 'First' (Plates 55 and 56). An enamelled version of this pattern in full was Number 4169, *c.* 1825. It was also printed in brown, pattern B138.

58 UNION WREATH, 'THIRD' *New Stone Plate, 9¾in. Mark 7*
The pattern is also found on earthenware. The centre of this pattern was obviously not designed for its border which, with a small mixed floral centre more complementary to it, was produced as Pattern 3813 printed in purple, *c.* 1822. The pattern illustrated is probably the one described by Jewitt as 'Union', 1822. It was very popular.

59 FONT ('GIRL AT WELL') *Earthenware Plate, 9⅞in. Marks 4 and 16a*
Mr Richard Newton pointed out that this pattern is undoubtedly the 'Font, 1821' in Jewitt's list since productions in the same pattern are known by other manufacturers and some of these bear this name.
The pattern has the same border as Union Wreath, 'Third', Plate 58. It was produced in a full enamelled version, Number 3661, *c.* 1822.

55

 56

57

58

 59

60 MILKMAID *Earthenware Plate, 10in. Mark 3*
See also Plates 98 and 99. Jewitt dates the introduction of this pattern to 1814. It uses the same border as Tower, Plate 70.

61 WOODMAN *Earthenware Dish. Mark 4*
See also Plate 98. Jewitt dates the introduction of this pattern to 1816.

62 'COUNTRY SCENE' *Reproduction Plate, 9in. From an original copper engraving at the Spode Factory*
Authentic marked Spode pieces are known.

63 WATERLOO ('ITALIAN CHURCH') *Earthenware Plate, 7⅜in. Mark 4*
Jewitt dates the introduction of this pattern to 1818. Its first enamelled version was Number 3395, *c.* 1820.
The building depicted is the church in the village of Waterloo, a fact ascertained by Mr Michael Newsom. Its portrayal is very similar to that on a dessert plate in the Duke of Wellington's Berlin Service, *c.* 1817.
In ignorance of this, the pattern had been given the name 'Italian Church'. The researches of Robert Copeland had previously established that the pattern which was at one time thought to be Waterloo was not the one meant by Jewitt. This pattern, depicting scenes of battles and occasions in the life of the Duke of Wellington, was definitely a Copeland and Garrett introduction. Seven of the scenes it uses were first published between 1839 and 1841 in a three-volume biography of the Duke by W.H.Maxwell.

64 'VILLAGE SCENE' *Earthenware Covered Toilet Pot, 2¼in. high. Mark 16a*
This small piece, which belonged to Major A.J.Bather, is one of the very few examples of this pattern known to me.

65 'GOTHIC CASTLE' *Earthenware Plate, 10in. Mark 3*
See also Plate 100. The border was taken from the same source as Indian Sporting, Plate 72. The pattern was produced in an enamelled version, Number 1966, *c.* 1812. The authentic name is not known, but it is much more likely that this is the pattern referred to by Jewitt as 'Castle', 1806, than the one illustrated in Plate 67—although the date still seems a little too early.

60

61

62

63

64

65

66 ITALIAN *Earthenware Plate, 9⅞in. Mark 4*
See also Colour Plate III. The most famous of all Spode's blue printed patterns,
Italian is still produced today in very large quantities. It has not yet proved possible
to trace the original source for the centre scene, which is very reminiscent of several
Pirenesi prints. The border, of Imari design, was frequently used for enamelled
patterns; but its first appearance as such was with the Italian centre, complete, in
Pattern 2614, *c.* 1816. Jewitt dates the introduction of the pattern to that year.
Examples are sometimes found with the 1816 Wheal Sparnon Mine inscription (see
note on Plate 24).

67 CASTLE *Earthenware Plate, 9⅞in. Mark 4*
See also Colour Plate III. The centre of the pattern is taken from aquatint engravings
of The Gate of Sebastian at Capena which appeared in *Merigot's Views of Rome and
its Vicinity*, published 1796–98.[293] Jewitt dates the introduction of Castle to 1806,
but see note on Plate 65.

68 LUCANO *Earthenware Plate, 9¾in. Marks 4 and 16a*
The centre scene was taken from an aquatint engraving of The Bridge of Lucano
near Rome which appeared in *Merigot's Views of Rome and its Vicinity*, published
1796–98.[294] The pattern was popular with other manufacturers. Jewitt dates the
introduction of it by Spode to 1819.

69 ROME *Earthenware Plate, 9¾in. Mark 16b*
The centre decoration was taken from aquatint engravings of The Castle and Bridge
of St. Angelo and Trajan's Column in Rome which appeared in *Merigot's Views of
Rome and its Vicinity*, published 1796–98.[292] The pattern is sometimes called Tiber.
Jewitt dates the introduction of 'Roman' to 1811. This is confirmed by a letter to
Wedgwood at Etruria, dated 22nd February 1812, reporting that 'A lady in our
rooms a few days ago stated that she had seen Mr Spode's new blue pattern of the
bridge at Rome over the Tiber, and she thought it very handsome'.[117]

70 TOWER *Earthenware Plate, 9¾in. Mark 3*
See also Plates 97 and 99. The centre scene was taken from an aquatint engraving of
the Bridge of Salaro, near Porta Salara, which appeared in *Merigot's Views of Rome
and its Vicinity*, published 1796–98.[293] Jewitt dates the introduction of the pattern
to 1815. The border was used in an enamelled pattern, Number 3166, *c.* 1820. The
border was also used for Milkmaid Pattern, Plate 60.

71 DRESDEN BORDERS *Earthenware Plate, 9in. Marks 4 and 16a*
This border was sometimes used for heraldic centres. It was also a popular gilt design
for china. See Plates 207 and 213.

66

67

68

69

70

71

72 'INDIAN SPORTING' *Earthenware Plate, 9⅞in. Marks 4 and 16a and 'Death of the Bear'*
See also Plates 94 and 300. S.B.Williams deals with this pattern in great detail. The several scenes used are taken from illustrations in *Oriental Field Sports, Wild Sports of the East* by Captain Thomas Williamson, the publication of which began in 1805.

73 'CARAMANIAN' *Earthenware Plate, 10in. Mark 3*
See also Plate 93. A Copeland pattern was produced with these centres but a different border and was known as 'Turk'. Jewitt dates the introduction of the pattern he calls 'Turk' to 1813, and this may have been the name used during the Spode Period. Jewitt's date seems to be disproved by evidence quoted by S.B.Williams[290] concerning a dinner set documented as having been given as a present in 1809. The several scenes used in the pattern are taken from three volumes by Luigi Mayer: *Views in Egypt* and *Views in the Ottoman Empire chiefly in Caramania, a part of Asia Minor hitherto unexplored* and *Views in Palestine*. They were published in 1801, 1803 and 1804 respectively.[291] The border is taken from the same source as Indian Sporting Pattern (see the note above on Plate 72).

74 GREEK *Earthenware Plate, 10in. Mark 4*
See also Plates 91 and 92. The main source for the large number of designs found in this pattern was *Outlines from the Figures and Compositions upon the Greek, Roman and Etruscan Vases of the late Sir William Hamilton; with engraved borders. Drawn and engraved by the late Mr. Kirk*, which was first published in 1804.[296] This was probably the first multi-scene pattern introduced at the Spode Factory. The first enamelled version was Number 1111, *c.* 1806. The pattern was subsequently used in eight other enamelled versions, Numbers 1307 to 1314.

75 AESOP'S FABLES *Earthenware Plate, 10in. Marked with a Copeland and Garrett mark and Mark 24 with the Spode obliterated*
See also Plates 89 and 90. The pattern was introduced at the very end of the Spode Period. Examples in blue are very rare and a more popular colour appears to have been green. The researches of Robert Copeland have established that the several scenes used for the pattern were taken from a book by Samuel Croxall, D.D., *Fables of Aesop*, published in two volumes on 4th June 1793.

76 PORTLAND VASE *Earthenware Soup Plate, 10⅛in. Copeland and Garrett mark*
The pattern is known on marked Spode pieces. The first enamelled version was Number 5057, *c.* 1831

77 WARWICK VASE *Earthenware Plate, 9¼in. Copeland and Garrett mark*
It is not certain that this pattern was produced during the Spode Period. I have never seen a piece marked Spode.

72

73

74

75

76

77

78 GERANIUM BORDER *Earthenware Dish, 10¾in. long. Mark 16a*
Device of a Dutch company in the centre.

79 LATTICE SCROLL BORDER *Earthenware Dinner Plate*
Unidentified coat of arms in the centre.

80 GERANIUM BORDER *Earthenware Soup Plate, 10in. Marks 4 and 16a*
Arms of the Confederation of Colombia in the centre. See Page 73.

81 GERANIUM BORDER *Earthenware Divided Dish, 11½in long. Marks 16a and 3 and a printed circle enclosing the initials 'TG', surrounded by the legend 'Master 1821, 22'*
The arms are those of the Skinners' Company of London.

9 China

BODY AND POTTING

The point has been made in Chapter 3 that bone china could, and can, be successfully made with very large variations in the proportion of the ingredients. This is readily illustrated by early formulae. Of the five given below, the first three are Spode recipes in use before the introduction of felspar. The fourth is the first Spode Felspar Porcelain recipe, which is dated 20th November 1821, and which was substantially altered no fewer than nine times between that date and 1836.[100] The fifth is given for interest's sake and is what would be regarded today as a first-class formula, producing bone china of a high quality. Quantities are all given as percentages; but the very minute quantities of blue stain, added in most of the formulae to improve whiteness, have been excluded.

	(1)	(2)	(3)	(4)	(5)
Bone	35·5%	26%	50%	46%	49%
China clay	23·5%	15%	19%	31%	25%
Blue clay	11·7%	11%	6%	—	—
China stone	17·6%	37%	19%	—	23%
Felspar	—	—	—	15%	3%
Flint	11·7%	11%	6%	—	—
Sand fritt	—	—	—	8%	—

The first formula is the one referred to in Chapter 4, which was copied out by Henry Daniel, c. 1817. It bears some resemblance to the second one which, in the Factory recipe book, is noted as being for 'Fluted Temple China, etc'. This, when made up, would have been a little deficient in whiteness and fineness; but it was relatively inexpensive in its constitution and was calculated to pot and fire well, giving a minimum of trouble. All in all, it was well designed for inexpensive teaware of fluted shape decorated with blue prints. The third formula would have produced a much higher grade of china than the first two, and this would have been reserved for more expensive shapes and decorations.

Some collectors, conditioned by the near-magical powers of identification claimed by certain porcelain pundits, may learn with horror of the existence of more than one body on a factory at a time. It must be accepted with equanimity by anyone interested in nineteenth-century china, since it was a universal practice. References to 'the best body' of a factory are not infrequent in the works of earlier authorities, and where there was a best there would also have been a worst—and several in between, no doubt. Earlier potters were not obsessed by ideas of standardisation. To them, it was only common sense to make their lives a little easier by 'knocking up' a special body for a special purpose. A typical practice was the addition of an extra amount of highly plastic ordinary clay, like the common blue clay,[80] at the expense of the very 'short' china clay when making large articles like chamberpots. Tips relating to formulae were as important as the formulae themselves: after the one he noted down, Henry Daniel added 'to thirty of the above add one Blue Clay. Will make it work a deal better and make no visible difference in the Colour. Makes it better to place the flat ware'.[101]

The practice of having several china bodies in production at the same time makes the identification of early examples of Spode bone china difficult at times. Frequently, a piece which has some of the characteristics of early date is just a lower grade of china, made with price mainly in mind. In addition, seconds ware was not destroyed at the Factory but was decorated with inexpensive patterns and sold off—the usual Potteries practice. For this purpose, bat printed patterns were the most frequent choice, and examples of the popular Pattern 557 (Plate 260) are often found in which the excellence of the china body itself is only equalled by the number of potting and firing defects crowded into it.

Having given ample warning of the dangers which abound, it is still possible to state that Spode china has certain general features which serve to identify it. The first of these is its whiteness—an outstanding feature even in the earliest examples and one which improved throughout the period. Although earlier pieces are frequently found with iron specks in the body, the general texture is excellent, indicating that the raw materials were well chosen and carefully prepared. Translucency varies widely, and early pieces are markedly lacking in it. A tea service like the lustre one illustrated in Plate 257 has all the marks of uneven firing—a factor which affects not only the translucency of pieces but also their shape. The cans in this service are of unequal size, and several are severely flanged out at the top. Earlier potting tended to be thick, as a form of defence against the hazards resulting from a barely understood firing technique for china, but this was rapidly overcome and most Spode pieces are remarkable for the fineness of their potting and their high translucency.

The introduction of felspar into the mix in 1821 is discussed in detail in Chapter 5. It brought about a real improvement in the body and a much greater uniformity of quality throughout the product. The texture of the china was almost faultless; and the glaze, also made with felspar, was of a quality never seen before and never bettered since. It was applied thickly but very evenly, and the word 'luscious' has been aptly used to describe it. Its appearance is usually distinctly creamy.

Most of the interest in Spode's china inevitably centres on the decorations rather than the quality of the material itself. As with every great china manufacturer, the glory of Spode's decoration was fine painting. What little is known about the artists and the decorating establishment in which they worked has been told in Chapter 4. For the rest, the illustrations given—which have been arranged by subject—must speak for themselves. More will now be said about some other aspects of Spode china decoration.

JAPANESE INFLUENCE

The outside influences on the designs produced by Spode were several. In the first two decades of the century, the shapes and patterns produced in earthenware and, later, in stone china were influenced by the Chinese. Influenced is too weak a word: they were dominated. The Orient never occupied such an exclusive, commanding position with Spode china, having to share it with some European factories, particularly Sèvres; but two Japanese styles of decoration—the Kakiemon and the Imari—exerted a very strong influence. The second, which shows itself some years after the first, in about 1805, was the more important of the two; but Kakiemon decorations were never completely ousted.

Kakiemon, a Japanese potter of the mid-seventeenth century, gave his name to a distinctive style of enamelled decoration which was extensively taken up by Meissen and the English eighteenth-century porcelain factories. The first patterns of this kind to appear in the Spode pattern books are Numbers 281 and 282. The second of these proved very successful and had a strong influence, over many years, on the development of other patterns. It is illustrated in Plate 225, and one of the many patterns derived from it features in Plate 226. As late as Pattern 2038, which is a repeat of the original 282 with slight modifications, this early design was still holding its own. Later and very popular patterns owing a great deal to Kakiemon influence were Numbers 868 and 715 (Colour Plate VI and Plate 230).

If Kakiemon decorations may be described as asymmetrical, Imari can only be called disorganised. Exported from Arita in the Province of Hizan in the first half of the eighteenth century, they were commonly called 'japans' in England. In the nineteenth century, the variety known as 'brocaded Imaris' were those most favoured by the English, whose home-produced kind was characterised by the sprawling use of underglaze cobalt blue; areas of red, and sometimes green; and flashing gold tracing over all. Gaudiness was of their very nature: they looked a lot for the money. Their popularity was phenomenal. John Haslem described them as 'good candlelight patterns'.[192] And so they are. But the description—since he took a jaundiced view of the slapdash fashion in which they were later executed by his own factory, Derby—could be imagined to have a double meaning. Bloor Derby patterns of this kind require all the flattery which poor light can give them.

The first Spode pattern of distinctly Imari type is Number 944, but it is too 'organised' to be typical. Pattern 963, illustrated in Plate 233, is much more representative of the type, having all the proper characteristics. The next pattern, Number 967, is also typical; and it was this one which provided the Factory with an almost complete answer to the public's taste for this kind of decoration. It remained in production well over a hundred years, subsequently for earthenware as well as china, and was extensively copied by other potters in the late nineteenth century. It probably decorated a greater volume of ware than the scores of other Spode Imari patterns put together. Examples are illustrated in Plates 232 and 247 and Colour Plate VIII. Its success must have been immediate, for there are very few new entries for patterns of this kind until Number 1216 (Plate 234). But from then on, fresh ones were introduced with great rapidity and it is evident that Imari decorations were accounting for a lion's share of the Factory's china business.

In about 1818, there was a distinct falling off in the number of new pattern-book entries for Imari designs. Patterns for the new product, stone china, were often indebted to the style, and the popular Mosaic border (Plate 287) was pure Imari in design: but new patterns for china were markedly less frequent than in the earlier period. Among those that did appear, a large proportion were of a very detailed, expensive kind like Pattern 2508 (Plate 235). This may have been a shrewd reaction to what was happening at Derby, where Bloor was busily engaged in cheapening the market.

Haslem describes how, to raise the funds to pay the instalments on his purchase of his factory in 1811, Bloor decorated vast quantities of seconds ware with cheap, showy patterns. He recruited paintresses in Staffordshire who could 'paint different Japan patterns, borders, etc.' and the finished products were sold off in large quantities up and down the country at public auctions.[187] In the short term, he solved his problem—but he signed the old Derby factory's death warrant in doing so. Spode II made no attempt to compete on this ground, which was not of his choosing. His decorations are skilfully executed, on good china, with gold of the best quality. The gilding is frequently the best feature of the whole.

GILDING

The esteem in which Spode II's china wares are held today is due in part to the excellence of their gilding. Even Professor Sir Arthur Church, who found little to say about them, commented, 'the gilding on Spode's wares is of great solidity and smoothness, quite the best of his day'.[159] This is more a compliment to the

quality of the gold used and to its sound firing than to the gilders; but all were of a remarkably high standard. We can agree with the factory poet that 'the ornamental gilders they have charms'—high enough praise from a painter—and it is still wonderful for 'strangers to behold the different forms in which they pencilled gold.'

Frequently, the gilders had little scope for displaying their talents. The solid gold background, which features in several well-known Spode patterns, tested their capacity for painstaking labour rather than their artistry. Best known is Pattern 711, which incorporates fine flower, and sometimes fruit, painting: examples are illustrated in Colour Plate V and Plate 215. The first pattern to appear with such a background was Number 652 (geometrical motifs reserved in white and traced in red), and the style was at the height of its popularity c. 1805. Flowers were always the most popular subject for use with it, but ornamental scrolls are found in Pattern 706. In Pattern 867, a floral decoration on a solid gold background was combined with solid bands of silver lustre. I have never seen a piece in this pattern, but the effect must be dazzling. One dreads to think of the price which an example of it would command today.

Another type of gilt background which required little more than hard, tedious labour from the gilder was that made up of hundreds of tiny dots. The best known pattern incorporating this is Number 2009 (Plate 219), with its conventional floral sprays; but its first use was in Number 802—a much richer pattern with bold, free, flower groups typical of those being used with backgrounds of solid gold. Pattern 2610, similar to Number 2009, is illustrated in Colour Plate VIII.

Solid gold backgrounds tended to go out as ground colours, particularly cobalt blue, gained more favour. With these, the gilder still held his own. If anything, a cobalt ground with scale gilding looked even richer than solid gold. The best known example of this is the famous 1166, for years the most sought-after of all Spode patterns (Colour Plate VIII and Plate 221). This scale gilding called for extreme skill since the scales were beautifully gradated in conformity with the shapes of the articles. Scale gilding was used on several other patterns, among the best known being Number 1139 (Plate 220), where it appears on a white background. The style was introduced earlier than this, however, and the first use of it I have traced is on Pattern 882.

Although some of the heaviest gilding appears early in the period, the bulk of early teawares were simply gilt. Not every gilder was capable of a master-piece, nor could every customer pay for such expensive work. This is not a thing to be regretted since the most pleasing gilt effects are usually not the heaviest. The simplest mark a gilder can make with gold on china looks like a leaf. This explains both the name and the variety of 'leaf form' borders and motifs on early English china. They flowed naturally and quickly from the gilder's pencil (brush) and variations came easily and in profusion. This did not prevent many of them from being used time and again. A few of those often encountered on Spode china are illustrated opposite with sketches, and even this small selection demonstrates how the simplest theme could be embroidered. Their execution on the wares varies considerably, according to the skill of the gilder and the pace at which he was working. Their use was not restricted to gold and they can be found partially or entirely completed in enamels.

Early on, the leaf form was used to build up a weight of decoration heavier than the simple or even the complex free-flowing borders. The most widely used result, 'all over leaf', is exemplified by Pattern 2136, illustrated in Plate 274. First introduced *c.* 1803 with Pattern 531, it continued to reappear in new versions at the Spode Factory for one and a half centuries. I have traced more than twenty for the Spode Period alone. When used on rich grounds—particularly on cobalt blue, as it was in three instances—it shows off the quality of Spode's gold as few other decorations can. Backgrounds favoured for this kind of gilding were, in addition to cobalt blue, the white undecorated china, red, and turquoise. In some of the versions, a plain coloured band was substituted for the border of diamond motifs which was usually employed with it.

Another, more ambitious, gilt design which was very extensively employed is the one sketched above. Its first use was as a border for teaware patterns like Number 878, illustrated in Plate 274. With these, the border finished at the bottom of the teacup handle. It was not until its eighth version, Pattern 1020, that it was first enlarged to cover the whole of the cup exterior. It was then used extensively for items other than tea sets, such as matchpots, gardenpots and rich dessert plates. Complete all-over designs were evolved from it, like Pattern 1168, which decorates a sandwich set illustrated in Plate 155. It still continued to appear on teawares, frequently in its original, narrower version. The dominant central flower motif is often reserved in white, sometimes traced out in gold or a colour, and the accompanying gilt forms vary in shape according to the style of individual gilders and the piece to be decorated. Invariably used with one or more rich ground colours, the effect is always lush and expensive and the design produced some of the most successful of Spode's richer china wares.

Twenty-three versions have been identified, their introduction concentrated into a brief period of about two years—*c.* 1805 to 1807. The design was not finished with them, but its use later was with very much more complex gilding or with marked differences in the whole drawing.

The three borders sketched here are frequently encountered. The first, the very simple 'Cross and Dot', was introduced *c.* 1805. It was subsequently used as a frame for the panels of cobalt blue which feature in gold bat printed teaware patterns, like Number 1699, illustrated in Plate 276. It was also used with a gold line at the edge for painted centre decorations.

The second border, 'Dontil Edge', is common to all English factories and is supposed to have been devised by a decorator named Dontil at Worcester. An unlikely tale, in view of its popularity at Sèvres in the eighteenth century and the fact that the French word for denticulated is 'dentelé', which describes it perfectly. It is termed 'French edge' in the Spode pattern books. Apart from a simple gold line, dontil edge is probably the most frequently met of all gilt finishes and its popularity has never ceased. It appears on the earliest Spode china as an inner or supplementary border, but it was not widely used in its more usual form, at the edges of articles, until *c.* 1815.

The third border, 'Egg and Dart', is virtually a Spode hall mark and is often found with expensive decorations on important ornamental pieces. Its first use was, oddly enough, for a teaware pattern, Number 1269, where it appears complete with the secondary border consisting of 'three dots and a dash' normally found with it. For examples see Plates 180, 202 and 278.

The gold on gilt wares straight from the decorating kiln is light brown in colour and rough in texture. It is smoothed and brought to a proper gold appearance very easily and quickly by rubbing with fine sand; but to obtain a really brilliant sheen, it is necessary to compact the surface of the gold by burnishing. Today, for reasons of taste as much as expense, most gold decorations are only sanded; but in the nineteenth century, all expensive china was burnished. Burnishing is a woman's trade, but it is one requiring considerable physical strength and great energy. The gold has to be well fired and thick, often applied in two coats, to withstand the battering it receives from the burnisher's blood-stone or agate.

A burnisher's stone drawn across a gold surface which has not been sanded will make a bright line against the duller background. When the possibilities of this were realised, the art of 'chasing' was born. Where and at what date it was first practised is uncertain, but this method of decorating was certainly in use at the Chelsea and Sèvres factories in the eighteenth century. Chasing was never left to burnishers. It was, at the least, a gilder's craft. In Victorian times, and probably in the Spode Period also, the foremost painters did not disdain to

chase their own pieces. Chasing seems to have become popular at the Spode
Factory in about 1818, when a series of patterns featuring it appeared on ornamental pieces, each pattern having six versions, one for each of the ground
colours used: rose, purple, yellow, green, blue and black. The subjects were
various and included figures, landscapes, festoons of flowers, fables and shells.
These chased patterns form one of the richest classes of decoration produced at
the Factory. Three of them are illustrated in Plate 222.

Another, later, refinement in gilding was 'raised gold' decoration, which is
sometimes confused with chasing. Raised gold means what it says: the gold is
in relief. When this is encountered on eighteenth century Sèvres porcelain it is
not so much an effect as a fact, the relief having been achieved by a build-up of
solid metal. The method employed in Staffordshire, invented by Henry Daniel
and still in use, sought to produce this effect at far less expense. Relief ornaments were built up with a brush on the glazed surface, using a paste of fluxed
yellow colour and ground-up china wasters. These were allowed to dry slowly,
to prevent cracking, and were then fired prior to being gilt over in the normal
way.[100] The results can never compare with the real thing: the reliefs are too
high, and they are devoid of the delicate modelling which alone justified such a
lavish use of precious metal at Sèvres. The substitute technique could succeed
with simple decorative effects, as in Pattern 4028 (Plate 266); but it was more
often employed without restraint, with repugnant results. It was extensively
used for teawares towards the end of the Spode Period, but it made its début
with more than a score of patterns between Numbers 3916 and 4056, most of
which are found on ornamental wares. The favourite subjects for ornaments
were Chelsea-style Oriental figures or birds, and a very fine, dark crimson
ground colour was popular for them. Patterns 3993 and 3982, which are of this
kind, are illustrated in Plates 243 and 244; and Plate 174 illustrates a sumptuous
decoration using raised gold.

It was Simeon Shaw who attributed the invention of the technique to Henry
Daniel, in a badly worded passage which has caused considerable confusion:

> About 1822, Mr. Henry Daniel, the enameller, already mentioned, commenced
> the manufacture of a different kind of Porcelain, at Stoke; and in 1826, the Stone
> China, at Shelton; the shapes and patterns being of the improved kind, so much
> preferred by the public. But, in addition to the various methods of enamelling
> then practised, he introduced the practice of laying grounds, of different colours,
> and ornamenting them with gilding, both burnished, and embossed, or frosted
> work as applied to plate. His efforts have been very successful; and the Porcelain
> fabricated at the manufactory of H. and R. Daniel, will bear a comparison for
> excellence, and elegance of ornament, with that of any other manufacturer.[265]

This passage has been widely misinterpreted and has been responsible for a ridiculously late dating for the introduction of ground laying. If it is read carefully, it will be noticed that the date 1826 refers solely to Daniel's production of stone china. The other date, 1822, refers to his becoming a china manufacturer.[48] The practise which he then introduced (for his china) was not laying grounds but *laying grounds and ornamenting them with raised gold*. To make confusion absolute, in a previous passage Shaw stated:

> His enameller, Mr. Henry Daniel, here [the Spode Factory] first introduced, in 1802, the present method of ornamenting Porcelain, in raised unburnished gold, much similar to embossed dead gold, or frosted work, on plate. A Porter Cup then made, is a fine specimen, of Mr. Spode's Porcelain, and of the artist's ability.[256]

The date 1802 is certainly a slip of the pen or a compositor's error for 1820; more probably 1822. Even so, Shaw reveals uncertainty about whether raised gilding was invented by Daniel just before or just after his departure from the Spode Factory in August 1822. The Spode pattern books suggest that it was immediately after. The first pattern using it, quickly followed by ten more, was Number 3916. The date of introduction of a pattern shortly before this one, Number 3794, can be pinpointed to October 1822 (see Page 86).

PRINTING

Today, printed patterns on china are, almost without exception, applied on the glaze; but in the early nineteenth century, it was not unusual for them to be underglaze. When they were, the technique employed was exactly the same as that described in Chapter 8 for earthenware, and the same method of obtaining and transferring prints was employed for most on-glaze printing. Spode II produced numerous patterns on china by this method—not only blue printed designs, which aped their earthenware counterparts, but also a variety of different borders and outline designs for subsequent enamelling. Because of their similarity to earthenware, these cannot claim the same attention as one distinct type of decoration, associated mainly but not exclusively with china and achieved by the gentle art of bat printing. In bat printing, the printer employed bats of glue, not pieces of paper, to transfer his designs from the copper engraving to the glazed surface of the ware, in a way described by William Evans in 1846:

> A definite quantity of good glue is soaked well some hours in water; it is next put into a large jug, and by the heat of boiling water evaporated during four hours; afterwards it is poured out on large well-glazed flat dishes, to the thickness of one-eighth of an inch, and left to cool. The glue is next cut into pieces, technically called papers, corresponding in size to the [copper] plates. The printer rubs his colour, in the state of an impalpable powder, well in a saucer, with a lock of carded cotton, well dried. He, with rosin, fixes his plate to a wood prism, as a handle,

then rubs into the engraving his oil, (a mixture of cold-drawn linseed oil, and oil of turpentine, or Barbadoes tar,) and, with much pressure, the glue paper abstracts the oil out of the engraving, and being immediately laid carefully on the ware, previously wiped very clean, the oil, by a gentle pressure, adheres; he next with a sponge cleans the paper, and leaves it to dry, while he applies the powdered colour, by the cotton to the oiled design. With a series of papers he proceeds successively till his complement of ware is finished; and afterwards, commencing with the vessels first printed, with silk rags he cleans off all the superfluous colour from the design, and wipes all the other parts clean from whatever might be likely to adhere to the glaze, while being baked in the muffle.[167]

Compared with normal transfer printing, the method was troublesome, but it was the only way then available of obtaining prints of great delicacy. Every refinement at the engraver's disposal, every nuance he achieved, could be captured by this means. Various colours were used, but any colour other than black is extremely rare on Spode pieces. The universal popularity of this colour for the process gave rise to its being generally called 'black printing', causing a certain amount of later confusion with earlier, eighteenth century black transfer printing.

Spode bat printing was almost entirely confined to teawares, and the results are among the most aesthetically satisfying ever produced at the Factory. The very limitation of the method was its greatest advantage. Obviously, it was impossible to produce fitted borders or all-over designs. Only relatively small areas of print were available, suitable for centres or border panels. These smaller areas were complementary to the delicacy of the engravings themselves and also ensured that a welcome expanse of white china would show its own beauty. As the process was relatively cheap, compared with the freehand painting more usual on china, most patterns were kept inexpensive by having only slight gilt decorations to finish them. There was thus a veritable conspiracy against ostentation, and to add to the attraction of the patterns was the interest of the subjects used. Not only were they varied—landscapes, country houses, coursing scenes, fruits, flowers, allegorical subjects—but each pattern was also provided with a large number of different engravings, so that it was possible to buy a tea set and find hardly one piece decorated with the same scene as another.

The most popular subject for Spode bat printed patterns was landscapes. Number 557, illustrated in Plate 260, was produced in quantity. It is still possible to find almost complete services in this design: a large one survives which belonged to Hester Savory.[82] Later landscape patterns had fewer scenes. The best known of these is Number 4406, illustrated in Plate 262. Of the patterns which employed subjects other than landscapes, Numbers 500 and 1922 (Plate 259), were probably the most popular.

N

An interesting, later, development in bat printing was its use for gold, on which Shaw commented:

> In 1810, Mr. Peter Warburton, for the New Hall Company, took out a Patent for Printing Landscapes and other designs, from Copper Plates, in Gold and Platinum, upon Porcelain and Pottery. The appearance is extremely beautiful; but a great oversight in the first introduction of the method, has prevented its acquiring the celebrity to which it is entitled. The Copper Plates employed were those previously used for Black Printing, engraved in a very fine manner, and not containing sufficient oil to receive adequate strength of the pulverized gold. One or two Specimens, from very coarse plates, possess great beauty and elegance. There is every probability that this branch of ornamenting will again be introduced for the bottoms of tea saucers, and sides of the cups.[263]

Warburton enrolled a specification, in February 1810, for three distinct methods of printing precious metals.[125] The first, and the least remarkable of the three, was exactly the same as normal bat printing but with the substitution of powdered gold for colour.

Quite how or why Spode II came to be using this technique at the very time Warburton obtained a patent for it is a mystery: but it was certainly employed by him in the production of nine patterns which can, from their numbers, be dated to c. 1810. Each of these uses fruit, landscape or animal subjects—numbers 1692, 1701 and 1703 on a white background, and numbers 1691, 1693, 1696, 1697, 1699 and 1700 on a background of cobalt blue borders or panels (Plates 276, 277 and 278).

The cobalt blue decoration is interesting in itself. A close examination reveals that it was not produced by the ground-laying process normally associated with such broad areas of colour but was printed from a very coarsely engraved copper. This would have been a less costly method and one which the notorious fluxing qualities of cobalt could be relied upon to disguise. The use of this dark colour as a background was an effective counter to the problem mentioned by Shaw: the excessively thin deposit of gold resulting from the fineness of the engravings used. Spode used normal bat coppers, which were not coarsened in any way, and the light weight of gold in the decoration is all too apparent in most surviving examples, which show considerable wear. But pieces in good condition are extremely effective visually, due to the contrast between the gold and the blue behind it. Indeed, the fact that pieces in any of the three patterns without the blue background are so rare (I have never seen a single such example) suggests that, without this contrast, they were commercial failures and were abandoned.

An odd characteristic of these patterns is that they never seem to have any accompanying marks. Every piece that I have seen decorated with them has been not only without the Spode name but also devoid of its pattern number.

LUSTRE

In 1846, John Hancock Senior wrote to the *Staffordshire Mercury*:

> Sir,
>
> In the notice of the death of Mr. John Booth, of Well Street, inserted in your last week's paper, it is stated that he was the inventor of lustre for earthenware. I beg to state that this is incorrect, as I was the original inventor of lustre, which is recorded in several works on Potting, and I first put it in practice at Mr. Spode's manufactory, for Messrs. Daniel and Brown, and continued to make it long before Mr. Booth or any other person attempted to do so.
>
> If Mr. Booth's friends should doubt the truth of this statement, I shall be very happy to furnish them with proofs on the subject, or answer any questions which they may think proper to ask. Perhaps Mr. Booth's friends are not aware that I am still alive, although at the advanced age of 89. By inserting this you will oblige one whose character is at stake.
>
> JOHN HANCOCK
Etruria.[189]

The credit is freely accorded to him by Simeon Shaw, who adds the interesting aside that he made the process of little value to himself 'for the recipe could be obtained from him by any person, for a small sum of money'.[261] Exactly what the 'lustre' was that Hancock invented and that subsequently developed into such a large and interesting branch of pottery decoration is not clear from Shaw:

> The first maker of the Silver Lustre properly so called, was Mr. John Gardner, (now employed by J. Spode, Esq.) when employed by the late Mr. Wolfe, of Stoke; and the next were, Mr. G. Sparks, of Slack Lane, Hanley; and Mr. Horobin, of Tunstall, (now of Lane End.) A person named Mr. John Ainsley, recently dead, introduced it at Lane End; and since 1804, it has been practised with varied success, thro' the whole of the district. The Gold Lustre is regarded as having been first produced by a Burslem Artist named Hennys, then resident in London; where for some years he thus ornamented the Chalk body ware made by Mr. Wilson, of Hanley. This Lustre is the solid kind. The method of preparing a Gold Lustre which could be applied by the Pencil, is very different every way; and was discovered by Mr. James Daniel, of Pleasant Row, Stoke.[261]

Since the original invention of lustre took place in the Spode Factory and John Gardner—the apparent inventor of silver lustre 'properly so called'— was subsequently employed there, we should expect lustre decorations to feature largely among Spode wares. Yet they are rarely encountered and are more troublesome to investigate than any other class of the Factory's products. Lustre wares are normally associated with small factories and, whatever their present day value, a cheap class of merchandise designed for bulk sales. The earliest kind of lustre which can be traced in the Spode pattern books is the silver variety, which was used not on earthenware but on china—and in expensive decorations, at that. Patterns containing this lustre can usually be identified in the books by the dark grey water colour used to depict it. Thirty-three have been counted between and including Numbers 800 and 949. One of these, Pattern 822, is illustrated in Plate 257. They invariably have gilt finishes and frequently have enamel decorations too, and were used for items such as spills and covered chocolate cups as well as teawares.

All of these patterns were introduced within a very short space of time, c. 1805. Together with the arrival at the Spode Factory of John Hancock in August of that year (see Page 39) and Henry Daniel's known use of platinum there by November (see Page 43), they substantiate the former's claim to his invention. Platinum is the metal normally associated with silver lustre, which was generally used in Staffordshire on earthenware, often of brown body. When employed on a white background it assumes a darker hue, which has been well described as having the appearance of lead rather than silver.[210] Spode china decorated with it has this characteristic dark colour, which is extremely attractive and which, rather unexpectedly, successfully combines with gold in the decoration.

The rarity of known Spode silver-lustred earthenware is hard to explain, particularly as the only silver lustre recipe of Daniel's which survives is, from its title, 'silver for cottage ware', not intended for china.[101] This mixture contains no platinum, consisting solely of four parts of prepared silver to one of calcined tin. Plate 119 illustrates two sales samples of earthenware border patterns which contain silver lustre. I have not yet encountered actual examples of these, or any others similar.

Gold lustre invariably employed the metal its name implies and came in two main varieties: gold proper, ranging from a very light to a very dark tone, and pink. Pink is the natural fired colour of a very thin smear of gold on a white body. It was lustre with these two colourings, used in large mottled areas, which appeared in the Spode pattern books, c. 1806. Once again, the body used was china and the decorations were of an expensive type. Seven patterns were initially introduced and seem to have been designed primarily for teaware. Their numbers were 1091, 1103, 1172, 1173, 1194 (see Plate 217), 1221 and 1397. No other entries for patterns using this type of lustre can be identified in the pattern books until an isolated entry for numbers 2357 and 2358, c. 1814, which are described as containing 'purple lustre'. An even longer period elapsed before the next and last entries, numbered 3745 and 3747. An earthenware vase in Pattern 3747 is illustrated in Colour Plate 11. Pattern 3745 is the same, with the addition of an enamelled red, white and green checkered band at the top.

What appears to be Daniel's first entry for a gold-based recipe is for china: 'mix well-made starch and a strong solution of gold equal parts—makes a pink lustre on china—works well with a pencil same as Hancock used for the Sphinx candlestick'. His next recipe is designed for earthenware: 'to lustre cottage jugs: make a strong solution of blue vitrol in water then mix equal parts of strong wort and the solution of vitrol. Mix above and a solution of gold equal parts— take care always to use new wort'. There was no excuse for not using freshly made wort, which was simply manufactured from a convenient material: 'take a pint of fine ale and boil it to half a pint'. Daniel's later gold-based lustre recipes for the period 1814 to 1818 are, on the whole, more conventional but raise the question of why new pattern entries had virtually ceased by that date. These recipes are similar to those employed generally in the nineteenth century, using balsam of sulphur and prepared solutions of gold and tin—sometimes lead.

As with silver lustre, the puzzle is why examples of gold-based lustre decorations on Spode are so seldom found. In earthenware they are even rarer than in china. One cannot escape the nagging suspicion that somewhere there should be a whole class of them waiting to be discovered, for it is difficult to believe that the technique was not exploited on a wider scale than present evidence suggests. At the very beginning of the Copeland and Garrett period, in 1833, a lustre pattern book was started using the prefix 'L' for the numbers. This contains approximately one hundred and fifty entries and they are all of an inexpensive type—teawares painted in purple lustre with sketchy peasant-style floral decorations, or underglaze prints partially or completely lustred over. It is difficult to believe that no wares of this kind were made in the Spode Period. Cheap and bright, they may have been useful export lines to the East; but it is improbable that they are what was meant by the lustres which Spode and Copeland wished to consign to Calcutta in 1822 (see Chapter 5): used alone, as a noun, the word 'lustre' usually meant a cut-glass pendant, and Spode and Copeland were glass merchants.

10 Stone china

In 1800, the sons of John Turner patented a ceramic body which appears to have been the first of the numerous stone chinas later produced by many Staffordshire potters, including Spode II. It is not easy to find a general description which fits this considerable array from many factories, but they are all characterised by a hardness far superior to ordinary earthenware—the best being highly vitreous. This was achieved without the expense and difficulty attending china manufacture since they could be fired along with ordinary earthenware and the body mix worked easily in the potter's hands, enabling large pieces to be manufactured without undue trouble. All are coloured a shade of grey, varying very considerably in strength according to the amount of cobalt stain added. The colour deliberately simulated that of late low-grade Chinese export porcelain, and the decorations employed were nearly always of Oriental type. Two further characteristics are usually attributed to stone china —thick potting and opacity. The first applies only partially to Spode's. Compared with other Spode products, the potting is sometimes coarse—particularly in the later wares, manufactured after the body had been reformulated and renamed Spode's New Stone—but they never suffered from the ungainly avoirdupois ('pudding' in potters' parlance) which characterised some of their competitors.[83] Spode pieces are also usually translucent to some degree; although with many pieces—particularly those in New Stone—the translucency is of a technical nature, only being apparent in strong artificial light. The question of translucency, a universal test for china, is of some interest since the description stone 'china' is often claimed to be a misnomer.[84]

According to the usual account, Spode purchased the Turner patent in 1805 on the bankruptcy of the two Turner brothers. Yet in 1817 *The Times* referred to Spode's Stone China as 'Newly invented', a description that was used again in 1819 (see Chapter 5). This is but one of several mysteries surrounding a most interesting class of ceramics which seems uniquely British and which has never attracted the attention it deserves from collectors.

At first sight, the Turners' patent specification[124] reveals that they had achieved the impossible and found a way of making pots without clay. They had apparently discovered 'a certain stone or stones or rocky substance called The Tabberner's Mine Rock' which, when mixed with an equal proportion of calcined Cornish stone, could be 'formed into vessels and other articles'. This mix they termed porcelain. For earthenware, the proportions were between six and ten of rock to every one of flint. A small amount of flint was also added to the porcelain mix, and this varied according to the size of the pieces being manufactured.

The problem of the absence of clay has to be solved by the nature of Tabberner's Mine Rock. The specification stated that it 'Contains silecious and argillaceous earth [clay], magnesia, lime and water'. In other words, it was a conglomerate substance not aptly described by the word 'rock' or 'stone'. Its clay content must, in fact, have been extremely high since the Turners claimed that their mixes were very ductile.

Although the specification draws a clear distinction between earthenware and porcelain, only one mark—'Turner's Patent'—is ever found, and sometimes pieces went unidentified except for a normal Turner impressed mark. The special mark used for the patent ware is in itself remarkable, being in large letters and executed painstakingly by hand in red enamel. One wonders why this costly and laborious method was used for the print and enamel patterns when it would have been so much easier and cheaper to engrave and print the mark, as was done by both Spode and Wedgwood.

It was Simeon Shaw who said that Spode II 'purchased the right to manufacture this patent stone porcelain'[262] from the Turners, and it was Jewitt who provided a date—1805:[207] perhaps an intelligent deduction, since the two brothers went bankrupt about then. Although pieces of Spode Stone China are often identical in appearance with those of Turner's Patent and share the characteristic of translucency, the story hardly stands up to examination. Shaw tells how the Turners were prevented from manufacturing their new ware after it had 'acquired celebrity'[263] because the Marquis of Stafford interdicted supplies of the stone which, presumably, they had been extracting from his land. Two alternative reasons are suggested. First, the Marquis was offended by their taking out a patent, particularly as their father had been so active in opposing the extension of Champion's. But since 'patent china goods' feature in their bankruptcy sale in June 1807,[204] seven years after they took out their patent, and since their father opposed Champion in 1775, the Marquis seems to have had a slowness to take offence matched only by the length of his memory. The second alternative, 'that the Marquis was wholly ignorant of the procedure', is equally odd. He was not an Oriental despot, deaf to all pleas, remote and unapproachable—particularly not to William Turner, a substantial local manufacturer and the very man who, about ten years previously, he had extricated from a Paris goal.[259]

Even if the Marquis had behaved in this 'authoritative and aristocratic manner', it is hard to see how this could have involved the Turners in any more trouble than changing their supplier. Tabberner's Mine Rock was, according to the 1800 specification, found in 'the coal mines in the said county of Stafford between a hard marle and an iron stone rock'. The word 'mine' was synonymous with vein or seam, and the Tabberner's Mine was one of more than thirty making up the North Staffordshire coal field. The rock was therefore available as a worthless waste product from any local coal master who mined this vein— and many who did owed no allegiance to the noble Marquis.

In truth, the use of Tabberner's Mine Rock seems not to have been difficult, original, or even particularly desirable; and the patent may have been, as Reginald Haggar suggests, a false one designed to deceive competitors. At the meeting of potters which was instigated by Spode II in 1800 to discuss the patent,[85] William Perry claimed that he had used Tabberner's Rock fifteen years before, and William Adams of Tunstall remembered using it as an apprentice.[184] One thing is sure: it was not an essential ingredient for making ware of the stone china type. Formulae dating from the early nineteenth century and used by a number of manufacturers are still extant. In fifteen I have examined, not one contains any Tabberner's Mine Rock. The four ingredients which seem to have been universally employed are the thoroughly reliable and well-understood china clay, china stone, flint, and blue or brown clays.[80]

In 1813, C.J.Mason, husband of Spode II's niece, burst upon the scene with his Patent Ironstone China. His magic ingredient, 'Prepared Iron Stone', was so outlandish and patented with a specification[126] so unlikely that at least one modern ceramic authority has expressed doubt concerning whether he ever used it all.[161] Be that as it may, he had secured what would today be termed a unique selling point and a name so good in its evocation of exclusivity (patent), strength (iron), durability (stone) and quality (china) that any up-to-date market research firm would be proud to provide it.

The success of Mason's product is legendary and its introduction marked the beginning of what may be called a stone china boom. It may have marked the beginning of the use of the very term 'stone china'. Hitherto, the word 'stone' seems to have been used only in conjunction with the word 'ware'. Staffordshire potters have always been as quick to borrow a good name as a good shape or pattern, but this was one which enjoyed a measure of protection. Pottery patents had always been relevant only to manufacturing and could not have been too troublesome to circumvent in the privacy of a factory. It would, however, have been an admission of illegality, in view of the Mason patent, to use the name Ironstone China. Stone china was a good second best.

It is noticeable that the Turners themselves seem never to have referred to their ware as anything else but 'Turner's Patent'. If Spode did buy their patent, it is remarkable that he never used this commercially desirable word—particularly as it is more than doubtful if he ever needed their formula. Only Shaw ever refers to Spode's Stone China as a patent body and is at pains to stress that Mason's body is not 'to be confounded' with the Turner one.[262] William Evans, writing in 1846, was almost certainly nearer the truth when he ignored the patent specifications and called Mason's body an imitation of the Turners'—and he mentioned nothing of Spode II having intervened.[164]

On the whole, there are good reasons for believing that the description in *The Times* of 1817 of Spode's stone china as newly invented was not wildly inaccurate. Evidence from the Spode pattern books suggests that its production started in or shortly after 1813. Examples of the ware decorated with patterns introduced before that date are rare in the extreme. I can recall seeing only one—a magnificent service in the freehand Imari-style pattern, 1409, introduced *c.* 1810. The plate without a pattern number illustrated in Plate 291 has an outline print which makes its last appearance as Number 1632; but neither this pattern nor any of the preceding twelve versions of it resemble this particular plate in colouring, and the absence of an entry for the decoration points to it being an abortive revival using an old existing engraving. There is, of course, no reason why patterns first produced before 1813 on china or earthenware should not subsequently have been used for stone china; but in contrast to the paucity of known examples of this, I have encountered twenty-one patterns between numbers 2053 and 2550 (*c.* 1813–16) on stone china—and there will be many more than this.

If the Turners did not sell their patent to Spode, a question is raised concerning what the end of it was. The likeliest answer is that it just faded away. But the announcement in June 1807 of the bankruptcy sale of their factory stock, which included 'Patent China goods', contained the news that 'the purchasers will also have an opportunity of matching and continuing the patterns' at the fresh manufactory started by William Turner in Lane End. William Turner may have retained the use of the patent for his new venture since he must have retained some things, like copper engravings, normally regarded as assets of a manufacturing partnership. His venture on his own continued until 1829; and although when his factory was eventually sold up there was no mention of the stock including patent ware, the use of the patent could have been abandoned by him at any time during a twenty-one year period.[204] There is a class of Turner wares which, in their lack of finish and quality, seem quite foreign to the high standards set by John Turner and—to judge from dated pieces—maintained by his sons when they worked together. Several marked pieces of the patent ware belong to this category, and the shapes used fit as happily into the period after 1806 as the one before.

If Spode did follow Mason into the market, that he did so with very little delay is revealed by a letter, dated 19th March, 1814, from Josiah Bateman to

Josiah Wedgwood Junior: 'Every one enquires for the stone china, made by
Spode and Mason and it has a very great run—I presume you know what it is—
it is a thick coarse china body, not transparent, with china patterns, but in
texture similar to old stone ware'.[113] Mr Bateman did not draw any distinction
in 'transparency' between the two products, but the difference in quality was
remarked on the next week: 'I send you one of Mason's stone china plates for
patterns—it is not equal to Spode's in quality I believe—I will endeavour to
get one of Spode's'.[118]

It is a remarkable fact that Mason's Ironstone was generally not equal in
quality to Spode's Stone China—in body, potting, or choice and execution of
the decorations. Remarkable, since it is almost a law of nature that with anything
new it is the second in the field who plays the cheapjack. From the start, Mason
seems to have set out for a mass market in which price would have been the major
factor. In this he was entirely successful. Finding normal methods of distribution inadequate for the volume of sales he wanted, like Bloor of Derby, he later
took to conducting public auctions of his wares up and down the country and
making extensive use of press advertising.[183] In April 1819, John Howarth,
Wedgwood's accountant in London, commented that stone china (which they
started to make the following year) was: 'Repeatedly enquired for but it appears
from the great quantity of this ware made and making by several manufacturers
and selling by auction and otherwise advertised for sale that the competition for
prices must be unprofitable'.[150]

Who will believe that Spode II found the business without profit? Mr
Howarth's sage and accountant-like comment overlooks the fact that the market
for nearly every commodity has a top, a middle and a bottom. Judging from
the number of pieces which have survived, Spode II achieved a very substantial
turnover in his better quality ware, certain to be welcomed by the better class of
retailers, who must have been incensed by Mason's public auctions. The visit
of Queen Charlotte to his London warehouse in 1817 (see Chapter 5) and her
interest in the new ware was just the kind of dignified publicity Spode required,
and its effect was not short-lived. Three months after the royal visit, a report
reached Wedgwood: 'Since the Queen went to Mr Spode's the stone china is
much enquired for, and is got more into repute indeed a dealer cannot be
without it, and a great deal is sold'.[150]

The Copeland and Garrett recipe book[100] contains two Factory recipes for
stone china which could date from the Spode Period. The first is named 'Old
stone china body' and the second 'New stone china body'. Although any definite
statement based on old formulae requires the greatest hesitation, it does seem
that they represent the difference between Spode's Stone China and Spode's
New Stone. The bodies were composed as follows:

	Old stone china body	New stone china body
Ball clay	21%	14%
China clay	nil	29%
Cornish stone	72%	34%
Flint	5%	23%
Patent ironstone	2%	nil

Ironstone could, apparently, be used as an ingredient in very small quantities. Its description as 'patent' ironstone in the Factory recipe book was doubtless an honest admission, which it was safe enough to make since the book itself had a lock and key and its normal home was the Factory safe. Interestingly, this seems to be the only formula ever discovered in which ironstone appears. Several early Mason formulae for his stone bodies are known but none of them contains it, although it featured as an improbable 20 per cent of the whole in his 1813 patent specification.

The first Spode body is more porcelainous in its construction and much more likely to produce translucency than the second one. The use of china clay in the second would have resulted in a body with a naturally lighter colour. But the shade of grey was really controlled by the amount of cobalt stain used and, although this could have been varied at will in the actual manufacture, the proportions given are one ounce of cobalt for every one hundred and twenty-two pounds of mix in the first formula, and an ounce for every one hundred and seventy-five pounds in the second. The naturally lighter tone of the New Stone was thus deliberately heightened, and these two formulae confirm the evidence of our eyes.

From the start, Spode's Stone China, with its mock Chinese seal mark (Mark 19: Appendix IV), had a very deliberate Chinese flavour, apparent not only in the colour of the body but in the shapes in which it was potted. Although the teaware shapes employed were those common to other factory products, the plates, meat dishes and covered dishes were all from models studiously taken from the Chinese. As with ordinary earthenwares, teawares are rare compared with dinnerwares. Vases and other semi-ornamental pieces are not common but, when they can be found, are almost invariably of pure Chinese form.

The suitability of Stone China for blue printed wares was obvious, and Chinese landscape patterns were inevitably produced. Plate 17 illustrates a pattern of this type which has always, in living memory, been known on the Spode Factory as 'Queen Charlotte'. It may have been the one purchased during the Royal visit in 1817, but I have yet to discover it on a piece of stone china. The piece illustrated is bone china. More distinctive than the landscape

patterns but equally Oriental was Grasshopper Pattern, which had a very long
life (Plates 22 and 296). The number of these blue printed patterns never
approached those for ordinary earthenware, probably because the ware was
more expensive. Much greater diversity was achieved in the polychrome patterns derived from the Chinese and executed by the print and enamel process in
the famille rose style. This particular decorating technique lent itself well to
patterns of this kind and in them reached a height of perfection hardly to be
found in the products of other contemporary factories (Colour Plate IX). For
the printed outlines of many of these patterns a sepia colour was used on the
glaze, which gave an admirable, crisp effect. The enamel colours are a tribute to
Henry Daniel's skill as a colour maker: the water greens and pinks, in particular,
are among the finest colours encountered on ceramics of any period from any
country. The execution of the decorations is characterised by the extreme
dexterity and care with which the paintresses filled in the printed outlines.

The numbers of the patterns indicate that the very first design efforts in
Stone China always remained the most successful. The two patterns which
probably still provide the largest number of extant Spode pieces are Cabbage,
2061, and Peacock, in its third version, 2118 (Colour Plate IX and Plate 285).
The former, which is sometimes called Tobacco Leaf in the antique trade, is
still (1970) in production at the Spode Factory. Peacock, if anything, proved
even more successful. Although production of it finally ceased in 1963, it had
enjoyed continuous and substantial sales for one and a half centuries. Other
early and long-lived patterns were Bude (Plate 283)—produced in at least seven
versions, not all on stone china—and Willis (Colour Plate IX). Successful patterns enjoyed not only long life but successive reincarnations. Cabbage is a
remarkable exception to this since it appears to have been produced only in its
original version throughout the Spode Period. But the permutations of Peacock
and Willis, used not only on stone china, were considerable: seventeen in one
and twenty-five in the other. One of the versions of Willis, 2647, illustrated in
Plate 287, has an entirely different border known as Mosaic. This very rich
Imari-type border was also employed with other centres. In numbers 3450 and
3452 it was used as a pattern alone, without a centre at all.

The most popular border of all, Ship, is ill-named. It takes its name from
Pattern 3067, illustrated in Colour Plate IX, in which a ship features as part of
the scene in the centre. This pattern, which had subsequent differently coloured
versions, numbered 3068, 3133 and 3134, is the first appearance of the border
as an outline print. But it was first used with the floral centre, for which it was
obviously designed, in Pattern 2272 (Plate 288). This was decorated completely
freehand and was followed by another freehand version, somewhat simplified,
number 3025. Once the border had been engraved for Ship Pattern, it became

one of the Factory's greatest stand-bys and was used on bone china and earthenware as well as stone china, on patterns rich and simple, with and without
centres, in at least fifty decorations.

Some stone china patterns were rich and must have been costly, particularly
when the decoration was applied without the aid of outline prints. A pattern
much in favour for elaborate gilt finishes, and widely used apart from stone
china, was Frog Pattern (Colour Plate IX)—so named from a resemblance in
the border. It appears first, fully engraved, as Number 3137. Other versions
were 3248, 4623 (particularly rich) and, on Gadroon Shape in earthenware or
china, 4233, 4274, 4275, 4653 and B113. The border was used by itself for
Patterns 3350 and 5411.

The new ware was ideal for providing replacements or additional pieces
for existing Chinese services, many of them crested. This class of business,
which would certainly not interest any potter today, does not seem to have been
unwelcome to Spode II. Sometimes these matching pieces can be discovered
accompanying the Chinese pieces they were originally sent to join, providing the
opportunity for the kind of comparison made in Plates 282, 297 and 299. Such
pieces were usually decorated entirely freehand and, having avoided the printer
in their manufacture, may be found to have no other mark than the simple hand-
lettered 'Spode' found on the bone china wares. The facility with which the
adaptable decorators of the day could copy an original, possibly for the sake of
one or two pieces only, is remarkable. Spode II's customers must have found
him endlessly obliging, for not only were decorations supplied to order—some
of them involving the concoction of special colours—but frequently the original shapes were matched as well. The wide distribution of the Chinese services among the English aristocracy, which provided the source for this
ostensibly trivial and uneconomic business, suggests a reason for the trouble
taken over it: some of the Factory's great oaks may have been produced by these
little acorns. One of the side benefits was the supply of a never-ending stream
of original artwork, and more than one successful Spode Stone China pattern
began life as a matching to a Chinese piece supplied for copying.

Individual variations in colour are naturally met with, but it is generally
true to say that the Stone China was distinctly grey and the New Stone distinctly
off-white. It was not only the colour of the ware that reflected less dependence
on the Orient: the introduction of the new body seemed to mark a general
coming of age. The printed Oriental seal gave way to a decidedly Occidental
impressed mark (Mark 7: Appendix IV), and patterns and shapes began to
appear which were no longer exclusively Oriental in character. The very
popular Bang-Up Pattern, 3504 (Plate 289), was purely Oriental. But there
could hardly be anything more native than the version of Union Wreath

illustrated in Plate 58, which became a popular underglaze blue printed pattern on New Stone, although found on earthenware also. Even the Flower Embossed Shape, so popular for china, was produced and given a typical china floral decoration with Pattern 4064 (Plate 301).

The date when New Stone replaced Stone China can be assessed with some accuracy. The plate in Frog Pattern, 3248, illustrated in Colour Plate IX, bears on the reverse the inscription illustrated below. It is marked Stone China. Whatever the reason for the inscription—to provide a unique commemorative piece for the firm or for use on quantities of the ware as sales promotion—it proves that the Stone China body and mark survived until after the middle of 1821. Another Stone China plate, produced about the same time for the Madras Horse Brigade of Artillery, is illustrated in Plate 300. The battle honour which features so conspicuously on this was earned by the Madras gunners in 1814, but it was not until December 1820 that they were authorised 'to bear on their appointments the word "Java" in commemoration of their services on the reduction of the island of Java'.[86]

Evidence that New Stone was in production very shortly after 1821 is to be found in the patterns used for its decoration. Ignoring popular patterns like Cabbage and Ship, which continued in production for decades after their introduction, patterns on New Stone seem always to be found with numbers higher than 3400. For example, of seven patterns on New Stone in the collection of Robert Copeland the lowest number is 3435. I have never seen a piece in the extremely popular Bang-Up pattern, 3504 (Plate 289), which was not New Stone.

The new body and name can safely be guessed as appearing in 1822. They continued into the Copeland and Garrett Period, after 1833, and pieces marked Spode's New Stone are frequently found with a Copeland and Garrett printed mark. Like most new bodies, its introduction seems to have had less to do with any technical advance than the needs of sales promotion. It may have been prompted by increased competition, following the entry of Wedgwood into the stone china field in 1820.[146]

Used at the Coronation of His Majesty George The 4th 19th July 1821.

Tablet of brown earthenware in the Spode Museum. Length 13½in. Mark 4. This is similar to those laid in the corner stones of Stoke parish church and mentioned by Simeon Shaw, who supplied a translation of the bas relief inscription: 'This Parish Church, at first well adapted to the few scattered Husbandmen, who, in early times, composed the Inhabitants of Stoke-upon-Trent, having given birth to Eight other sacred Edifices, but at length become inadequate to contain, within her Walls, the New Population, which the Local Manufacture, The Potters' Art, had gathered around her; was rebuilt from the Foundations, on an extended scale, as near to the Spot, where for more than Eight Centuries, Worship to God, in Christ's Name, had been paid, as a regard to the Ashes of the Dead would allow, by means of Resources, supplied;—partly, by the Voluntary Offerings of the Opulent, and among these most conspicuous a Gift of £3,000 from John Chappel Woodhouse, Rector, and of £500 from Josiah Spode, of the Mount; partly by a Parochial Rate; and lastly yet most worthy of record, by Contributions arising from the supernumerary Labours of the Working Classes spontaneously bestowed. The Corner Stones of the Foundations were laid the 28th of June, in the Year of Our Lord Christ, 1826,[233]

Other Spode slabs, made in four different bodies, are described by Shaw as having also been deposited in the corner stones of the church.

The succession

Most of the firms founded by contemporaries of the Spodes exist no more. Their ends are more clear cut than their beginnings. But if John Hassell, who visited the Spode Factory in 1819, were to return today he would find it on the same site, with many of the original buildings still in use. And he would not need to change one word of this part of his original description: '. . . one of the most complete establishments in the kingdom. . . . There are about 800 people, of all ages. . . . Here almost an endless variety of earthenware is made . . . China, too, has been brought to the greatest perfection, both as regards its colour and transparency, and the taste displayed in its decoration.'

The story of what happened after 1833 is beyond the scope of the present work, but there was no sudden change in the Factory's products or activity when Copeland and Garrett became its proprietors in that year. Nor in other years when its destiny was decided: 1847, when W.T.Copeland continued the firm alone; 1867, when he took his sons into partnership; 1931, when the Copeland family ceased to be solely responsible for running the business; 1966, when it became one of the international group of Carborundum companies.

During this long period, taste and demand have altered—as have production techniques. But such changes have been evolutionary rather than revolutionary and, throughout them all, the original shapes and decorations of the Spodes have shown a dogged persistence as large sections of the buying public continued to demand them. To the Factory, the Spodes' policy of innovation, competition and, above all, sound potting has proved one that it is too perilous to neglect. The result is that their name is no longer just that of a family, or even a firm. It has become attached to that most indestructible of all human achievements—an idea.

82 Spode I, 1733–97. From a miniature portrait. **83** Spode II, 1755–1827. From an engraving by W.Greatbach, after a painting by Keeling, dated 1806. **84** William Copeland, 1765–1826. From an oil painting executed shortly before his death. **85** William Taylor Copeland, 1797–1868. From an oil painting executed in 1836, when he was Lord Mayor of London.

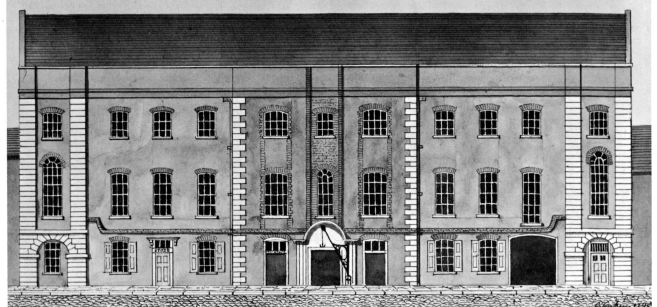

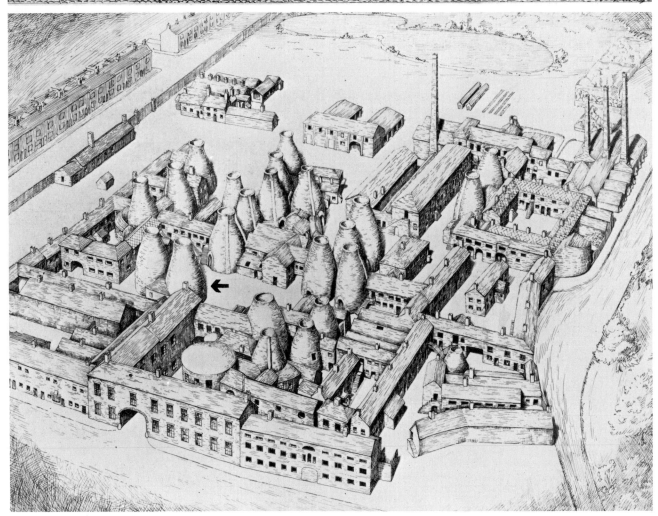

86 Watercolour, dated 1798, of Spode II's premises in Portugal Street, London; front elevation.
87 The Spode Factory in Stoke. From a drawing by Harold Holdway, based on a detailed map of 1833 and an early model of the factory in the Spode Museum.

88

88 The surviving bottle oven at the Spode Factory, from a pen and wash painting executed in 1965 by Leonard Brammer. The artist's vantage point is indicated on Plate 87 (opposite) by an arrow to the right of the two bottle ovens, lower left. The far one is the one which remains; the site of the other can be seen in the foreground of the painting.

BLUE PRINTED EARTHENWARE
Aesop's Fables Pattern. See also Plate 75. **89, 90** (left to right and top to bottom) Plate, 8in, 'The Dog and the Sheep'. Dish, 16in, 'The Sow and the Wolf'. Plate, 8in. Baker, 9in, 'The Dog and the Shadow'. Vegetable dish base, 'The Wolf and the Crane'. Dish, 10in, 'The Mountain in Labour'. Soup tureen: cover, 'The Hare and the Tortoise'; base, 'The Wolf, the Lamb and the Goat'. Dish, 19in, 'The Dog in the Manger'. Vegetable dish: cover, 'The Wolf and the Lamb'. The dishes 19in. and 10in. and the baker are impressed Spode. Other pieces are of Copeland and Garrett manufacture. *Major A.J.Bather.*

91

92

BLUE PRINTED EARTHENWARE
Greek Pattern. See also Plate 74. **91, 92** (left to right and top to bottom) Dish, 16½in. Dish,
14½in. Plate, 8in. Dish, 12½in. Soup plate, 10in. Covered vegetable dish. Dish, 18½in. Soup
tureen. Marks 3 and 4. *Major A.J.Bather.*

BLUE PRINTED EARTHENWARE
93 Caramanian Pattern. Soup tureen; dish, 21in; and sauce tureen. Marks 3 and 4. See also Plate 73. *Major A.J.Bather.* **94** Indian Sporting Pattern. Soup tureen: cover, 'Hunting an old Buffalo'; base, 'The Hog at Bay'. Dish, 18in, 'Dooreahs Leading out Dogs'. Marks 4 and 16a. See also Plate 72. *Major A.J.Bather.*

BLUE PRINTED EARTHENWARE
95 Floral Pattern. Covered vegetable dish; Dish, 18½in; and plate, 8in. Marks 4 and 23. See also Plate 48. *Spode Museum*. **96** Botanical Pattern. Dish, 18½in, and Covered vegetable dish. Marks 4 and 16a. See also Plate 54. *Spode Museum*.

97

98

BLUE PRINTED EARTHENWARE
97 Tower Pattern. Toy dinner service, and 21in. 'Well and Tree' meat dish. See also Plate 70. *Major A.J.Bather.* **98** Large jug in Woodman Pattern, 11in. high, capacity 1¾ gallons. Small jug in Milkmaid Pattern, 2¾in. high, capacity 2oz. See also Plates 60 and 61. *Major A.J.Bather.*

BLUE PRINTED EARTHENWARE
99 Giant teapot in Tower Pattern, 11in. high, capacity 2 gallons. Small teapot in Milkmaid Pattern, 2¾in. high, capacity ¼ pint. *Major A.J.Bather.* **100** Garden seat, 19 in. high, decorated with elements from three patterns: Group, Gothic Castle and 'Lattice Scroll'. Mark 5. See also Plates 43, 65 and 33. *Major A.J.Bather.* **101** Footbath in Lanje Lijsen Pattern, approximately 18in. high. See also Plate 23. *Major A.J.Bather.*

EARTHENWARE
102 Cream ware pot with hinged lid. A rare early piece, finely modelled and potted. Height, 10¾in. Mark 2a. *N.Bernard Esq.*

EARTHENWARE

103 Early cream ware, basket-weave embossed stand. Of similar quality to the pot opposite. Length, 10½in. Mark 1d. *H.Holdway Esq.*   **104** Early white ware dish or stand with blue enamelled edge. Length, 9¼in. Mark 1c. *Spode Museum.*   **105** Early blue-painted white ware dish strainer with holes pierced in a fleur-de-lis design. Length, 11½in. Mark 1d. See page 11. *Major A.J.Baker.*

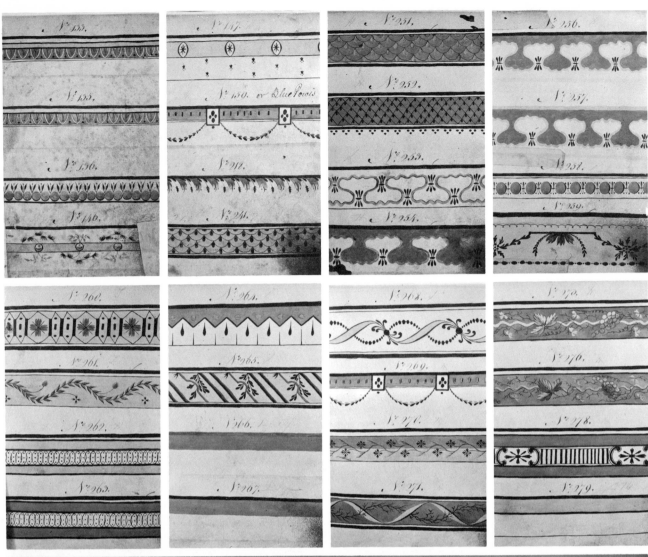

EARTHENWARE (see page 140)

106 The first eight pages of the first Spode pattern book, showing, left to right and top to bottom by page, Patterns 133, 135, 136, 146; 147,159 or Blue Powis, 218, 241; 251, 252, 253, 254; 256, 257, 258, 259; 260, 261, 262, 263; 264, 265, 266, 267; 268, 269, 270, 271; 273, 276, 278, 279.

107 Three pieces of white ware decorated with early patterns. The plate in the centre has Mark 3 and '136': the covered centre to the left is marked '254' only; and the egg stand has Mark 2a only but is Pattern 273. *N.Bernard Esq.*

110

EARTHENWARE

108 Barrel shape scent jar. Polychrome decoration on cobalt blue ground. Height, 9¾in. Mark 3 and '2217'. *Spode Museum*. **109** Very rare earthenware pastille burner. Cottage painted in yellow. Height, 4in. Mark 10. *Mrs N.Emery*. **110** Plate, 10in, and sauce tureen in white ware with blue enamelled edge—a later version of the shape and decoration in Plate 104. Mark 4. *Major A.J.Bather*.

EARTHENWARE: PRINT AND ENAMEL
111 Pierced basket and stand. Pattern 3909. *Spode Museum.* **112** Dinner plate and covered custard cup and stand. Pattern 2577. *Spode Museum.* **113** Dinner plate. White flowers on a red ground, identified as Pattern 1012. *Spode Museum.* **114** This decoration derives from a Chinese one known as 'Spinach and egg' or 'Tiger ware'. Mark 4 only, but identified as Pattern B353. NB. This plate is not printed and enamelled but under glaze painted in green, yellow and dark brown. *Spode Museum.* **115** An unusual decoration, expensively finished in gold. Mark 3 and '4207'. *Spode Museum.*

EARTHENWARE: PRINT AND ENAMEL

116 Dinner plate, 10in. Marked only with pattern number '1690'. This pattern is discussed on Page 86. *Spode Museum.* **117** Number 3716, one of the several versions of Tumbledown Dick Pattern. *Spode Museum.* **118** Pattern 3057, heavily enamelled with a gilt finish. *Spode Museum.* **119** Decorated plate rims for use as sales samples. The top one is 7in. long. The band and leaves are silver lustre, as are the darker areas of the bottom one. NB. These are freehand decorations, not print and enamel. *Spode Museum.* **120** Shell dish with black and yellow border. *Spode Museum.* **121** Pattern 3280, brilliantly coloured. *Spode Museum.*

EARTHENWARE: COLOURED GLAZE

122 Brown glazed earthenware, known in its day as 'Rockingham ware'. (left) A teapot in a shape also produced by Spode in red ware with a smear glaze. Mark 4. (right) A Cadogan teapot. This was filled through a hole in the base, the liquid then passing through an internal tube which reached within half an inch of the top of the pot. Height, 6½in. Mark 4. *N.Bernard Esq.*

123 Green glazed earthenware. Plate, 9½in, and pierced violet pot. Mark 3. *Spode Museum.*

124

125

126

EARTHENWARE: COLOURED PRINTS

124 Number B139, a brown print version of Fruit and Flowers Pattern. See also Plate 46. Diameter of saucer, 4½in. Mark 16a only. *Author's collection.* **125** Mug decorated with a view of Brighton Chain Pier, in brown print. Height, 3in. Mark 16a. *Spode Museum.* **126** Rare, late example of black printed cream ware in Aesop's Fables Pattern. Subject shown: 'The Leopard and the Fox'. Diameter, 11in. Mark 24. *H.Holdway Esq.*

EARTHENWARE: B PATTERNS

127 'Peasant' style, underglaze, painted decoration. The plate has Mark 4 only but is B1, the first entry in the 'B' pattern book. *H.Holdway Esq.* The cup is a Copeland and Garrett shard and has been identified as B384. *Spode Museum.* **128** Page from the 'B' pattern book. The pattern at the top, B223, is evidence that mocha decoration was employed in the Spode Period.

129 Pages from the 'B' pattern book showing the three kinds of patterns, all underglaze, which it contains. (top left) B24, a simple border; next, a print and enamel. The patterns following are 'peasant' style.

EARTHENWARE
130 White ware dish of early appearance, with painted decoration. Length, 10½in. Mark 2a.
Spode Museum. **131** Cream ware basket and stand. Length, 10½in. Mark 3 and '1611'.
132 Pierced basket-weave embossed plates, a shape made over a long period of time. The example fourth from the left is white ware; the others are cream ware. Second from the left is Pattern 304; fourth, Pattern 772; fifth, Pattern 1553. Diameter, 7½in. **133** Teapot in grey-coloured earthenware with white sprigged ornament of Egyptian subjects. Height, 4in. Mark 3.
Spode Museum.

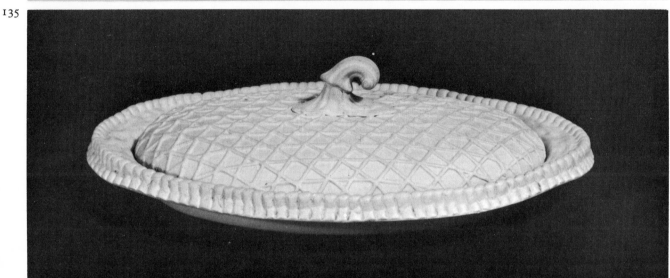

EARTHENWARE: COLOURED BODIES

134 (left) Jug in light grey earthenware with sprigged ornaments in dark blue. Mark 4. (centre) Antique Shape jug in dark green earthenware with sprigged ornaments in white. Height, 6in. Unmarked. (right) Jug in glazed cane ware. Mark 2a. See also Colour Plate 11   **135** Dish and cover in cane ware, made to simulate pie crust. Length, 8in. Mark 2a. *N.Bernard Esq.*   **136** Cane ware teapots. (left) Bamboo shape with blue enamelled decoration. Mark 2a. *Spode Museum.* (right) Decoration of blue, green and white enamel. Height, 5½in. Mark 2a. *N.Bernard Esq.*

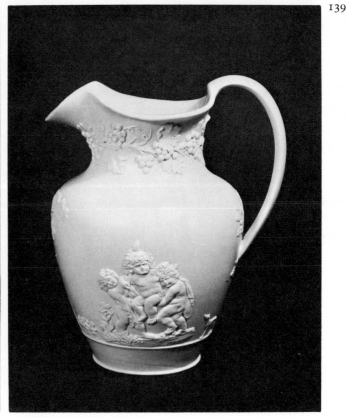

STONEWARE
137 Covered jug, 6in. high, and mug with sprigged fox-hunting ornaments. Smear glazed exterior and bands of dark brown. Mark 3. See also Colour Plate 11. *Spode Museum.*
138 Silver-mounted mustard pot with sprigged ornament. Smear glazed exterior and band of dark brown. Height, 4in. Mark 3. Silver hall mark: Sheffield, 1824, and maker's mark 'T.B & Co.' *Author's Collection.* **139** Antique Shape jug with sprigged ornaments. Fine white stoneware. Height, 8¾in. Mark 3. *Spode Museum.*

STONEWARE. BASALTS

140 Early flask in light grey stoneware. Function uncertain, perhaps for containing powder. Length, 6½in. Mark 1b. *Spode Museum.* **141** Stoneware jug with sprigged ornaments on a chocolate coloured ground. Smear glazed exterior. Height, 4¼in. Mark 2b. *N.Bernard Esq.* **142** Basalts teapot with very fine moulded and hand-tooled finish. Height, 4½in. Mark 2a. *N.Bernard Esq.*

143

144

145

BASALTS

143 (left to right) Low Egyptian Shape cream jug with sprigged decoration; cream jug, 3in. high, with engine-turned decoration; small teapot with glazed exterior. Mark 2a on all. **144** (left to right) Cream jug with moulded decoration; fine sugar box with sprigged decoration; sugar box and cream with moulded decoration, after Turner. Mark 2a on all. **145** Engine-turned decoration. (left) Cane Shape coffee pot. Height, 6½in. Mark 2a. *N.Bernard Esq.* (right) Egg Shape coffee pot. Height, 8¾in. Mark 2a.

146

147

148

149

RED WARE

146 Two-handled Antique Shape jar with sprigged decoration of basalts. Height, 6½in. Mark 2b. *N.Bernard Esq.* **147** Teapot, after a Yi Hsing stoneware original. The ball on the lid revolves. Height, 6½in. Mark 2a. *Spode Museum.* **148** Scent jar with basalts sprigged decoration and supporting figures in Egyptian style. Notice how, in the hands of a Staffordshire modeller, a sphinx becomes an English judge. Height, 9¾in. Mark 2b. *Spode Museum.* **149** Jug with polychrome enamel decoration. Height, 4¾in. Mark 4 and '3339'. *N.Bernard Esq.*

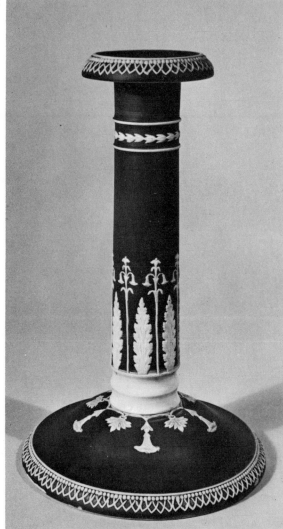

'JASPER'

150 White stoneware beaker with sprigged ornament in dark blue. Height, 4⅜in. Mark 3. *Spode Museum.* **151** Candlestick in 'jasper dip' with white sprigged ornament. Height, 10in. Mark 3. *Spode Museum.* **152** Small font in fine white stoneware. Symbols of the Holy Trinity at the three corners. Diameter, 7½in. Mark 4. *Author's Collection.* **153** Teapot in 'jasper dip' with white sprigged ornament. Height, 5in. Mark 3. *Spode Museum.* **154** Low Egyptian Shape sugar box in 'jasper dip'. Mark 2a. Jug in stoneware with sprigged ornament on a jasper blue ground. Height, 3⅜in. Mark 2b. See Plate 141. *N.Bernard Esq.*

CHINA: PRINCE OF WALES

155 Sandwich set in sumptuous decoration of gold, red and cobalt. The centre fitting contains four eggcups and a divided cruet in a holder, which fits into a china liner. Width of complete set, 21in. 'Prince of Wales' Mark 17 and '1168' on base of centre piece. *R.S.Copeland Esq.*

156 Page from a Spode pattern book showing No. 1112, gold on a red ground. **157** Dish in Pattern 1185, red and gold. Width, 8¾in. 'Prince of Wales' Mark 17. *Spode Museum.*

CHINA: HERALDIC DECORATION

158 Cream or sauce bowl and stand with a border of oak leaves and acorns in natural colours. From a service made for the Prince Regent. Mark 10. *R.S.Copeland Esq.* Plate, 9¾in, with device of George IV (formerly the Prince Regent) painted by the artist responsible for those on the tureen. Unmarked. *Author's Collection.* **159** Unhandled cup with portrait. Height, 2½in. Mark 13 and 'Futteh Ali Shah King of Persia'. *R.S.Copeland Esq.* **160** Reverse side of cup in Plate 159.

CHINA: HERALDIC DECORATION

161 Small bowl with armorial decoration in a style associated with Chinese export porcelain. Diameter, 4¼in. Mark 10. *Spode Museum.* **162** Icepail from service made for the King of Oudh. See Page 73. Mark 11. *The National Army Museum.* **163** Plate, 10in, with a border of raised gold motifs on a crimson ground and a royal coat of arms at centre. Mark 18c. *R.S.Copeland Esq.* **164** Plate, 10¼in, with the arms of the Hon. East India Company. Mark 18c and 'The London'. See Page 72. *Spode Museum.* **165** Plate, 10in, with apple green border and the arms of the Worshipful Company of Goldsmiths at centre. Mark 18c. *Spode Museum.*

CHINA: HERALDIC DECORATION

166 Plate, 10¼in, with gilt border on a cobalt ground and the Copeland family's arms at centre. Mark 3. *R.S.Copeland Esq.* **167** Plate, 9 in, with light blue border and badge of the 40th Regiment of Foot (The Buffs). Marks 18c and 9. *Spode Museum.* **168** Plate, 10in, with Union Wreath Border (compare Plate 56) and device of the 4th Queen's Own Light Dragoons at centre. Underglaze printed in brown. Mark 16a. *Spode Museum.* **169** Covered cup and stand with the conjoined arms of the Copeland and Yates families. Mark 10. *R.S.Copeland Esq.*
170 Coronation jar with gold printed Tumbledown Dick design on very dark cobalt. Height, 13¾in. Mark 10 and '3967'. *Spode Museum.*

CHINA
171 Punch bowl made for the Burns Society of Dumfries in 1819. See Note 75. Diameter, 18in.
Mark 10. *Dumfries Burns Society.* **172** Centre decoration of the bowl illustrated in Plate 171,
a painting of the Burns Mausoleum in St. Michael's Churchyard at Dumfries. **173** Portrait
slab. Length, 5¼in. Mark 13 and, in script, 'Marquis Wellington, from an original painting in
the possession of the Countess of Mornington'.

CHINA

174 Loving-cup with painting of the Good Samaritan and very rich, raised gold decoration on a crimson ground. The reverse of the piece has a painting of three druids in a grove and an inscription in gold which reads: 'This Cup presented the 14th March 1825 to the Rev'd Thos. Brooke by the United Lodges of Ancient Druids of Lane Delph, Stoke and Lane End as a mark of respect for his Urbanity and Kindness evinc'd towards them on all occasions'. Height, 8¼in. Mark 18c. *Spode Museum.*

CHINA: FIGURE PAINTING

175 Grecian Shape jars decorated in green, ground colour and burnished gold, with tavern scenes in natural colours. Height of large vase, 7⅛in. Mark 10. *R.S.Copeland Esq.* **176** New Shape French jar, cobalt and gilt with portrait. Height, 8⅛in. Mark 11 and, in script, a quotation from *A Midsummer Night's Dream*, beginning 'Oh me! for ought that I could never read . . .' *Spode Museum.* **177** Detail from companion piece to that in Plate 176. Mark 11 and, in script, an old ballad beginning 'A Merlin small, She held upon her hande . . .' *Spode Museum.*

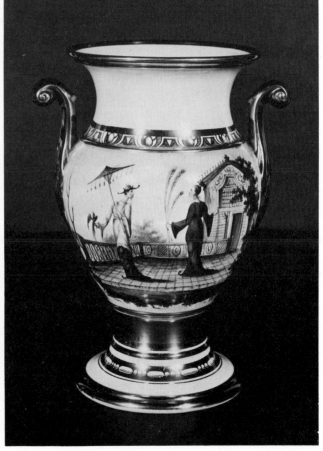

CHINA: FIGURE PAINTING

178 (left) Plate, 9½in, with scene of otter hunting. Mark 10. (right) Pierced plate, 8½in, with pastoral scene. Marks 13 and 9. *R.S.Copeland Esq.* **179** Beaded matchpot on claw feet. Figure of child with dog, gilt finish. Height, 6⅜in. Mark 10 and '3613'. *Spode Museum.* **180** New Shape jar with figures in chinoiserie style and gilt finish. Height, 7⅜in. Mark 10 and '1444'. *R.S.Copeland Esq.*

CHINA: FIGURE PAINTING

181 (centre) Pot-pourri bowpot with harvesting scene in brilliant raised enamels, cobalt and gilt finish. Height, 7⅝in. Mark 10 and '3234'. (left and right) Beaded, footed beakers with finely painted scenes. Pattern 1988. The scenes are described in script on the base of each article. *R.S.Copeland Esq.* **182** Beaded beaker matchpots, all painted by the same artist. Height, 4⅝in. Mark 10 on all. The centre two are also marked 'No. 1888' and have the scenes described thus: 'The Serpent and the Man', 'The Fowler and the Partridge'. *R.S.Copeland Esq.*

CHINA

183 Silver Shape cup (handle hidden from view) with figures, in Continental style. Height, 2⅜in. Mark 10. *N.Bernard Esq.* **184** New Shape French jar. Pattern 3243: painted figure after Adam Buck. Height, 5¼in. Mark 10. *Spode Museum.* **185** Two dessert plates, 9in, with finely painted river scenes and light yellow borders. Mark, in script, 'Blades, London' (see Note 16) and, left, 'Richmond Bridge', right, 'Maidstone Kent'. *R.S.Copeland Esq.*

186

187

188

CHINA: LANDSCAPE PAINTING
186 (centre) New Shape garden pot. Height, 6¼in. Mark 10 and '1926'. (left and right) French Shape garden pots with monochrome landscapes in sepia. Height, 4¾in. Mark 10 and '382'. *R.S.Copeland Esq.* **187** French Shape garden pot with monochrome landscape in sepia. Height, 5½in. Mark '384' only. *N.Bernard Esq.* **188** Covered cabinet cup and stand with view of Chigwell, Essex. Height, 4½in. Mark 11 and descriptions of views in script. *Spode Museum.*

189

CHINA: LANDSCAPE PAINTING
189 New Shape French jar with finely painted river scene and cobalt and gold finish. Height,
6¾in. No marks, only 'Llanrwst Bridge' in red script. *N.Bernard Esq.*

CHINA: LANDSCAPE PAINTING

190 Dessert plate, 8½in, with river scene and apple green border. Mark 10 and '2925' with 'Barskimming Bridge, Scotland' in script. *R.S.Copeland Esq.* **191** Urn with a view of Bath Abbey. Height, 5¼in. Mark 11 and descriptions of views in script. *Spode Museum.* **192** Footed comport with landscape and blue enamel rim. Length, 13¾in. Mark 11 and 'Kirkstall Abbey' in script. *R.S.Copeland Esq.*

CHINA: LANDSCAPE PAINTING

193 Antique Shape double icepail. River scene with cobalt and gold finish. Height, 13in. Mark
10 and, in script, 'Warkworth Castle, Northumberland'. View on reverse, not shown, 'Tremarton
Castle, Cornwall'. *R.S.Copeland Esq.*

194

195

196

197

198

199

CHINA: BIRD PAINTING

194 Flat candlestick with bright yellow ground. Mark '1578' only. *R.S.Copeland Esq.* Beaded matchpot. Mark 11 and '1629' with 'Yellow Wagtail' in script. *N.Bernard Esq.* **195** Plate, 8¼in, in Pattern 2423. Mark 10. *R.S.Copeland Esq.* **196** Twig-handled comport, brown border. Length, 11in. Mark 11 and '2102'. *R.S.Copeland Esq.* **197** Plate, 8½in, light blue border. Mark '1979' and, in script 'Grosbeak'. *Spode Museum.* **198** Cream bowl, yellow border. Height, 5⅜in. Mark 18b and '3672'. *Spode Museum.* **199** Plate, 9¾in. Mark 10 and description of birds in script. Cobalt rim. *R.S.Copeland Esq.*

CHINA: BIRD PAINTING

200 Plate, 8¼in, in Pattern 1723, painted in Chelsea style. This piece is unmarked. *R.S.Copeland Esq.* **201** Dolphin embossed plate, 8¾in. Mark '1724' only. *N.Bernard Esq.* **202** Icepail with apple green ground colour and painting of 'Tame Swan' (described on base). Height, 11¾in. Mark 10. *Spode Museum.* **203** Footed beaker with lavender blue ground. Height, 6¼in. Mark 10 and '2091'. *N.Bernard Esq.*

CHINA: FLOWER PAINTING

204 Plate, 10in, with 'Spear Leaf' embossment, intricately gilt, on a cobalt ground. Mark 10 and '3139'. *R.S.Copeland Esq.* **205** Detail from Plate 204. **206** Plate, 9in, and cream bowl and stand. Wicker embossment with a light blue ground and gilding. Mark 10 and '1182'. *R.S. Copeland Esq.*

CHINA: FLOWER PAINTING
207 Page from a Spode pattern book showing Number 3499. This pattern's centre is described as 'Sherwin's fruit and flowers'. **208** 'Envelope plate', 8½in, with Flower embossment reserved on a stone-coloured ground. Unmarked but identified as Pattern 2057. *Spode Museum.* **209** Superbly executed copy of a painting by Van Huysum, whose signature is reproduced in the bottom left-hand corner of the tray. Height, 13in; length, 18¼in. Mark 10. *R.S.Copeland Esq.*

CHINA: FLOWER PAINTING
210 Plate, 9in, crimson ground on rim. Mark 18c and '4673'. Ball shape jar with pierced cover. Mark 10. *R.S.Copeland Esq.* **211** Plate, 9in, and cream bowl from a dessert set in Pattern 4485, stone-colour ground on rim. *Spode Museum.*

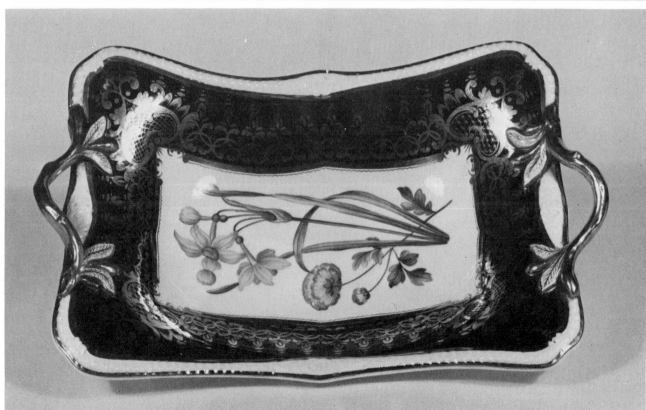

CHINA: FLOWER PAINTING
212 Twig-handled comport with exceptionally detailed gilding. Length, 13½in. Mark 10 and '3765'. *Spode Museum.* **213** Twig-handled comport with botanical style painted centre and surrounding cobalt ground, heavily gilt. Length, 11¼in. Mark 10 and '3663'. *Spode Museum.*

CHINA: FLOWER PAINTING

214 (left) Vase with baskets of flowers and gilt decoration. Mark 11. (right) Oval shape vase with cobalt ground. Mark 10 and '4313'. *N. Bernard Esq.* (centre) Tuscan jar, 10¼in. high. Mark 10. *Author's Collection.* **215** Two-handled Antique Shape jar, Pattern 711, solid gilt background. Height, 8⅜in. Mark 13 and the date '1814'. *Spode Museum.* **216** Very large embossed jug with a decoration of roses surrounded by gilt weed, also popular for teaware. Height, 12½in. Mark 10 and '2812'. *R. S. Copeland Esq.*

CHINA: FLOWER PAINTING

217 Chocolate cup and stand with enamel and gold border and all-over mottled purple lustre, similar in effect to the jar illustrated in Colour Plate 11. Height, 4⅜in. Mark '1194' only. *N.Bernard Esq.* **218** Pineapple stand with chased gold and flower painted decoration, Diameter, 8¾in. Mark 10 and '2778'. *R.S.Copeland Esq.*

CHINA: FLOWER PAINTING
219 Bow-handled incense burner. Height, 5¼in. Mark 10 and '2009'. *N.Bernard Esq.*

CHINA: FLOWER PAINTING

220 Pair of Beaded Vase Shape jars, and bottle and stopper with decoration of flowers and scale gilding. Height of jars, 4⅜in. Mark '1139' only. *Spode Museum.* **221** Group of pieces in the famous Pattern 1166, flowers and scale gilding on a cobalt ground. (left to right and top to bottom) Dolphin tripod incense burner, 6½in. high; letter rack; Beaded New Shape jar; flat candlestick; Image-Handled Antique Shape cup and turned down stand; Bottle Shape milk and stand. *Spode Museum.*

CHINA: CHASED GOLD

222 Group of pieces with chased gold decorations. (left) Beaded Dresden Shape jar with chased figure in various tones of gold and brilliantly burnished gold bands. Height, 6⅜in. Mark 10 and '2801'. (centre) Beaded Parisian Shape jar with chased figures on matt ground of intense electric blue: Pattern 2736. Height, 7in. Mark 10. (right) Cabinet cup and stand with chased landscapes on a black ground. Mark 10. *N.Bernard Esq.*

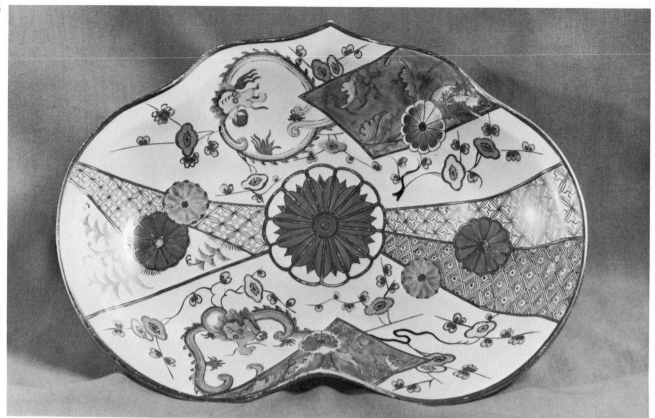

CHINA

223 Early dish of rare shape, painted in Japanese style, Pattern 287. Length 10½in. Mark 2a within two blue concentric circles. *Spode Museum.* **224** Early flower pot and stand. Polychrome flowers on a black background, bottom band in chocolate brown. Height, 4¾in. Mark '311' only. *N.Bernard Esq.* **225** Early dish in Spode's most popular Kakiemon decoration, Pattern 282. Length, 12in. Mark '282' only, within two blue concentric rings. *Spode Museum.*

227

228

229

CHINA

226 (left and centre) Basket and stand with blue printed decoration, derived from the border of Pattern 282 (see Plate 225 overleaf). Mark 2a, (right) Stand with hand-painted blue 'Chantilly Sprig' decoration. N.B. This piece is not china and is discussed on Page 139. Length, 9in. Mark 2a within two concentric blue rings. *Spode Museum.* **227** Footed beaker. Height 6in. Mark '2360' only. See also Plate 284. *Spode Museum.* **228** Swag embossed plate with blue painted decoration. Diameter, 10in. Mark 4 *N.Bernard Esq.* **229** Image-handled chocolate cup in Pattern 2638. *Spode Museum.*

CHINA: IMARI STYLE

230 Pattern 715, which owes more to the Kakiemon style than to the Imari. Painted in red with cobalt blue panels, this pattern was a popular one. Diameter of plate, 8in. *Spode Museum.*

231 Pattern 2214, a popular and very imaginative decoration. Diameter of dish, 7in. The marks provide a lesson in continuity: the saucer is Spode, the dish is Copeland and Garrett, *c.* 1840, and the cup is Copeland, *c.* 1870. All three pieces are marked, in addition, with the pattern number. *Author's Collection.*

232

233

234

CHINA: IMARI STYLE
232 Covered chocolate cup and stand—height, 4¾in.—in Pattern 2283, and two matchpots in
Pattern 967. **233** Diamond dessert dish in Pattern 963. Length, 10in. *R.S.Copeland Esq.*
234 Covered chocolate cup and stand—height, 4¾in.—in Pattern 1409 *N. Bernard Esq,* and
two matchpots in Pattern 1216. *R.S.Copeland Esq.*

235

236

237

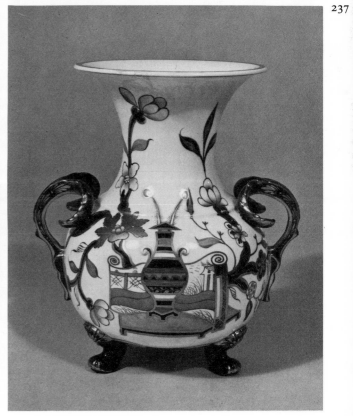

CHINA: IMARI STYLE

235 Beaker, 6⅜in. high, in Pattern 1946; plate, 9¾in. diameter, in Pattern 2508; bow-handled bucket in Pattern 2375. **236** Wine cooler. Height, 9¼in. Mark 10. *R.S.Copeland Esq.* **237** Vase, 7½in. high. Mark '3710' only. This peculiarly shaped vase is used to illustrate this pattern in the pattern book. *N.Bernard Esq.*

238 239

240

CHINA: IMARI STYLE
238 Porter mug in Pattern 2375. Compare Plate 235 overleaf. Height, 4½in. **239** Dessert shell dish in Pattern 1495. Length, 9 in. *Spode Museum*. **240** Footed comport in Pattern 1250. Length, 14⅜in. *Spode Museum*.

IMARI STYLE

241 Very tall vase, 14¼in. high, in fine quality earthenware. This important piece is marked
solely 'No. 1227' in red. There is no entry in the pattern books for this number, and both the
shape and the use of the prefix 'No.' are not characteristic of Spode—although the quality of the
decoration is. Its identity is established by a piece with the same decoration in the collection of
the late Dr Strachan. This is marked 'Spode', with this pattern number. *R.S.Copeland Esq.*

CHINA

242 Lamp pedestal and shade. The metal fitting which supports the shade is hollow, to contain the fuel. Decoration: ornate gilding on a crimson ground. Height complete, 27in. Mark 10. *Spode Museum.* **243** Covered jar with raised gold decoration on a crimson ground. Height, 10⅜in. Mark 10 and '3993'. *R.S.Copeland Esq.* **244** Beaker with raised gold decoration on a crimson ground. Height, 4⅝in. Mark 10 and '3982'. *R.S.Copeland Esq.*

CHINA

245 Pair of bottles with modelled lizards, painted in natural colours. Remarkable for the perfection of the white china. Height, 4¼in. Mark 10. Candlestick of shell shape with handle and ornament to resemble seaweed, painted red. Mark 10. *N.Bernard Esq.* **246** Ornamental piece, modelled on the 'Eel-Basket Vase' made at Chelsea. Height, 9⅝in. Mark 12. *Spode Museum.* **247** Penholder in Pattern 967. The dolphins are decorated to simulate bronze. Height, 5⅛in. *Spode Museum.*

CHINA

248 Lamp, elaborately decorated in different tones of gold. Height, 8¼in. Mark 10. *Spode Museum*. **249** Pair of pieces of uncertain function. Figures painted in natural colours, remainder of decoration gold. Height, 5¼in. Mark 11. *N.Bernard Esq.*

CHINA

250 Basket of modelled shells, polychrome painted. Height, 5¾in. Mark 10. *Spode Museum.*
251 Candlestick of elaborate form with painted sprays on a lavender ground. Height, 3in. Mark 12 and '4618'. *R.S.Copeland Esq.* **252** (left) Covered bowl with Coalbrookdale type of applied decoration. (centre) Cottage pastille burner; height, 4⅝in. (right) Covered bowl with applied flowers painted yellow and rose knob painted pink. All pieces, Mark 10. *R.S.Copeland Esq.*
253 (left) Low Dutch jug with light blue ground and white figures in relief. Height, 5½in. (right) Similar jug but with dark green ground. (centre) Indian Sporting figures on light blue ground. Marks 3, 10 and 10 respectively. *N.Bernard Esq.*

CHINA

254 Matchpot in Pattern 4649; jar, 9¼in. high, in Pattern 4650; and ewer in Pattern 4687. *Spode Museum*. **255** Pail custards with pierced covers, decorated by sprigged flowers painted in natural colours. Height, 3in. Mark 10 and '2910'. *Spode Museum*.

CHINA
256 Barrel Shape scent jar, white figures on light blue ground with a heavy gilt finish. Height, 7¼in. Mark 11 and '2063'. *Spode Museum.*

257

258

259

260

CHINA: TEA WARE

257 Old Oval Shape teapot, sugar box and slop bowl and Bute Shape teacup and can, decorated with silver lustre bands and gold border. Marked '822' only on a few pieces, and Mark 8 on sugar box and teapot. *Spode Museum*. **258** Old Oval Shape cream jug with Pattern 382, painted sepia landscapes. *G.Godden Esq.* **259** New Oval Shape cream jugs with bat printed decorations. (left) Pattern 1922; (right) Pattern 500. *G.Godden Esq.* **260** New Oval Shape. Bat printed in light black with Pattern 557. The only marked piece is the teapot, and this is marked only with the pattern number. *Spode Museum*.

CHINA: TEA WARE
261 Low Round Egyptian Shape teapot, sugar box and cream jug with Etruscan Shape teacup. Heavily gilt on a cobalt ground. **262** Tall embossed Pembroke Shape cup and saucer with accompanying major items. Pattern 4406; bat prints of landscapes in black. *G.Godden Esq.*

263

264

265

CHINA: TEA WARE
263 London Shape teacup and accompanying items in a shape the name of which is not known. Richly decorated with panels of cobalt. Mark 11 and '2637'. *Spode Museum.* **264** Beaded Déjeuner Shape. Pattern 2643, cherubs on clouds with a fawn background. The cup to the right is a different pattern with a decoration of chased gold. *R.S.Copeland Esq.* **265** Etruscan Shape with Pattern 3549. *R.S.Copeland Esq.*

CHINA: TEA WARE

266 Bell Shape cups and saucers with accompanying items in Octagon Shape. Border decoration of flowerheads, alternating in raised gold and dark green enamel. Mark 18c and '4028'. *Spode Museum.* **267** '4643 Shape'. All-gilt decoration on light blue ground. Mark 18c and '4738'. Plate and teapot stand bear Mark 9. **268** Gadroon Shape. Gilt decoration on a royal purple ground. Mark 18c and '4032'. *R.S.Copeland Esq.*

CHINA: TEA WARE

269 Pembroke Shape. Well-finished landscapes alternating with panels of yellow ground, gilt. Each scene is described in script on the base of the piece. Mark 11. *R.S.Copeland Esq.*

270 Etruscan Shape cups with Octagon Shape items. Brilliantly coloured enamels and outline black print. Mark 18c and '3863'. Some of the saucers in this service are numbered '3638'—a rare example of a decorator marking pieces with the incorrect pattern number. *Author's collection.*

CHINA

271 London Shape cups and Egg Shape coffee pot. Pattern 2352, azure blue enamel and gilt. A service of remarkable quality, destined for the Imperial Court at St Petersburg. See page 74. *Mrs Molla Kraft, Oslo*. **272** Vase Shape coffee pot, 10¼in. high, small Sweep-Neck Shape teapot and cream and can in Pattern 1429. *G.Godden Esq.*

CHINA

273 (left) Toy can and saucer and toy Oriental jug, 1⅞in. high, in Pattern 3644. (right) Toy Oriental jug and bowl in Pattern 3420. See page 214. *N.Bernard Esq.* **274** (left to right) Cream jug in Pattern 878, red ground; sugar box in Pattern 1709, cobalt ground; cream jug in Pattern 2136, cobalt ground. *Spode Museum.* **275** Bute Shape cans. (left to right and top to bottom) Pattern 959; can marked 'Spode 9674'; Pattern 374; Pattern 742; Pattern 960; Pattern 1128 (see page 214). The mark 'Spode 9674' is not a decorator's error. This number was not reached in the pattern books until many years after the Spode Period, and this piece, although early, is a fake. Note the slight difference in shape and handle from the other cans and the 'dirty body' of the china. *N.Bernard Esq.*

CHINA
Decorations in gold, bat printed on a cobalt ground. **276** Cup and saucer. Both pieces are completely unmarked; but the cup has been identified as Pattern 1699, coursing scenes, and the saucer as Pattern 1693, landscapes. **277** Dolphin embossed cream bowl and stand. Completely unmarked but identified as Pattern 1696, fruits. *Spode Museum.*

CHINA

278 Three bottles, decorated with gold bat prints on a cobalt ground. Completely unmarked but identified as Pattern 1697, landscapes. Height, 6¼in. *Author's Collection.* **279** Beaded beaker with decoration of shells in natural colours, Pattern 3236. Height, 6in. *R.S.Copeland Esq.*
280 Beaded matchpot, panels of bright green, Pattern 1388. Height, 4⅜in. *Spode Museum.*

281

CHINA

281 Part of a service of several hundred pieces made for the Lubbock family. Each piece is painted with a design composed of two botanical species, no species being used more than once. Botanical names are given in script on the back of each article. Marks vary as the service was added to and pieces were replaced over a period of more than forty years. *Present owner or owners unknown.*

STONE CHINA
282 (left) Plate, 9¾in, in Landscape Pattern—underglaze blue print and polychrome enamels and gold. Mark 19a and '2857'. See also Colour Plate IX. (right) Chinese export porcelain plate, hand-painted.   **283** Part of a dinner service in Bude Pattern, blue and gold. Length of 'Well and Tree' dish in centre, 18¼in. Marks 19a and '2219'. *Spode Museum.*

STONE CHINA

284 Punch bowl. Pattern 2360: printed and enamelled, famille rose colours with gold. Diameter, 17¼in. Mark 19a. See also Plate 227. *R.S.Copeland Esq.* **285** Part of a breakfast service in Cabbage Pattern. Height of coffee pot, 11in. Mark 19a and '2061'—except teapot, which has Mark 7.

286

287

288

STONE CHINA

286 (left to right) Plate, 9in, in Pattern 2372, which has Grasshopper border; Pattern 2086; Pattern 2053. All with Mark 19a. **287** (left) Plate, 9½in, in Pattern 2976, which has Mosaic border. (right) Pattern 2647, Mosaic border and Willis centre. Both with Mark 19a.

288 (left) Plate 9½in, in Ship Pattern. Mark 19a and '3067' (see Colour Plate IX). (centre) Freehand painted plate in Pattern 2272, the original for Ship border. Mark 10. (right) Soup plate in Pattern 3702, Ship border and Star centre. Mark 7 and a Copeland and Garrett printed mark.

STONE CHINA
289 (left) Plate 9½in, in Pattern 2886. Mark 19a. See Colour Plate IX. (right) Bang-Up Pattern, a later and very popular adaptation with entirely different colours. Mark 7 and '3504'.
290 (left) Plate, 9½in, with Star centre. Mark 19a and '2407'. (right) Pattern 3435. Mark 7.
291 (left) Plate, 9½in. Mark 19a. (right) Plate with Ship border and arms of the City of Bristol. Mark 7. *R.S.Copeland Esq.*

STONE CHINA
292 A group of Stone China cups and saucers. **293** Taper jar, with rich decoration of iris in natural colours on a cobalt ground with gilt finish. Height, 19½in. Mark 19a. *Spode Museum.*
294 Beaker with snake handles in Pattern 3143. Height, 12in. Mark 19a.

STONE CHINA

295 (left) Figure, 6⅛in. tall. Mark 10. (right) Similar figure in Chinese porcelain. *Spode Museum.*
296 Fly-handled cream bowl and stand in Grasshopper Pattern but with a gilt finish. Mark 19a.
R.S.Copeland Esq. **297** (left) Plate, 9in, in Chinese export porcelain with (right) Spode matching piece bearing Mark 14. (centre) Armorial plate with blue printed border. Mark 19a.
R.S.Copeland Esq. **298** Plate, 9½in, in Pheasant Pattern. Mark 19a and '2240'. **299** (left) Cup with blue hand-painted landscape. Mark 10. Both decoration and shape executed to match a Chinese service, a specimen from which is to the right.

300

301

302

STONE CHINA
300 Plate, 10in, with Indian Sporting border, polychrome enamelled, and the device of the Madras Artillery. Mark 19a. *Royal Artillery Institution, Woolwich.* **301** Plate, 8½in, in Flower embossed shape with deep blue enamel border and gilt finish. Mark 7 and '4064'. *Spode Museum.* **302** Freehand painted dish in Imari style. Length, 19in. Mark 9 and '2283'.

Appendixes, notes and references

1   The Spode family

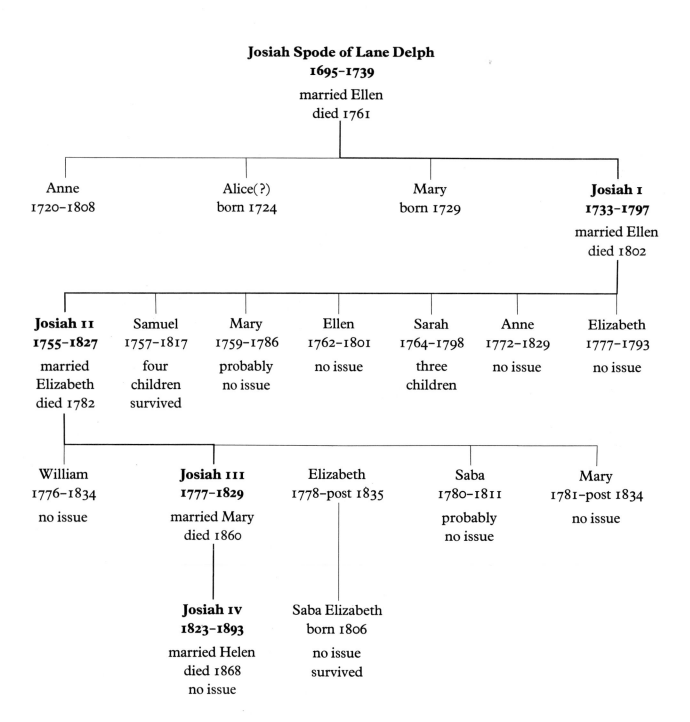

Josiah Spode of Lane Delph
1695–1739
married Ellen
died 1761

Anne	Alice(?)	Mary	**Josiah 1**
1720–1808	born 1724	born 1729	**1733–1797**
			married Ellen
			died 1802

Josiah 11	Samuel	Mary	Ellen	Sarah	Anne	Elizabeth
1755–1827	1757–1817	1759–1786	1762–1801	1764–1798	1772–1829	1777–1793
married	four	probably	no issue	three	no issue	no issue
Elizabeth	children	no issue		children		
died 1782	survived					

William	**Josiah 111**	Elizabeth	Saba	Mary
1776–1834	**1777–1829**	1778–post 1835	1780–1811	1781–post 1834
no issue	married Mary		probably	no issue
	died 1860		no issue	

Josiah 1v	Saba Elizabeth
1823–1893	born 1806
married Helen	no issue
died 1868	survived
no issue	

The information contained in this appendix has been gleaned from many sources. Foremost among these have been the Stoke Parish Register and documents kindly made available by Hawkesyard Priory. Unless otherwise stated, all quotations relating to entries of births, deaths and marriages are from the former. The gravestones mentioned are all at Stoke Parish Church. Mr John Yates, a descendant of Spode I's son Samuel, and Mrs Joyce Hanson, a descendant of Spode I's daughter Sarah, have both generously made available the results of their own extensive researches.

JOSIAH SPODE OF LANE DELPH, 1695–1739

The entry of his burial—'8th April 1739 Josias Spode, Lane Delph, pauper'—is the only entry relating to Spode I's father in the Stoke registers. The family seems to have originated in Biddulph, where Joseph Spode, son of Richard and Joan, was born on 26th March 1657. Joseph and his wife Mary had nine children baptised there between 1679 and 1699: Mary, Elizabeth, Martha, Joseph, Jane, Sarah, Josiah (on 15th December 1695), William and Samuel. The occurrence of all three boys' names and three of the girls' names subsequently used in the Spode family is significant.

Biddulph is a village, nine miles north of Lane Delph. Concerning the period before 1740 and the growth of the potting industry through the ever-increasing demand for white stone ware, Simeon Shaw noted that: 'workmen for the different branches, were so much in requisition, that persons from distant parts, and especially from the neighbouring villages, were hired and settled in the towns, increasing the number of parishioners, and ultimately the mass of parochial burdens'.[243]

No entry occurs in the Stoke or Biddulph registers for Josiah's marriage, and his wife's surname is unknown. She was buried on 29th November 1761: 'Ellen Spode, Lower Lane, widow'. Lower Lane was west of and adjacent to Lane Delph.

JOSIAH SPODE I, 1733–1797

Baptised '25th March 1733 Josiah Spode of Josiah and Ellen de Lane Delph'. His gravestone reads 'Josiah Spode Potter died 18th August 1797, aged 64'. He married Ellen Finley at Stoke on 8th September, 1754. Her gravestone reads 'Ellen, wife of Josiah Spode who died 17th January 1802, aged 76'.

JOSIAH SPODE II, 1755–1827

Baptised '25th May 1755, Jossiah of Jossiah and Ellen Spode of Stoke'. Believed to have been born 8th May. His gravestone reads 'Josiah Spode of the Mount who died 16th July 1827 aged 72'. Marriage: '9th July 1775 Josiah Spode Potter and Elizabeth Barker Spinster both of the Parish of Stoke'. Elizabeth was buried on 7th June 1782, and the entry in the Register of St Giles, Cripplegate, states that she died of fever. Of the thirty-five deaths recorded that month, nine were attributed to the same cause.

JOSIAH SPODE III, 1777–1829
His monument in Stoke Church states he was born 22nd August 1777, and died 6th October 1829. He married Mary Williamson of Longport, Staffordshire, at Clapham on 11th April 1815, the Rev. Edward Whieldon, Rector of Burslem, officiating.[137] Mary's marriage portion from her mother was £3000, and Spode III was provided by his father with an estate at Great Fenton and an annuity of £500 during their joint lives. Mary was the daughter of Anne Williamson, née Henshall, by her second marriage to Robert Williamson, earthenware manufacturer of Longport: her first husband had been James Brindley, the eminent engineer.[279] Mary's brother, Hugh Henshall Williamson, was one of the two trustees of Spode III's estate on his death.

JOSIAH SPODE IV, 1823–1893
Born on 12th August 1823; only child and sole heir of Spode III. He left Stoke as a child with his mother, lived the rest of his life at Hawkesyard, near Armitage in Staffordshire, and had no connection with the Factory. He married Helen Heywood in 1848 but had no issue and died a widower in 1893, leaving his fortune to found a Dominican Priory, which still thrives. Helen Gulson, his niece, who had lived with him many years prior to his death and had, like him, been converted to the Roman Catholic faith, bequeathed the collection of Spode and other ceramics she inherited to the Victoria and Albert Museum.

OTHER CHILDREN OF JOSIAH SPODE OF LANE DELPH
Anne Her baptismal entry remains undiscovered, but she was born in 1720. Spode I left her an annuity of £20 and a house 'now erecting near to the Mill in the Meadow in Stoke' at the time of his death. Her married name was Gallimore. She had married a blacksmith who, in 1764, bought a property in Stoke from John Turner; but she was left a widow some time before 1778. Buried '19th May 1808 Ann Gallimore, 88, Stoke'.
Alice Baptised '6th October 1724, Alice Spode of Josiah and Anne'. The mother's name is unfamiliar but no other entries for Spodes occur at this time. Anne may have been Josiah's first wife and Ellen his second.
Mary Baptised '25th November 1729 Mary Spoad of Josiah and Ellen'.

OTHER CHILDREN OF SPODE I

Samuel Baptised 28th October 1757. His gravestone states he died 26th January 1817, 'in his fifty-eighth year'. The entry of his marriage to Robert Garner's daughter, Sarah, is undiscovered. She died at Lane End 'awfully sudden, in a fit of apoplexy' in February 1824.[132] Her gravestone states she was aged sixty-three. Their first child was born in 1784 and died an infant. Four children reached maturity: Elizabeth, 1785-1862; Sarah, 1788-1842; Josiah, 1790-1859; and Samuel, 1798-1845.

Elizabeth was left £1000 in Spode II's will and died a spinster. Sarah married Charles James Mason in 1815.[182] Josiah and Samuel, who were left £2000 each by Spode II, both went to Tasmania. Josiah settled there, eventually becoming Chief Magistrate, but returned to England before his death. Samuel's stay was short, and on his return he practised as an attorney-at-law. There are living descendants of Josiah.

Mary Baptised 12th August 1759. Marriage: '16th December 1783 Richard Rivers Newcastle Surgeon and Mary Spode Spinster'. Witnesses to the marriage were Robert Garner Junior and Margaret Garner. Entry of burial: '5th June 1786 Mary Rivers'.

Ellen Baptised 3rd January 1762. She died a spinster and was buried on 27th June 1801.

Sarah Baptised 19th December, 1764. Marriage: '16th September 1787 Richard Rivers of Newcastle Surgeon and Sarah Spode Spinster'. Witnesses to the marriage were Sam Poulson and Sam Brindley. For this marriage to Mary's widower, special dispensation must have been obtained: it was not until the Deceased Wife's Sister's Marriage Act of 1907 that the law was changed so that 'No marriage between a man and his deceased wife's sister shall be deemed void or voidable as a civil contract by reason only of such affinity'. Sarah died in 1798 and her husband in 1802. They had three children: Josiah, baptised on 3rd June 1789, and in 1813 described as 'of Penton ville in the County of Middlesex Gent'; William, baptised 27th August 1790; and Anne.

Ellen Spode's will was proved on 8th October 1801. In it, she left £1,000 to the children of her late sister Sarah. Josiah Rivers was his mother's heir at law, inheriting the portion she had inherited from her father, Spode I. William Rivers was left £2,000 by his uncle Spode II, and his children were also left £2,000 between them. He was married twice: first to a Miss Mollart and then, in 1824, to a widow named Mary Guest at Hanley. His three children, one christened Josiah Spode, were all the issue of his first marriage. He worked at the factory for Spode II and in 1813 wrote to Josiah Wedgwood at Etruria for an assortment of Hibiscus Pattern 'for my uncle'. He later manufactured on his own account at Bedford Row, Shelton.[171] There are living descendants.

Anne Baptised 30th December 1772. Died 5th July 1829. In her marriage settlement she was described as living in Liverpool. Her brother, Spode II, provided her with a marriage portion of £3,000 and an annuity of £250, the income on a further £5,000, when she married Thomas Fenton of Stoke Lodge in August 1808. The marriage had no issue. Thomas Fenton was one of the two trustees of Spode III's estate on his death.

Elizabeth Baptised 21st January 1777. Her gravestone reads 'died 1st July 1793 aged sixteen years'.

OTHER CHILDREN OF SPODE II

William Baptised in Stoke Parish on 8th March 1776. He died a bachelor on 27th May 1834, at the home of his sister Elizabeth in Park Square, London. From 1805, he was equal partner with William Copeland in the London business, which went under his name, but he entirely withdrew from it on 31st December 1811. In March 1815, in Spode III's marriage settlement, of which he was a trustee, he was described as 'of Ashe, Surrey Gentleman', where he lived until his death—but his name was still Spode. In 1831, he withdrew his trusteeship and it was noted that he had 'since by Royal License exchanged his name for Hammersley'. This happened before 1825, since he was called by his new name in the will which his father drew up in October of that year. The reason for this change of name has not been discovered, and another mystery surrounds how he disposed of the fortune left him by Spode II. Already in a position to retire in comfort in 1811, when only thirty-five, he inherited a fortune of more than £100,000 on his father's death in 1827. He left his entire estate to his sister Elizabeth and this was finally sworn for stamp duty in November 1835 as being worth 'under £16,000'. In contrast, the estate of his younger brother, Spode III —whose inheritance had been no greater—was valued in 1832, three years after his death, at £162,576.

Elizabeth Born 15th December 1778, 'daughter of Josiah Spode Hardwareman and Elizabeth' (Register of St Giles, Cripplegate). The entry was also made in Stoke Register with the incorrect date 15th October 1778. She married Broad Malkin, 'late a major in His Majesty's 21st Regiment of Light Dragoons', in 1805, when she was provided with the income (£400 a year) on £8,000 which was settled on her by her father. On her father's death, her fortune was augmented by a further £32,000. Described on 24th March 1829, as a 'widow of Henrietta Street, Cavendish Square, St. Marylebone, Middlesex', she had lost her husband some time prior to 1827. By 1834 she was married again, her second husband being a Dr Bree. She outlived her brother William and inherited what remained of his fortune. Her only issue was a daughter, Saba Elizabeth, by her first marriage.

Saba Elizabeth seems to have died before her mother. In 1825, when she was nineteen years old, her grandfather, Spode II, provided a marriage settlement of more than £10,000 for her. This was increased by a further £20,000 on his death. Her marriage, to the Rev'd Bidlake Bray of Brompton Row, Middlesex, may not have been a happy one since in her will, dated 3rd January 1828, she left £8,000 to her uncle, William, as 'a tribute of affectionate gratitude for his constant kindness and protection from my infancy particularly for the recent instances of it which I have experienced since my separation from my husband'. This may, of course, mean only that he had died. Their only child died at the age of five months.

Saba Born 6th March 1780, 'daughter of Josiah Spode China man and Elizabeth' (Register of St. Giles, Cripplegate). The entry was also made in Stoke Register. On 9th November 1809, she married George Whieldon, 'Bachelor and Gentleman' at Stoke, the witnesses being her sister Mary and her father, who had provided a marriage settlement of £10,000. She died soon after, on 29th July 1811, and no issue of the marriage has been traced. Her husband, who married again in 1817, was the son of Thomas Whieldon, the man for whom Spode I had worked as a youth.[153]

Mary Born 23rd November 1781, 'daughter of Josiah Spode Warehousekeeper and Elizabeth' (Register of St Giles, Cripplegate). The entry was also made in Stoke Register with the incorrect date 23rd December. In 1821, she married Edmund John Birch and her father provided £500 a year, secured by £30,000 on his own death. The sum was made up to £40,000 by his will in 1827. She outlived her husband and in about 1834 was residing in Leamington. There was no issue of the marriage.

Edmund John Birch was a successful manufacturer of high quality black basalts and jasper wares who appears to have disposed of his factory in Shelton in about 1814.[216] Spode II, at the time of his death in 1827, was under contract to purchase Fradswell Hall and its extensive surrounding estates from his son-in-law. The Hall is located in Staffordshire, twelve miles south-east of Stoke. The sum to be paid was £63,000. The transaction subsequently went through with his executors. Arthur Hayden lists an Edward John Birch as a signatory to the enrolment of Spode II's Pottery Troop of Cavalry in 1798: the first Christian name may be an error.[197] The original document cannot be traced.

11   The London business

The main sources for the information contained in this appendix are three articles of partnership in the Spode archives dated 29th May 1813; 19th July 1824; and 1st March 1826. After 1805, the London business was quite distinct and separate from the Stoke Factory. The various partnerships relate only to London. The Factory remained entirely under Spode II's control until his death and then passed to his son, Spode III, and finally his son's executors.

Bill head used in 1790

JOSIAH SPODE II, 1778–1805

Details of the first premises occupied by Spode in Fore Street, Cripplegate, are given in Chapter 2. In 1795, he was still listed in Kent's Directory as being at No. 45, Fore Street; but the following year his trading address was given as Portugal Street. It was not until 1802 that he purchased the freehold of the new property. The premises, which had an insured value of £10,000, were in two parts: the warehouse itself at No. 5, Portugal Street, and the living accommodation adjacent at No. 37, Lincoln's Inn Fields. Spode II never relinquished their ownership, and the successive partnership concerns paid him £400 a year rent for them and were responsible for their maintenance. After he returned to Stoke, the house was occupied by his son William, and later by William Copeland, and then by *his* son William Taylor Copeland; but a sitting room and bedroom were always reserved for Spode's use when he visited London.

Until 1805, Spode II continued to own the whole of the London business, although it was under the management of William, his eldest son, and William

Copeland. Simeon Shaw says of this period: 'The connections gradually increased, after he [Spode II] settled here [in Stoke], and his satisfaction with the attention to his interest by a confidential servant in town, was evinced by a most substantial mark—a present of £1,000; and as a further reward for his assiduity and integrity, by a share in the London business; still [1829] enjoyed by his son.'[255]

Bill head used in 1800

WILLIAM SPODE AND CO, 1805–1811

This became the title of the London business in 1805 when Spode II relinquished it entirely to his son and William Copeland, who became co-partners. In directories of the period, they are described as 'Porcelain, Earthenware and Glass Manufacturers' and later as 'Potters and Manufacturers of Stoke Porcelain to HRH the Prince of Wales'. On 31st December 1811, the partnership was dissolved by mutual consent. William Spode, having made over his entire share to William Copeland, seems to have retired from business altogether.

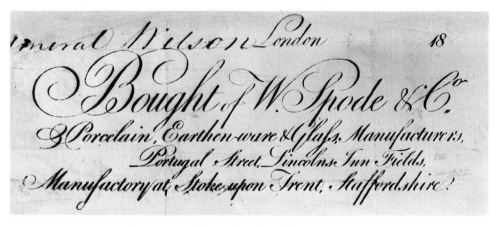

Bill head used in 1809

SPODE AND COPELAND, 1812–1823

Immediately William Spode retired, his father, Spode II, entered partnership with William Copeland—but they were not equal partners, the latter retaining three-quarters share of the whole. On 1st January 1812, the London stock and fixtures were valued at £32,534 and Spode II paid Copeland £8,133, thus purchasing a quarter share. The extent of the stock figure is remarkably high, especially since all agreements relating to London provide that the value of its stock should be taken at the selling wholesale price in London less 20 per cent.

In the partnership agreement of 1812 and the two subsequent ones of 1824 and 1826 two interesting points were made. The first concerned restraints: the London partner was bound actively to supervise the business there and could not, without consent, be involved in any other trade or business; but Spode II had no responsibility to concern himself with its affairs beyond what he chose, and he suffered no restrictions on his other activities. The second related to the Factory at Stoke: all agreements state that the Portugal Street business had always been closely connected with and 'principally supplied' by it and had become the established medium of sale for its products in London. Each had 'essentially promoted the other', and this was to be perpetuated by the partners giving 'to each concern the utmost extent of preference', the London business continuing 'to vend as much as possible, goods of the manufacture of Josiah Spode'.

In other directories of the period, the partnership business is described as 'Spode and Copeland, Potters and Manufacturers of Stoke Porcelain to HRH the Prince Regent' (after 1820, 'HM the King'). But in Lowndes Directories it is simply 'Spode & Co.'

Bill head used in 1822

Stoke Factory bill head used 1812–1826

SPODE, COPELAND AND SON, 1824–1826

On 1st January 1824, William Copeland's son, William Taylor, who was then aged twenty-six, was admitted to the partnership. This was achieved by a gift to him from his father of a quarter share. The holdings thus became a half held by William Copeland and a quarter each held by his son and Spode II. In 1824, the London stock valuation was £28,200.

Bill head used in 1827

SPODE AND COPELAND, 1826–1833

William Copeland's death on 20th January 1826, made a new partnership agreement necessary. The deceased's share was taken up equally by the surviving partners, making them equal co-partners. The style of the firm reverted to what it had been before 1824. The new partnership began on 1st March 1826, and was to run for seven years. The agreement provided that in the event of Spode II's death it should be continued for the remainder of this term by his

executors. This is exactly what happened. On 1st March 1833, William Taylor
Copeland and Thomas Garrett, his new partner, acquired complete control of
not only the London business but also the factory at Stoke. Portugal Street
continued to be the base for the London business until 1849, when a move was
made to 160, New Bond Street.

Bill head used in 1836

III Invoices and prices

INVOICED 1771: TO MESSRS. JOSIAH AND THOMAS WEDGWOOD.
Bought of SPODE AND TOMLINSON.

1771							£	s	d
Sep. 7th.	33 Dozen Table plates					@ 1/6d.	2	9	6
21st.	16 dozen flat plates and 4 Dozen Soops					@ 2/–d.	2	0	0
	4 (?Seconds) Long feathered dishes 20in.					@ 2/–d.		8	0
	6	–do–	–do–	–do–	–do– 18in.	@ 1/6d.		9	0
	6	–do–	–do–	–do–	–do– 16in.	@ 1/–d.		6	0
	6	–do–	–do–	–do–	–do– 14in.	@ 8d.		4	0
	6	–do–	–do–	–do–	–do– 12in.	@ 5d.		2	6
	6	–do–	–do–	–do–	–do– 10in.	@ 2½d.		1	3
	6	–do–	–do–	–do–	–do– 13in.	@ 6d.		3	0
	8	–do–	–do–	–do–	–do– 11in.	@ 3½d.		2	4

The ware invoiced was almost certainly cream ware. 'Feathered' will refer to the ornament at the edge of the dishes. This was one of the most popular cream ware shapes among all manufacturers. A dish is illustrated (No. 19) in the Leeds catalogue of 1783,[271] which also states that they were available in sizes from 20in. to 6in. The description of the 'Long feathered dishes' is indistinct but could be 'Sec'd', meaning seconds quality. *Wedgwood MS 20838-29.*

INVOICED SHELTON 23 JUNE 1774: TO JOSIAH WEDGWOOD & CO.
Bought of MOUNTFORD AND SPODE.

2 Dozen 3 (?pints) Chamberpots   4   0 (? pounds)

The price seems excessive for the time unless they were elaborately decorated, which is unlikely. On the other hand, if the '4' refers to shillings they seem far too cheap compared with the prices charged for dishes in 1771. *Wedgwood MS 9409-11.*

INVOICED LONDON 17 JULY 1800: TO MR. EVERETT.
Bought of JOSIAH SPODE.

4 Blue & White square Dishes & Covers   £1   2   0

Wedgwood MS 2201-12.

INVOICED LONDON 27 NOVEMBER 1809: TO HENRY STYLEMAN ESQ.
Bought of W. SPODE & CO.

				£	s	d
18 Elegant Cabinett Cups & Saucers Stoke China rich various patterns				£7	7	0
18 Cans and Saucers				7	7	0
1 Canoe Shape Sugar Box					14	6
1 Milk Ewer					12	0
1 Pint bason					12	6
2 Cake Plates				1	13	0
1 Round Ink Stand				2	2	0
1 Two Handled Chocolate Cup & Stand				1	16	0
1	–do–	–do–			15	0
1	–do–	–do–		1	1	0
1	–do–	–do–		1	4	0
1	–do–	Henley Pattern		1	1	0
1	–do–	flowers squares & gold festoons		1	1	0
Box					5	0
				£27	11	0

Henry Styleman was a wealthy Norfolk gentleman. It is to be regretted that
pattern numbers are not given on this invoice since, from the prices, the decorations are elaborate ones. It has not proved possible to identify either 'Henley
pattern' or the one described beneath it. 'Canoe shape' is an alternative name for
the New Oval Shape sugar box (see Plate 260). For 'Stoke China' see Appendix
IV. *From the original in the possession of C.A.Meadows Esq.*

INVOICED LONDON 1810: TO ADMIRAL WILSON.
Bought of W. SPODE & CO.

1810	Enamelled Green Edge			
Feb. 10	1 Vegetable dish		9	0
	6 Large plates		3	0
	6 Dessert plates		2	0
	2 Butter boats		2	0
	1 Blue & White soup tureen		10	0
	5 Square covers		13	9
	Package		2	0
April 27	To Goods as p. Bill	9	4	6
June 2	1 Large Blue & White dish		6	0
	Rivetting 4 dishes and 1 plate		5	4
	Mending 2 tureens		3	0
June 23	1 Cut glass cover to sugar basin		2	9
		£12	3	4

The charges for repairing broken ware are interesting, as is the cut glass cover. *Spode MS.*

INVOICED STOKE 15 JULY 1813: TO STEPHEN TEMPEST ESQ.
To JOSIAH SPODE, Potter & English Porcelain Manufacturer.

				£	s	d
30 China poringer handled bowls and						
30 saucers No. 1922 dark black & edge			1/6d.	4	10	0
18 China Cans	–do–		9d.		13	6
18 „ Can saucers	–do–		8d.		12	0
36 „ Muffins 7in.	–do–		1/6d.	2	14	6
12 „ 8½in. Dessert Plates			3/–d.	1	16	0
5 „ Bowls	–do–				11	6
2 „ 24s Dutch jugs	–do–		3/–d.		6	0

Pattern 1922 was a popular bat printed one and is illustrated in Plate 259. *From a transcript among the Spode MSS.*

INVOICED LONDON 1822 (?): TO HIS MAJESTY THE KING.
TO SPODE & COPELAND.

> Elegant Royal Blue Grounds gold chased figures
> and ornaments with Compartments of Historical
> Paintings, viz,—
> 1 Very Large Vase, with the Figure of Cleopatra
> 2 – less – Perseus and Andromeda   £51 10 0

The invoice is undated but the Keeper of the Privy Purse obtained a receipt for payment of the account on 2nd August 1822. It has not proved possible to trace these three vases, which must represent outstanding examples of their kind. Details of three other notable royal commissions are given in Note 89. *Royal Archive 26450. By gracious permission of Her Majesty The Queen.*

JAMES WORDLEY, the Liverpool dealer, was invoiced by Spode II for goods delivered from Stoke in February, April and September 1826 at the following prices, on which a discount of 10 per cent was allowed.

CHINA

Pattern 885	Bute teacup @ 1/11d. and saucer @ 1/11d.
967	Toy oriental jug and bowl @ 5/6d. complete and a 4in. round basket with pierced cover @ 7/6d.
1128	Bute teacup @ 1/8d. (*see Plate 275*).
1978	Large can @ 2/4d. and 8in. bread and butter plate @ 6/6d.
2768	Teacup @ 10d.
3420	Toy oriental jug and bowl @ 3/6d. complete (*see Plate 273*).
3644	Rose spouted tea tasters @ 1/9d. and toy ones @ 1/6d; oriental toy jugs @ 1/–d. and handbowls @ 1/6d; Paris toy teacups, cans and saucers all @ 6d. (*see Plate 273*).
3689	Embossed teacup @ 1/11d.
3886	Ring stands with knob pillars @ 2/9d.
3975	Bow handled, flanged basket 5in. @ 7/6d. (*see Colour Plate VIII*).
3993	Round wafer box @ 3/6d.
4001	Rose tea taster @ 3/6d.
4003	An Etruscan tea set without teapot and stand @ £8.8s.6d.
4039	A Gadroon tea set @ £6.0s.6d.
4070	Teacups @ 2/6d, Saucers @ 2/6d, Cans @ 2/8d, Tetragon plates @ 7/6d, Slop Bowl @ 6/6d. (All Gadroon Shape).

Flower Embossed Shape with a gold dontil edge: Teacups @ 9*d*, Cans @ 10*d*,
     Breakfast cups @ 1/2*d*, Bread and Butter plates 8in. @ 3/–*d*.
     and 7in. @ 2/6*d*.

EARTHENWARE
Pattern 1690   China shape double icepail @ 21/–*d*. (*see Plate 116*).
     3807   Herculaneum Scent Jar @ 20/–*d*.
Blue Italian Muffin plates 6in. @ 2*d*. (*see Plate 66*).

STONE CHINA
Pattern 2240   Twifflers (8in. plates) @ 8*d*. and Baking Dishes 11in. @ 3/6*d*.
     and 9in. @ 2/–*d*. (*see Plate 298*).
A small cover, pierced, with fruit knob, blue grounds and gilt to pattern @ 1/6*d*.
Wedgwood MSS. 12–2230, 31 and 32.

It is sometimes erroneously assumed that finely decorated china and good earthenware were relatively cheaper in the early nineteenth century than they later became. It is difficult to relate money values to the present day, but the price Henry Styleman paid in 1809 for just one of his chocolate cups and stands—£1.16*s*.0*d*.—was exactly equivalent to two weeks' wages for Joseph Turner, the enameller and gilder, in 1805 (see page 55). William Outrim, the senior executive at the Spode Factory, was paying £10.0*s*.0*d*. a year rent to Spode III's executors for his Stoke house in 1832—ten shillings less than the price of a complete tea set in Pattern 1002 in 1810.[269] This would have been a good house and he would probably have had at least one servant. The rent paid by less exalted employees for less impressive homes was between three and six guineas a year. George Bell, the bat printer,[87] paid five guineas, so his weekly rent was less than the price of one of the dessert plates he probably produced daily by the score in Pattern 1922 (see Tempest invoice). The highest paid of all potters on the Factory were the throwers. Spode II was paying his throwers 5/–*d*. a day in 1820—so the price of an icepail decorated in Pattern 1690 (Wordley invoice) would have paid four days' wages for the man who potted them. In 1825, a good labourer's wage for a day was 2/6*d*.[10] Even Spode I's price of 2/–*d*. for a 20-inch dish, in 1771, does not look so low in relation to a price for coal of little more than this for half a ton (see page 21).

Manufacturers in Staffordshire worked to common price scales and supplied similar compositions. Spode II's price lists have not survived; but one produced by Job Ridgway & Sons of Cauldon Place, on 1st January 1813, has been rescued by Reginald Haggar, by whose courtesy it is partially reproduced on

U

the page opposite. It consists of twenty-one gradually rising scales from which five have been selected.

That these scales and these compositions were both used by Spode is proved by an invoice of 8th October 1810, to a Thomas Brown from W.Spode & Co, London, for a tea set in Pattern 1002, itemised exactly as the composition given opposite for a 'complete set' and charged at £10.10s.0d, the twenty-first scale.[269] Slight discrepancies are revealed, however, between the scales and the prices in the invoices given above, particularly in the Wordley invoices of 1826. One of the reasons for deviating from the scales by this late date may have been the popularity of fancy and embossed shapes by then—account having to be taken of the extra expense of producing these as opposed to plain shapes. The tea set in 4039 in the Wordley invoices is £6.0s.6d. (cf. the thirteenth scale) and the one in 4003 without a teapot and stand is £8.8s.6d. (cf. the twentieth scale). The large and small plates in the scales are what Spode termed 8-inch and 7-inch Bread and Butter Plates, deep and saucerlike in shape, often called 'biscuit dishes' in the antique trade. Some of the items in Pattern 1922 in the Tempest invoice tally with the fifth scale, as do some in the Wordley invoice for plain white Flower Embossed shape with a gold dontil edge. This scale is possibly the lowest one employed by Spode for decorated china, but he certainly used higher scales than those produced by Ridgway. This is indicated by the Styleman invoice, and many Spode patterns were very much more costly than number 1002 which in 1810 was charged on the twenty-first scale, Ridgway's highest.

The composition of a basic complete set did not include, at this date, any small tea plates. These were introduced later and appear not to have become popular until the 1830s. The teapot was frequently dispensed with in wealthier households in favour of silver, and so were the cream jug and sugar box at times. Coffee and chocolate pots in china never seriously competed with their silver and metal counterparts, which explains their comparative rarity. The absence of hollow-ware pieces from the Tempest invoice, except bowls and jugs, is noteworthy.

MANUFACTURERS' SCALES FOR CHINA AND BREAKFAST SETS, 1813

	First			Fifth			Thirteenth			Twentieth			Twenty-first		
	£	s	d	£	s	d	£	s	d	£	s	d	£	s	d
Twelve Cups & Saucers		9	0		19	6	2	9	0	3	18	6	4	3	0
Twelve Cans		6	0		9	9	1	4	6	1	19	3	2	1	6
Teapot		3	6		5	6		11	9		18	0		19	0
Teapot Stand		1	0		1	9		4	3		7	0		7	3
Sugar Box		2	0		3	3		8	0		12	9		13	6
Cream		1	0		1	9		5	6		8	6		9	0
Slop Bowl		1	2		2	9		7	3		10	10		4	0
Large Plate		1	6		3	3		8	6		13	6		14	3
Small Plate		1	3		2	6		7	3		11	2		11	9
COMPLETE SET	1	6	5	2	10	0	6	6	0	9	19	6	10	10	0
SET—8 CANS	1	4	5	2	6	10	5	17	10	9	6	6	9	17	2
Breakfast Bowl & Saucer		1	3		2	6		6	0		9	6		10	0
Muffin 7in.			10		1	6		4	0		6	6		7	0
Covered Muffin		2	6		4	3		9	9		15	0		16	0
Butter Tub & Stand		2	6		4	3		9	9		15	0		16	0
Eggcup			6			9		2	4		4	1		4	4
Pint Milk Jug		2	0		3	0		7	0		10	6		11	0
Roll Tray		7	0		9	6		17	6	1	4	7	1	5	6

Impressed marks	**Painted marks**

SPODE
1a

SPODE
1b

SPODE
1c

SPODE
1d

SPODE
2a

Spode
3

SPODE
2b

SPODE
4

SPODE
5a

5b

StokeChina
6

SPODES
NEW STONE
7

527
8

16
9

SPODE
10

Spode
11

Spode
12

Spode & Copeland
13

SPODE.
Stone China.
14

Printed marks

Spode

15a

SPODE

16a

16b

17

15b

16c

18a

18b

18c

18d

SPODE
Stone-China

19a

21a

Floral

SPODE

23

SPODE
Stone China

19b

21b

𝕾pode's
𝕴mperial

20

B. Nº

22

24

IV Marks

The illustrations given on the previous two pages are all actual size—although most marks vary in size from piece to piece. Painted marks naturally show very considerable variation from one to the other, in style as well as size.

Something has been said on the subject of marks and marking in the main body of the book, particularly in Chapter 6. The marks given in the illustrations have been grouped according to the process used to produce them: impressed in the clay before glazing, painted by hand, or printed. The numbers allocated to them cannot, therefore, provide any guide to the date of any particular mark.

Of all methods of marking, the one to be preferred is impressing in the clay. Not only are impressed marks completely permanent but also they cannot be faked by subsequent decorators. Obviously, they cannot be employed for pattern numbers—only for the manufacturer's name or the name of a particular body. Their limitations do not end there since only very simple marks can be impressed successfully, and they have the disadvantage of failing in their object if they are not applied with care. The most elaborate impressed mark used by Spode was Mark 7, and this is simple enough. The method was the one mainly employed at the Factory for earthenware, stoneware, red ware and basalts. China tewares are rarely found with an impressed mark, although very early pieces—particularly teapots—sometimes have Mark 2a. The Factory's normal practice was at first, presumably, carried over to the new product. Later on, impressed marks seem to have been used for china, on jugs and other pieces with sprigged decoration of the kind illustrated in Plates 253 and 256.

Whether to use a painted or a printed mark was basically decided by the process employed for the decoration. If this were freehand painted, a painted mark was almost inevitable. If printed, a printed mark, engraved on the same copper as the pattern, was both neater and cheaper. So cheap and easy, in fact, that many pieces of printed Spode earthenware have a printed mark as well as an impressed one, making assurance doubly sure. An interesting comment on the relative cost of the two methods, c. 1800, is contained in the notebook of an anonymous pottery manufacturer which is among the Spode Archives. He noted: 'Molly Poulson charges 2d. per dozen for lettering plates at the bottom with names'. On the same page he recorded that 'Minton & Co. pay 3d. per dozen viz. 1d. a dozen more than common ware' to their transferrers for doing Lily Pattern (see Plate 31). Thus, it was as expensive to paint a name on a piece as to fit a complete printed decoration to it.

It is doubtful whether, as a general rule, 'a Molly Poulson' was employed
at the Spode Factory for lettering. A more convenient arrangement, where
pattern numbers needed to be added, was to let the men or women responsible
for the decoration also be responsible for the marking. The great variation in
styles of lettering to be found in Spode marks indicates that this was the
practice there as it was at Derby, where a palette was kept in the decorating
shop especially for the purpose but was not always used—painters being the
unregimented breed that they are.[193]

Notwithstanding the cheapness of printed marks and their guaranteed
uniformity, they were very rarely used on Spode china before 1821 unless the
decoration itself was partially or completely executed in print. Derby introduced
printed marks after complaints about the carelessness of their painted ones; but
although fear of demarcation disputes would not have prevented their painters
from taking off their own prints, one can imagine that both their dignity and
convenience were adversely affected by the innovation. The sheer bother of it
probably accounts for the extreme rarity of the Prince of Wales Mark 17. This
mark highlights the advantage of print, since nothing as intricate or neat, with
such a potent message, could have been hoped for from hand decoration. The
next attempt at 'sales promotion by back-stamp' was more determined and not
so easily defeated. In 1821, the massive Felspar Porcelain Mark, 18a, was
introduced, and printed marks on freehand decorated china arrived to stay.

MARK 1
Mark 1a appears on a piece illustrated in Plate 3; Mark 1b in Plate 140; Mark 1c
in Plate 104 and Mark 1d in Plates 103 and 105. Each of these marks is different
in detail from the others, but they have three things in common: a primitive
appearance, large size, and association with pieces which seem to be of early
date. It is reasonably safe to accept them as the first marks used, relating to the
productions of Spode I. Their rarity is only to be expected. Spode I, like most of
his contemporaries and unlike his son, was almost certainly an occasional and
casual marker. It must also be remembered that the scale of his production was
only a fraction of that which was later achieved by Spode II and that he worked
that much farther away from us in time.

MARK 2
Mark 2a, sometimes very tiny but always neat, is mainly associated with blue
and white printed ware of an early type (see Page 144). But it is also sometimes
found on basalts, pieces in coloured earthenware bodies, and some other wares,
including very early pieces of china. It is not unlikely that this was the Factory
mark in 1797, when Spode II took over, and that it was continued for some time
after this.

SPODE
1a

SPODE
1b

SPODE
1c

SPODE
1d

SPODE
2a

SPODE

2b

Mark 2b, usually but not always with the slight curve as in the illustration, is a larger version of Mark 2a. It is very rarely found on ordinary earthenwares but is encountered on red wares and the various stonewares.

MARK 3

Spode

3

Mark 3 is found on all of the bodies which were made at the Spode Factory. It is the most confusing of all the marks since its use must have extended over a period of more than twenty years, beginning *c.* 1800. At one end, it overlaps the use of Mark 2; and at the other, Mark 4. In blue printed earthenware, it is mainly found on patterns introduced between 1810 and 1820.

MARK 4

SPODE

4

Mark 4 is the latest of the impressed marks, introduced *c.* 1815 or a little later. When of small size, it can easily be confused with Mark 2a; but it can always be identified by the serifs on the capital 'S' of Spode. These are not always as pronounced as in the specimen mark illustrated, but they are always present. This mark was used until the end of the Spode Period in 1833.

MARK 5

5a   5b

I have encountered Mark 5a only twice, in both cases on garden seats. It appears on the one illustrated in Plate 100, and on one in Blue Italian which is in the Spode Museum. A crown was a very popular device with many manufacturers and one extensively used by Copeland & Garrett. Mark 5b appears on the base of the ice pail illustrated in Colour Plate I.

MARK 6

StokeChina

6

This mark is known on an early piece of very fine white earthenware with a clear glaze, decorated with Pattern 282 and marked with this number. On the grounds of pattern, shape, potting and material, this piece has to be accepted as of Spode manufacture. It is discussed on Page 139.

A London invoice of 1809, given in Appendix III, refers to '18 Elegant Cabinett Cups and Saucers Stoke China rich various patterns £7. 7. 0.' From the date and the price, it is very doubtful if this refers to articles made in this superior earthenware body, which was probably a precursor to china. From 1808 until 1824, the Post Office Annual's entry for the Spode London business contained the description 'manufacturers of Stoke Porcelain'. This refers to Spode china, and almost certainly that is what was meant in the invoice.

MARKS 7, 14, 19

Mark 19 is the earliest Stone China mark, *c.* 1813. Marks in imitation of

Chinese characters were old favourites with English potters, and impressed square seal marks are often found on eighteenth century Staffordshire red ware of Elers type. Miles Mason made extensive use of printed marks of this kind for his china, sometimes incorporating his name. But to the best of my knowledge, the only potter who, in addition to Spode, used one for stone china was Johnson of Hanley, with a mark very similar to 19b. The stone china marks of most other manufacturers followed C.J.Mason's, using a crown. Evidence from the wares themselves suggest that the two versions, full seal and half seal, were used contemporaneously—but Mark 19b is far less often found than 19a. The larger one obviously represents the first complete design, and the smaller one a subsequent abbreviation. Mark 7, which superseded Mark 19, was introduced *c.* 1822. See Pages 195 and 196.

Mark 14 is rare. Pieces of handpainted stone china with Marks 10 or 11 are sometimes found, but it was most unusual for the marker to describe the body as well.

19a   19b

SPODES
NEW STONE

7

SPODE.
Stone China.

14

MARKS 8, 9

These are but two from the endless variety of workmen's marks to be found on Spode products. With very early factories, where the employees were numbered by the dozen not the hundred, the study of individual makers' and decorators' marks may be rewarding and, indeed, in the absence of anything else, necessary. But with Spode, I have found it singularly without profit. Finely decorated wares very rarely have any such marks, and the commoner ones abound with them. The most frequently encountered are numbers such as 25, 30 and 45. These are impressed below Mark 4, and are potters' marks. The numbers 6, 12, 24, 36, in isolation on hollow-ware pieces, are usually not makers' marks at all but refer to the size of the article according to the potter's count. Marking of this kind was not common at the Spode Factory. Printers favoured individual letters of the alphabet, in capitals, for their personal marks; but earlier blue printed pieces are often found with various symbols. The universality of these and their consequent unreliability in serving to identify the work of any one factory are fairly well known.

Marks 8 and 9 have been selected because they are reasonably distinctive and may help in the identification of certain pieces. Mark 8 has been encountered on early china Old Oval Shape teapots and sugar boxes (Plate 257). The numbers vary—sometimes two figures, not three—but the mark is distinguished by a good central position on the base of the article, an extremely deep impression, and the small diamond preceding the figures. Mark 9 is a maker's mark which occurs very frequently on pieces of Felspar Porcelain.

◇527

8

16

9

Spode
10

Spode
11

Spode
12

MARKS 10, 11, 12

These are the marks usually found on Spode china before 1821. They were usually accompanied by the appropriate pattern number, which only very rarely has the prefix 'No.' before the figures. The commonest colour employed was red—the easiest to apply and about the cheapest. Often, the decorator would use any colour that was easily to hand, frequently the last one he had used on the pattern. The Factory probably had no strict rules about this, although the use of gold would have been discouraged for reasons of expense. Gold marks are consequently unusual.

Marks 10 and 11 were probably always used contemporaneously, but Mark 12 is normally associated with later patterns.

Spode & Copeland
13

MARK 13

Spode and Copeland was the title of the London business from 1812 to 1823 and from 1826 to 1833. As explained in Appendix 11, at no point did the Stoke manufacturing business go by this name. Pieces marked 'Spode & Copeland' must therefore have been destined for sale in or through London. But the use of such a mark could not have been common since examples are so rarely found. It was possibly reserved for special, important commissions. Pieces bearing it always seem to be fine productions. Examples are illustrated in Plates 173, 178 and 215. To have used a special, distinctive mark on the bulk quantities of ordinary wares destined for sale through London would have made the task of warehousing at the Factory extremely complex and difficult. An impressed mark in script, 'Spode and Copeland fecit,' appears on a bust of the Duke of Wellington which is in the Spode Museum. The bust was formerly in the collection of T.G.Cannon and is illustrated in his book.[156] Jewitt illustrates a Spode & Copeland mark described as 'both impressed and printed'.[208] I have never seen it, or met anyone who has. Another mark he gives—'Spode Son & Copeland'—may well be a mistake since neither the Stoke nor London business ever had such a title. 'Spode Copeland & Son' was the title of the London business for the brief period from 1824 to 1826.

MARK 14

See Mark 7 above.

MARK 15

Spode   *Spode*
15a   15b

Mark 15a is the companion printed mark to the impressed Mark 3, used contemporaneously and often in conjunction with it on earthenware. It is frequently the only mark on blue printed china tewares. Mark 15b is a curved variant very rarely found.

SPODE

MARK 16

Mark 16a, the commonest of all printed marks on earthenware, is often found in conjunction with impressed Mark 4, which it predates. It was in use *c.* 1810 and can be found in conjunction with Mark 3. It continued until the end of the Spode period in 1833. Mark 16b, encountered on blue printed wares, is of similar date to 16a but did not continue in use as long. Examples are rare. Pieces in Rome Pattern (introduced *c.* 1812) nearly always bear this mark, and it has been found on other patterns of similar date. It provided the centre design for Mark 19. Mark 16c is very rare but has been found with blue printed patterns, notably Blue Italian.

16a

16b

16c

MARK 17

Two pieces bearing this very rare mark are illustrated in Plates 155 and 157. Its significance and date, 1806, are discussed on Page 85.

MARK 18

The story of Felspar Porcelain and the relevant dates concerning it will be found in Chapter 5. Mark 18a, the first one used, bears a certain similarity to the Felspar mark introduced by Coalport in 1820, but the fashion for these large, circular, carefully designed marks incorporating a full address was probably started by Flight, Barr and Barr at Worcester. Examples with Mark 18a are hard to find. The date may have been omitted soon after 1821 had expired, producing the next mark, 18b. Two versions of this are known, but the only difference is that the one not shown has Stoke-upon-Trent in lower case type, not script. The next mark, 18c, is the common mark for Felspar Porcelain, and this was certainly in use by 1825 (see Plate 174). Spode Felspar Porcelain marks are always printed in purple.

I have never seen a piece bearing Mark 18d. The illustration is reproduced from an old copper engraving at the Spode Factory. See the note above on Mark 13 for 'Spode and Copeland'.

All pieces marked Felspar Porcelain are undoubtedly so, but the converse is not true. The usual practice with tea sets was to use the printed mark for all

17

18a

18b

18c

18d

20

21a

21b

B . N.°

22

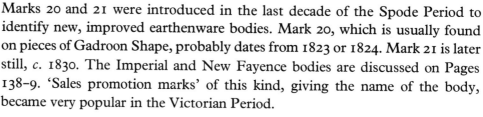

23

24

or most of the major pieces and to let the pattern number alone suffice for the teacups and saucers. Pieces of Felspar Porcelain are also not infrequently found with Marks 10, 11 and 12.

MARK 19 See Mark 7 above.

MARKS 20, 21

Marks 20 and 21 were introduced in the last decade of the Spode Period to identify new, improved earthenware bodies. Mark 20, which is usually found on pieces of Gadroon Shape, probably dates from 1823 or 1824. Mark 21 is later still, *c.* 1830. The Imperial and New Fayence bodies are discussed on Pages 138–9. 'Sales promotion marks' of this kind, giving the name of the body, became very popular in the Victorian Period.

MARK 22

Mark 22 is usually found in conjunction with Mark 21. Following it, the pattern number is added by hand—although this, also, is printed in certain cases. A simple 'B' alone was sometimes printed. The reason why the pattern number was not always engraved and printed is that many of these coppers were used for outline prints which were subsequently enamelled to produce differently coloured versions, each with a different identifying number.

'B' Patterns are frequently unmarked, except with an impressed Spode mark, and the prefix 'B' was not always supplied when the pattern number was put on by hand. If collectors find themselves with an obviously late underglaze decoration which has a number below 400, this will be the explanation. (See Page 89.)

MARKS 23, 24

These, to my knowledge, are the only Spode marks which incorporate the name of the pattern. Floral pattern is illustrated in Plates 48 and 95, and Aesops Fables Pattern in Plates 75, 89 and 90. The use of marks of this type was a late development. Floral Pattern was introduced *c.* 1830, and Aesops Fables at about the same time or even a little later. Marks with the name of the pattern in an elaborate cartouche became popular among nearly all manufacturers of printed wares during the Victorian Period. They reveal an awareness of the importance of pattern names as a means of sales promotion as well as identification. Earlier, patterns were known by a number, if they had one, or nicknames developed on the Factory and in the trade.

WORK MARKS See Marks 8 and 9 above.

SPECIAL MARKS

Special marks are always of the greatest interest. The commonest are the
descriptions sometimes given in script on painted pieces: with flowers, the name
of the botanical species; with landscapes, the name of the scene; with figures, a
piece of appropriate verse or a description relating to the subject painted. This
was the common and praiseworthy practice of the age, and an artist's lettering
was often as accomplished as his painting. Special marks relating to the reci-
pient or retailer are very rare and, particularly if they provide dates, are of great
interest. Pieces with marks of this kind are illustrated in Plates 2, 81 and 185.

FAKE MARKS

Fake marks do not represent a problem to Spode collectors—yet. The notorious
Samson of Paris seems never to have extended his activities to Spode; and the
interest of the less reputable members of the antique trade in earlier days was
limited to laboriously removing painted Spode marks from pieces in Pattern
1166—in the hope of selling the mutilated results as the products of some then
more fashionable factory. One of the cans illustrated in Plate 275 is an interesting
curiosity of a kind which any collector would be well advised to acquire if he
got the opportunity. It is an undoubted English fake of a very early date, and
rarer than any Spode piece. I have seen a piece of Japanese porcelain, manufactured in the 1930s, marked only with an impressed Spode in letters half an
inch high—so unlikely in every way that it could have been intended as a joke.
It is probably a reminder of unhappier times, before the Japanese manufacturers
themselves instituted a meticulous control on copying which now puts their
English counterparts to shame.

LATER MARKS

The later marks used at the Spode Factory, after 1833, fall outside the scope of
this book. The word 'Spode' often features in these, but always with the addition
of Copeland & Garrett (1833-1847) or Copeland and/or England.

In 1833, the new partnership, Copeland & Garrett, made a clean sweep of
the Factory's marks. There is ample evidence that, as a deliberate policy, they
lost no time in substituting their own names for Spode, which was obliterated
from existing coppers. Examples of Copeland & Garrett productions in Aesops
Fables Pattern are often found with Mark 24—but the Spode in the bottom
left-hand corner is always punched out. Only Mark 7, used in conjunction with
a Copeland & Garrett printed mark, seems to have been retained for a while—
either because of large stocks of biscuit ware, or because 'Spode's New Stone'
was more a brand name than a manufacturer's identification.

Notes

1 When Josiah Wedgwood and John Turner visited Cornwall in 1775 they were warned of the danger of attack from the tinminers. Pewter could contain up to 75 per cent tin and the price and demand for it dropped as earthenware sales increased. There are accounts of tinminers rioting and destroying stocks of earthenware. (See Geoffrey Wills, *Proceedings of the Wedgwood Society*, 1957, No.2, p.83 and 1966, No.6, p.106.)

2 Whieldon's Notebook. The book was discovered by Llewellyn Jewitt and is now in the collection of Stoke-on-Trent Museum and Art Gallery (Hanley Museum). I am indebted to Arnold Mountford, the Museum's Director, for allowing me to inspect and illustrate it (see p. 1) and for drawing my attention to two other relevant documents (Refs: 102 and 103).

3 The indenture of apprenticeship between William Shaw and Spode II which is illustrated on p. 37 was drawn up on 11th November 1799, although it was not signed until 23rd February 1801. The words 'and China' were deliberately inserted on the printed form after the description of the trade to be learned: 'Handling and Pressing of Earthenware'. *Spode MSS*.

4 Indenture of 11th November 1772, between Spode I and Thomas Mountford. This can no longer be traced but, fortunately, it is given in full by T.G.Cannon, *op. cit*, pp.70 to 82. Spode I's wife's business in Stoke as a haberdasher was reserved from his undertaking to have no other business interests.

5 The baptismal entries in Stoke Parish Register are very specific. Of sixty-six baptisms in the year 1755, only two are given as being from Stoke itself. Lane Delph had five.

6 The land was purchased on 10th September 1758, from William Lovatt and Thomas Ashley, and the property was still in the Spode family in 1831, when it was described as fronting on the north side of Church Street and occupied by Thomas Holdgate, Ironmonger (*Spode MSS*). In 1864, a William Holdgate was listed as an ironmonger at No.14 Church Street (*Jones' Mercantile Directory of the Staffordshire Potteries*, pp.123 and 203).

7 See Bevis Hillier, *The Turners of Lane End* 1965, p.4. Mr Hillier informs me that the only evidence of the date of Turner's birth in 1738 is his tombstone at Brewood, Staffordshire. His date of death is established beyond all doubt as 1787 (*op. cit*, p.62). The point has needed pursuit in view of Shaw's comment (*History*, p.173) that he 'died in 1786, at an advanced age'.

8 See John Mallett, *John Baddeley of Shelton*, ECC Vol.6, Pts.2 and 3. This detailed study shows that Baddeley's porcelain-making venture belonged to his earlier partnership with Reid and Co, which went bankrupt in the spring of 1761. Stocks of porcelain seem to have remained and may have been sold off at the beginning of his entirely new partnership with Fletcher of Newcastle, which started on 31st July 1761 (see

p.192 of above). This could account for Shaw's mistake.

It is difficult to understand how Baddeley had premises available for Spode I, since he never discontinued manufacturing himself. Even after his death in 1771, his son, Ralph, continued the partnership with Fletcher; and when it finally ended, in 1775, the factory (on the site now occupied by Messrs Ashworth) appears to have remained in the Baddeley family. A possible explanation is that on his bankruptcy, or when his new partnership was starting, John Baddeley was tempted to let part of his commodious premises. No trace of such a lease has been discovered, but such an arrangement would also explain why Spode I remained resident in Stoke and why, since Baddeley's fortunes recovered quickly, it did not last long.

9 Simeon Shaw states that Turner left for Lane End in 1762 (*History*, p.172), but Bevis Hillier (*The Turners of Lane End*, p.5) has found evidence that he was resident there in 1759.

10 The bill for the building of the original Meadow Oven survives. It is dated 1st June 1825. The job was done by Obediah Greatbatch and his men at a 'Whole cost including Brick Dressing and Labouring' (but not materials) of £10.3s.5½d. Excluding Greatbatch himself, thirteen men and boys were involved in the construction, at various rates of pay. The labourers earned 2/- or 2/6d. a day and a total of fifty-four man-days' work was charged for. *Spode MSS*.

11 The subsequent careers of Spode I's two partners remain a mystery. A Thomas Mountford was one of the forty-two proprietors of the Newcastle Canal Company in 1795. A William Tomlinson established a pottery at Ferrybridge, by Knottingley, and subsequently took into partnership Ralph Wedgwood, marking his ware Wedgwood & Co. (See Chaffers, *op. cit*, p.806.) William Tomlinson has been confused with John Tomlinson, Spode II's lawyer, one of Stoke's wealthiest and most prominent citizens.

12 Richard Ward's indenture of 12th February 1783, has been preserved (*Spode MSS*) but there is no trace of this apprenticeship, or one for William Copeland, in the Apprentice Books at the Public Record Office. These are a record of Inland Revenue receipts of the stamp duty instituted in 1709: sixpence in the £ on premiums of less than £50 and a shilling in the £ on those over. Richard Ward's premium was only one penny and, presumably, 'de minimis non curat lex'.

13 Wedgwood Manuscripts. MS 2198-12. The collection is now housed at Keele University and Josiah Wedgwood and Sons Limited, Barlaston. I am indebted to the latter for permission to quote from various documents. To the researches and generosity of J.K. and Una des Fontaines, I owe my awareness of the piece referred to in Note 36 and ten others (References 109 to 118).

14 See Lewellyn Jewitt, *The Ceramic Art of Great Britain*, Second Edition, 1883, pp.381 and 382. Jewitt's account of the early history of the London business is, in general, highly inaccurate. He states of William Copeland: 'Previous to this time [1784] Copeland, of London (a native of Stoke), who travelled in the tea trade, made the acquaintance of Spode and offered to undertake a commission to sell his tea-ware and other goods to his customers'. Neither Shaw nor Ward, or the lengthy article in the Art Union of 1846, or any other early record mentions any connection with the tea trade. Jewitt continues 'the enterprise was successful, and a warehouse was taken in Fore Street, Cripplegate, for the sale of Spode's goods'. Since Spode II was established there by March 1778, we are to believe from this that William Copeland had left Staffordshire, obtained a business appointment, negotiated a working arrangement with Spode II (who was ten years his senior) and helped to put him on his feet in London—all before he had reached the age of thirteen. According to Jewitt, it was William Copeland who, in 1779 (when he was fourteen), purchased the premises in Portugal Street. In fact, Spode II did not obtain these until 1796 and retained full control over them until 1805 (see Appendix II).

15 The display of Catherine the Great's service caused such a problem at Wedgwood's showroom in 1774. See N.McKendrick, *op. cit*, p.422.

16 There is varied evidence of the supply of goods to other manufacturers and merchants. Several records of Spode transactions with Wedgwood in London survive; and on 10th January 1795, Joseph Lygo, Derby's agent in London, wrote to Richard Eagan, the china dealer in Bath, 'I have this day sent some gilt goods of Spode's' (ex. inf. Geoffrey Godden).

Among the Spode MSS is a day-book, with entries from 25th April 1792, until 14th February 1793, for the firm of Trimbley Bell and Harris. This firm was listed as Toy Merchants of 23 St Martin's Lane in London directories between 1778 and 1798. 'Toy man'—or woman—was an early term for a china dealer, and although many of the transactions listed concern pottery 'toys', most are for tableware and glass. The presence of this book among the Spode MSS suggests that the firm may have received supplies from the Factory or Spode II's warehouse, or both. The sparse descriptions in the book do nothing to refute this and include 'Buffalo' dishes, 'Temple' dishes, 'Willow' dishes, green and blue edge dishes and plates, queensware, red glazed teapots and painted and gilt goods. Customers included Turner Abbott & Co, Neale & Co and Messrs Wedgwood, as well as many private individuals.

The plates illustrated in Plate 185 are marked only with the words 'Blades, London' in script but are of undoubted Spode manufacture, and other pieces, similarly marked, are known. John Blades was listed in London directories between 1800 and 1830 as a 'glass manufacturer' of 5 Ludgate Hill. He may, in addition to being a customer, have been one of Spode II's suppliers for glass.

17 In *The China-Mender*. The girl, explaining the predicament of her mistress's suitor, who had sat down on a table of treasured china ornaments, says:

'If he sent her up whole crates full, from Wedgwood's and Mr. Spode's,
He couldn't make amends for the cracked mandarins and smash'd toads'.

18 A characteristic of the pot pedlar was that he was usually prepared to accept old clothes in payment for his wares. See Bevis Hillier, *Two Centuries of China Selling*, ECC, Vol.7, Pt.1, p.6.

19 The possibility cannot be ruled out that some of these changes of address were due to renumbering in the street, but I have been unable to discover any evidence of this.

20 The original theatre, dating from 1662, was rebuilt by John Rich and opened with 'The Recruiting Officer' in 1714. It became known as the Devil's Theatre after a performance by Foote, whose portrayal of the Devil is said to have caused such terror in the audience that in the ensuing panic many lives were lost. The last performance there was in 1733, after which the premises had various uses. Immediately prior to Spode II's occupation, they were being used as a china warehouse by Caughley. The site is now (1970) occupied by the Royal College of Surgeons. See *Art-Union*, November 1846, p.288; *The Hornet*, 22nd April 1868, p.96; A.Hayden, *op. cit*, pp.20 and 21.

21 This was a large consignment and would have gone by water from Winsford to Liverpool. In 1833, it was estimated that a crate would hold about 72 dozen dinner plates or about 60 dozen unhandled teacups (*Spode MSS*). Larger pieces would, of course, occupy much more room eg. only about seven dozen teapots to a crate. Donovan was later an important customer of Minton and was dealing with him in 1799. He appears to have decorated Minton blanks and marked them with his own name. See Geoffrey Godden, *Minton, op. cit*, pp.4 and 11.

22 In the draft lease of 1802 for a coal mine referred to on page 34, references to quantities of coal are made in stacks 'such stack not to contain or consist of more than 25 hundred weight, each hundred containing 120 pounds'. *Spode MSS*.

23 See Simeon Shaw, *History*, p.149. The enormous benefit of canal transport can be judged by the maximum statutory charges fixed for the Newcastle Canal in 1795: 1½d per ton per mile for coal, stone and iron and 2d. for all other goods. Geo. III, Cap.87, LXI.

24 The Spode Factory Costing Book of 1833 (*Spode MSS*) reveals some interesting facts about the relative consumption and cost of coal and clay. It was calculated that 1500 dozen blue printed dinner plates required 11 tons of coal to fire to the biscuit state and a further 15 tons for 'hardening on' the prints and the final glost fire. So 26 tons were needed in all—roughly, one ton for every 60 dozen. One ton of clay mix would make 160 dozen dinner plates. Thus, by weight, nearly three times as much coal was required as clay. With holloware pieces, like teapots, the ratio was much higher: up to six to one. This was for the simplest two-fire earthenwares and the ratio further increased for more ambitious wares. Most china productions have at least three fires, some four or five. Clay mix, ready to supply to the potter, was costed at £3 per ton, but this included the cost of labour and preparation. Coal was costed at only 8s.10d. per ton.

In the late eighteenth century, the relative consumptions of the two raw materials may have been even more dramatically in favour of coal. By 1833, ovens were larger and fuel was probably being used more economically.

The fact that coal was more important than clay was often overlooked, not least by the Staffordshire potters themselves—when they were protesting about freight charges and the onerous disadvantages they suffered from being so far away from the source of their clay, the West Country (Ref.102). But their factories were built on top of some of the richest coal seams in Britain.

25 See *Victoria History of the County of Staffordshire*, 1963, Vol.VIII, p.219. None of the primary sources given as references throws any light on the description.

26 The dispute was widely publicised throughout the Potteries and aroused high feeling. A handbill, dated April 14th 1791, was circulated by Lane End pottery workers sympathetic to Samuel Spode's men. It began with the following allegation: 'Whereas a part of Mr. Spode's Journeymen Potters at the Folly, are at this time very ill treated by their said Master in refusing to employ them except they will comply with every unreasonable demand he thinks proper to make; four of whom he has by unjust proceedings lately lodged in Stafford Gaol, because they would not submit like Slaves to his imperious authority in going to dinner at an hour when neither Mr. Turner's Men, nor any Men about the neighbourhood go, except one Work which is of little account near the Toll-Bar, and tho' they have offered their Services, desiring to work Peaceably, observing the same Rules with their neighbours, he has been so far from listening to the distress of Poor Men who have got Families, that he has absolutely toss'd their Clothes into the Lane and trod them in the dirt, threatening them if they came upon the Bank; neither would he give them their discharge, and has kept them from work now about a Month.'

These charges were rebutted by Samuel and his supporters in another handbill, which was followed by yet a third from the workers. At this distance in time, it is impossible to say who was in the right—but the workers certainly put up the more convincing case. The three handbills are in Hanley Reference Library.

27 See Simeon Shaw. *History*, p.217. One wonders how this figure was obtained thirty years after the event. It sounds more like a profit figure for the late 1820s (see Chapter 5), but it could be correct: in 1812, the London stock figure was higher than in the later period (see Appendix 11).

28 Fenton Hall was built by Thomas Whieldon and was situated in Whieldon's Grove (see John Ward, *op. cit*, p.49). Whieldon had died in 1795. The Hall was still Spode II's address in February 1804 (Spode Grant of Arms: *Spode MSS*) but his obituary (Ref.131) states that he moved into the Mount that year.

29 Alexandre Brongniart, the great Sèvres Director, in his *Traités des Arts Ceramique* (1844, Vol.II, p. 446) paraphrased Shaw's passage, which he acknowledged to him. His paraphrase and translation are very accurate but the reference to bones in porcelain (*History*, p.218, the only one Shaw made to a subject as unfamiliar as it was interesting to a French ceramicist) failed to satisfy him. So: 'il [Spode] introduisit ou au moins perfectionna l'emploi des os calcinés dans la pâte'. Leon Arnoux, in 1851, and M.L.Solon, in 1903, both followed the man they regarded as their master.

30 The only current ceramic use for bone is in china, but this has not always been so. Enoch Wood claimed to have been the first to make 'use of bone in earthenware' when an apprentice with Palmer of Hanley (see Hayden, *op. cit*, p.100). Well he might, since bone features largely in recipes for what passed as jasper in the early nineteenth century (see Chapter 8).

31 See Eccles and Rackham, *Analysed Specimens of English Porcelain*, 1922, p.11. The authors group English porcelain into four classes, one being 'bone china', as distinct from early pastes containing bone.

32 See John Mallett *op. cit* (Note 8), p.142. On 16th August 1758, John Baddeley paid 'Carriage of Bone Ashes from Winsford £14.3s.6d.' I have heard the suggestion that they may have been used for manure: but this use does not appear to have been understood until the publication of Liebig's researches in 1840.

33 From an early nineteenth century transcript of an undated and unnamed practical treatise on potting (*Spode MSS*). The advice is sound: ox bones are the only satisfactory ones. In their advertisement for bones, in 1770, the proprietors of a porcelain company in Philadelphia offered to buy both horse and ox bones—and at the same price. They went out of business two years later (Ref.200).

34 Total annual production of bone china in the United Kingdom in 1969 exceeded £14,000,000, considerably more than half of which was directly exported. Ex. inf. British Pottery Manufacturers' Federation.

35 Report from *The Staffordshire Advertiser*, 20th September 1806. Prior to Spode, the appointment as Potters to the Prince of Wales had been held by the Turners of Lane End, whose bankruptcy was announced on 5th July 1806. The royal appointment was retained by Spode when the Prince became Regent in 1811 and again, in 1820, when he became King

George IV. Details of three notable commissions from him are given in Note 89. On his death in 1830, his brother, William IV, formerly the Duke of Clarence, ordered his Coronation Service from Davenport (see John Ward, *op. cit,* p.157) which the two of them had visited the day following their visit to the Spode Factory. Copeland and Garrett were still styled Manufacturers to the Royal Family in 1836 (see Appendix II).

36 See Wolf Mankowitz, *op. cit,* pp. 133 to 138. On page 138, mention is made of orders being received at Etruria for bone china as late as 1822, but Eliza Meteyard (*op. cit,* p.390) states its manufacture was abandoned about the middle of 1815 'and henceforth Spode executed any matches for customers'. The following extract from correspondence, dated 9th September 1815, may be relevant: 'Mr. Spode sent a note the other day to ask the loan of the copper plates to do some china plates no. 590, it is no doubt those you refused to do for somebody the other day as the quantity agrees'. (Wedgwood MS. 20.17760.)

37 Arthur Hayden (*op. cit,* pp.126 and 127) mentions the 1816 partnership in the Cornwall Clay and Stone Company and a major coalmining partnership of the two men, at Stokeley Colliery. My source of information for the Cornish ventures is the detailed account provided by R.M.Barton, *A History of the Cornish China-Clay Industry,* 1966, pp.37–40, 45 and 83. The same book (p.44 and Plate i) gives information on the activities of William Rogers, who promoted the Cornish clay industry by presenting elaborately decorated and suitably inscribed bowls to well-chosen persons in public life. At least one of these bowls was made by Spode—in 1813 for the British Museum, where it is still. It is the subject of an article by Hugh Tait in the *Connoisseur,* May 1970.

38 After Spode III's widow left the Mount, it was leased to Lewis Adams and after that became a school. Since 1897, it has been part of the North Staffordshire Blind and Deaf School and still stands, with many alterations and additions and without its former extensive grounds. Many of the houses built by Spode in Penkhull survived until about 1966.

39 Announcement made, *Staffordshire Advertiser,* 14th June 1806. Daniel and Brown, Hanley, appear in a directory for 1802 which, in addition to one hundred and thirty-nine potters, lists fifty-eight men in trades connected with pottery. (See Chaffers, *op. cit,* p.643.) They appear again in Holden's Triennial Directory for 1805. In this, one hundred and seven manufacturers are listed (Haggar and Mankowitz, *op. cit,* p.272). In these two trade directories, they are described as enamellers and there is no mention of their being potters or gilders. Gilders they certainly were, but we may doubt if they actually manufactured pottery, as opposed to purchasing it and selling it after decoration.

40 In the Chamberlain account books there is an entry of 2nd January 1796, for a quantity of tableware in Bridge and Temple pattern, supplied by Daniel and Brown. Another entry

occurs on 1st February 1796, 'for short service Bridge and Temple £4.12s.3d. Sundry Cream Coloured Ware 11s. 0d. Short service best nankeen £5.12s.9d.' Other references appear for 21st May 1796; 4th December 1797; 2nd September 1795 and 21st May 1796, and yet other notes of cash paid etc. appear up to 1801. Ex. inf. Geoffrey Godden.

41 At the end of 1812, Henry Daniel drew up a will. The real estate at his disposal consisted of six houses and a parcel of land in Shelton and a house, with brewhouse attached, in Stoke. All of these were occupied by tenants, and at this date he was living in a house rented from Spode II (*Daniel MSS*). He was still there in May 1833, when it was described as being on the south west side and fronting on High Street, Stoke (*Spode MSS*).

42 John Ward's account (*op. cit,* p.283) differs from Shaw's. He says that Daniel of Cobridge was a master potter who employed the Dutch enamellers and moved his workshop to Bagnall, three miles away, to preserve secrecy. Shaw simply states that Daniel of Cobridge was the first 'native' to practice enamelling and does not describe him as a potter. He implies that the Dutchmen themselves located their own muffle at Bagnall. He neatly overcomes the fact that Thomas Daniel only followed in the path shown him by Warner Edwards by crediting him with (on) 'glaze enamelling' and his master with underglaze enamelling ('biscuit painting'). These attributions cannot be taken too seriously, but it can safely be concluded that Thomas Daniel was very early in the enamelling field.

43 Simeon Shaw. *History,* p.167. On page 143, Shaw refers again to the 'papers left by Mr. Thomas Daniel'. He must have known Henry Daniel quite well and Henry was one of the executors of Shaw's father-in-law. Edward Simpson of Shelton, shopkeeper, died on 7th April 1812, leaving his friends, Henry Daniel, enameller, and William Goodwin, builder, to act as executors, with his widow Ann. It was not until May 4th 1825, that Simeon Shaw, along with the other five beneficiaries, received £30.13s.0d. as his equal share of the legacy, which was subject to 10 per cent duty since he was a stranger in blood to the deceased (*Daniel MSS*). His wife, Elizabeth, had died at some time between 1812 and 1825 (see *History,* p. 217: 'the younger Mr. Spode experienced a bereavement, conceivable by those only who have been similarly bereft').

44 A note unsigned and undated, reads 'H.Daniel was born in 1765. Thomas Daniel his father in 1742, H.Daniel Grandfather 1707, H.Daniel Great Grandfather 1677' (*Daniel MSS*). The date given for Henry Daniel's birth, 1765, is perfectly correct but that the other dates are in the nature of approximations is revealed by the rest of the note: 'H. Daniel the elder, who made his will leaving the estate, was born about the year 1677 and was about 30 years old when his son was born (1707). His son Henry was about 35 years old when his grandson Thomas was born (1742) and his grandson Thomas was 23 years old when his great grandson Henry was born (1765)'. On 23rd October 1739, a Thomas Daniel, son of Henry and

Nancy Daniel, was christened at Stoke. Henry Daniel himself was christened at Stoke on 29th September 1765, and his parents' names were given as Thomas and Fanny. He died on 14th April 1841, from 'decay of nature'.

45 The 1822 balance sheet (Pages 40, 41) contains an item of £27.12s.6d. 'to ½ year's rent of House, Chandlers Shop etc. in Mr. Thomas Daniel's possession' and among the Daniel MSS is an account book belonging to 'Thomas Daniel, Grocer, Stoke upon Trent'. Entries appear from 30th July 1814 to 12th February 1823 and reveal a sizable business but they are not in the handwriting of Henry's father and it is almost inconceivable that the business was his. Nor could it have belonged to Henry's son, Thomas, who was only fourteen in 1812 and working with his father. It may have been a relative who paid his rent through Henry as a matter of convenience.

46 The oldest document among the Daniel MSS is an indenture dated 7th February 1750, in which 'Richard Dyer, Son of John Dyer of St. Margaret's Westminster in the County of Middlesex' put himself apprentice for seven years to 'Nicholas Sprimont of Chelsea in the county of Middlesex aforesaid, Gent.' to learn the art of 'painting in enamel'. The indenture is in the usual form. Some of the entries are indistinct, since the document has received a great deal of wear—perhaps from being carried and produced as a reference. The description 'painting in enamel' is itself barely discernible but Dyer's signature is clear enough and those of the two witnesses: Henry Porter and Susanah Protin (On 13th November 1742, Sprimont married 'Ann Protin of Kensington, Spinster', see F.Severne MacKenna, *Chelsea Porcelain: The Triangle and Raised Anchor Wares*, 1947).
Dyer's connection with the Daniels is further established by an entry in the Chamberlain (Worcester) account books for 30th July 1798: 'By Rd. Dyer colours from Daniel and Co. £1.8s.0d'. Presumably, this transaction is quite distinct from the many they had with Daniel and Brown, and Daniel & Co. means Thomas Daniel acting on his own account, possibly with Henry involved. On 16th April 1799, there is an entry, 'paid Thomas Daniel for colours £4' and again on 10th August 1799, 'paid Mr. Daniel senior 5lb. of green, full, £1.10s.0d'. (See Note 40). On 2nd July 1843, the second son of John Daniel (youngest of Henry's three sons) was born. Henry's grandson was christened John Dyer Daniel, which provides an indication that Dyer was either an extremely close friend of the Daniel family or, more probably, the two families married into each other. John Dyer Daniel's mother's maiden name was Rhead, but that of Henry's own wife has not yet been established: they do not appear to have been married in either Burslem or Stoke Parishes.
R.W.Binns (*A Century of Potting in the City of Worcester*, 1877, p.88) stated that when Sprimont avowed his intention of ceasing his activities at Chelsea, in 1763, Worcester took the opportunity of employing several of his painters of the exotic bird and blue scaled ground decorations. Three of these—Dyer, Mills and Willman—were, according to Binns, remembered by a James

Plant, 'a workman lately employed on these works who has been nearly fifty years in the manufactory'. No dates are mentioned or suggested for Plant's recollection and it is not clear whether Binns received his information direct from him or from somebody that had worked with him.
S.W.Fisher (*The Decoration of English Porcelain*, 1959, pp.101 and 102) states that James Giles, the London decorator, was known to have employed a large staff which included Richard Dyer, and he mentions that the Bowcocke Papers record that Dyer worked for Bolton, the Lambeth enameller. He makes the interesting tentative suggestion that Dyer may have been the painter of what Honey referred to as the 'wet' (as opposed to 'dishevelled') style of bird painting found on Chinese, Chelsea and Worcester pieces.
There thus seems some evidence that Richard Dyer, after leaving Chelsea, worked in London and then obtained employment in Worcester. Quite how he came to become connected with the Daniels, and in what capacity, remains a mystery and we are left tantalised by this evidence of a link between them and the Chelsea Factory.

47 Thomas Daniel was supplying Minton in 1803 and his address, given as Hanley, was probably Daniel and Brown's premises. See G.A.Godden, *Minton op. cit*, p.162.

48 Articles of partnership between Henry and Richard, his second son, were not signed until 5th January 1827, but in them it is mentioned that the two have been in business together 'these three years and upwards', which reveals 1823 as the latest possible date for their start (*Daniel MSS*). G.A.Godden (*British Pottery and Porcelain 1780-1850*, 1963, p.47) states that Henry's name first occurs as a manufacturer in the Stoke Rate Records for 1823 (2nd rate, July 14th).

49 Five letters from Henry to John in Liverpool, dated 1820 and 1821, reveal that he was aware that the career intended for his son was not going according to plan. John, in fact, asked to join his father but was told that there was no situation available at the time which 'would do him any good'. *Daniel MSS.*
Why John was intended for a career so out of keeping with the rest of the family is something of a puzzle. Probably because, being the youngest, he had had a better education than his brothers. There is evidence of this among the Daniel MSS: he could write Latin. The opportunity may have come through Thomas Daniel, the grocer (see Note 45): Threlfall of Liverpool was one of his largest suppliers, of coffee and caraway seeds among other goods.

50 The letter is undated but is watermarked 1823. It is addressed to 'Messrs. Daniel & Son, Stoke China Works, Staffordshire Potteries'. The postmark is indistinct but could be 1823, which is the likeliest date (see Note 48). *Daniel MSS.*

51 These hiring agreements related, of course, to Daniel's own factory. They included some for a number of potters, as distinct from decorators. *Daniel MSS.*

52 Simeon Shaw, *History*, p.228. On the same page, Shaw mentions that the invention, 'the application of gold in a liquid state, in place of the leaf gold used upon size', had been attributed to Henry Daniel, who, 'far from arrogating the merit to himself, very explicitly avowed his complete ignorance of the person by whom the invention was made'.

53 From *A Representation of the Manufacturing of Earthenware*, 1827. This tiny, delightful book consists of twenty-one prints showing pottery processes and is supposed to have been published for Enoch Wood of Burslem. It is very rare and I am indebted to the British Ceramic Research Association for making their copy available to me.

54 *The Ruin of Potters and the Way to Avoid it, stated in The Plainest Manner, in the following lines, addressed, after thirty years experience, to the consideration of all in the Trade, by a Manufacturer*. Anonymous. Printed by T.Orton, Lane End 1804. It was later published, as a letter received, by *The Pottery Gazette*, 3rd January 1825, at a time when the controversy over sizes was again at its height.

55 On 22nd March 1826, W.T.Copeland wrote to Josiah Wedgwood Junior, seeking his support for opposition to proposed legislation on pottery sizes. (Wedgwood MS. 20837-29.) The support was denied. The Mason brothers were also in favour of state intervention (See R.Haggar, *op. cit*, p.36).

56 A notebook compiled by T.Shaw, a turner for Spode II, dated 1817. *Spode MSS*.

57 Thomas Ryan, in his account (Note 58), mentions the antiquity of the mine. The exact location of it was at Bulthey Hill, in Alberbury, one of those parishes half in England and half in Wales. The mine was last re-opened in the 1914-1918 war for barytes, and 2,700 tons were extracted. Ex. inf. Michael F.Messenger FLA, Shrewsbury Borough Librarian and Curator, and Miss M.C.Hill, MA, Salop County Archivist.

58 Wedgwood MS 21874-29. This is a lengthy handwritten account of Ryan's discovery of the deposits at Middletown Hill and the subsequent history of the company he formed. The document is unsigned and undated, but is written in the first person singular and Ryan himself must have been its author. It corroborates the sparse information given on the subject by Simeon Shaw (*Chemistry of Pottery*, 1837, p.437) and the fuller account given by William Evans (*op. cit*, p.7).

59 See *The Repertory of Arts*, vol.42, 1823, p.235. With this cheap, porous ware, sold in huge quantities to the labouring classes, the lead glaze was liable to prove soluble with vinegar etc. The cumulative effect of a diet of lead-tainted food over many years can be imagined.

60 Who this relative was remains a mystery.

61 From an extract from Mary Bagot's Journal, reprinted in *Links with the Past*, 1902, by Mrs Charles Bagot. The extract begins, 'Mr. Spode, the great china Manufacturer died lately, and we heard today a most interesting and credible account of him from his partner'. The date given for this—27th August 1824—is obviously a misprint. Many nearby extracts are dated 1827. Mary Bagot was the daughter of the Reverend Walter Bagot, brother of Lord Bagot. Walter Bagot held the family living of Blithfield and Leigh for many years. Mrs Charles Bagot was, by her own account, on friendly terms with Spode IV from 1866 to 1870.

62 Even in 1969, the highest price for the finest imported felspar did not exceed £27 per ton. In his account (Note 58), Ryan later mentions 'plenty of orders' from the Potteries at £2.10s.0d. per ton. Presumably, this was the 'cheaper sort' he mentions as having been purchased by Mayer, Minton, Ridgway and others.

63 Simeon Shaw, *History*, p.219. Shaw's date may be wrong. Ryan gave his expenses (Note 58) up to the end of 1820 as £3,196.1s.6d. Included in this was £200 for 'Pottery at Stoke' (presumably the one he engaged for experiments) and £105 for 'Porcelain Vase for George IV'. This entry could, however, relate to a quite different, unrecorded, vase made by Rose.

64 William Copeland's will contained legacies of £2,000 for each of his two nephews and his niece: William, James and Hannah Astbury (sic). They were the children of his only sister, Hannah. *Spode MSS*.

65 India Office Records. Miscellaneous letters received 1821, vol.144, p.294. This entry and others relating to Spode (Refs. 104 to 108) were discovered, and additional information supplied, by S.J.McNally Esq, Assistant Keeper, and made available to me by Robert Copeland. Unpublished Crown-copyright material appears by permission of the Secretary of State for Foreign and Commonwealth Affairs.

66 Ex. inf. J.F.Ware Esq, National Army Museum.

67 Between 1842 and 1854 (but not before), an extremely comprehensive record was kept by the Hudson's Bay Company of all shipments to Canada: HBC A 25/7. This record gives the exact value of every cargo, together with the type of commodity and the supplier's name. All entries for tableware are for Copeland and Garrett and, later, Copeland. The first evidence of Copeland and Garrett supplying them is an invoice (HBC.A.67/27 Fo.401) dated 15th June, 1836, for £145.7s.4d.

68 See Louis R. Coywood, *Final Report Fort Vancouver Excavations*, United States Department of the Interior, National Park Service, 1955, p.52. In an article on the excavations, in *The Oregon Historical Quarterly* of June 1948, Mr Coywood refers throughout to Spode ware but uses the expression in the generic rather than the historical sense.

69 Ex. inf. R.Newton Esq.

70 Translation from the original Norwegian of a note written in 1901 by Henrietta Rosenkilde's daughter, who was thirty-two when her mother died. Miss Rosenkilde was married on 21st January 1817, but very long engagements were typical of the place and period and the present was probably made in 1814, which is indicated both by the pattern number, 2352, and the circumstances of the arrival of the service in Christiansand. Napoleon was exiled to Elba in May 1814, in which month Norway declared her independence. The capture may have been made, however, by an American privateer. The Treaty of Ghent which officially ended the Anglo-American war was not ratified until February 1815.

The service is now owned by Mrs Molla Kraft, to whom I am indebted for the information concerning it.

71 The closure was announced in 1828, but the great sale of stock lasted into 1829. See Eliza Meteyard, *op. cit*, p.391.

72 See G.A.Godden, *Minton op. cit*, 1968, p.8. This may have been a bad year for them since the turnover seems low in relation to their size. In June 1833, the Factory Inspector reported that he had 'inspected the works of Messrs Copeland and Minton, each employing about seven hundred hands . . . I examined minutely both these establishments and found them in the best order' (Factory Inquiry Commission, Cass 1968, Report by Mr. Spencer of 28th June 1833, B2, p.78). A turnover of about £62 per capita, which is all that could have been achieved in 1841–42 if they still employed this number, was not good in relation to their likely labour costs. The old rule of thumb in the Potteries (which can still be heard among the older generation) was 'packing should equal twice the wage bill'. On 29th January 1837, W.T.Copeland wrote to his factory complaining that 'The wages last week seem very large—£900' (*Spode MSS*).

73 Probably Newcastle High School, as it is now known. The Headmaster, Mr John Roberts, MA, informs me that his school was originally known as the Free Grammar School, Newcastle, but in the eighteenth century was referred to simply as 'The Grammar School'. Popular usage may have continued to be the earlier form.

74 See the Factory Inspector's Report quoted in Note 72.

75 This bowl played an important part in forming the first Burns Society in the world. On 25th January 1819, a group of Burns' admirers, having finished their second annual dinner to celebrate the poet's birthday, decided to open a subscription for the purchase of a china punch bowl to be used on all similar occasions. The bowl was duly delivered, and on its foot each subscriber's name was given in full. They met on the 18th January 1820, and a minute survives from this meeting which records 'the china bowl made by Spode of Staffordshire of excellent workmanship with elegant emblematic devices

(capable of holding three gallons), a handsome silver punch spoon and three dozen glasses, purchased from the amount of the subscription, were produced to a meeting of the subscribers, this 18th January 1820 and very much admired'. It was at this meeting that the subscribers to the bowl formed themselves into a Society which, since that date, has been known as The Burns Club of Dumfries—the first of many throughout the world. The bowl and four Spode jugs of similar decoration can still be seen in Burns House, Dumfries, except for one day in the year, Burns' birthday, when they are in use.

76 Only a small minority of the pages in the pattern books bear watermarks and the dates of these are not always in sequence. Patterns 251, 281 and 322 are dated 1799 but Pattern 286 has 1797. Between Patterns 341 and 558 six marks occur, all 1794. Pattern 565 marks the beginning of the use of a slightly larger size of paper. Patterns 567, 569 and 974 are marked 1804 and then, in isolation, Pattern 1057 has 1806; but following this, the marks revert to 1804, occasionally interspersed with 1803. These two dates occur twenty-one times between Patterns 1224 and 3690. Obviously, if a pattern is on a page marked with a date earlier than that of a prior one then, despite this, it cannot be dated before its predecessor. Thus, although the watermark 1794 appears for Patterns 341 to 558, the date is without significance since 1799 occurs before. Similarly, Pattern 1057 being on a page marked 1806 removes all interest from the subsequent dates of 1803 and 1804. The page bearing Pattern 3693 introduces a yet larger size of paper and the watermarks occur, with one insignificant exception, chronologically. Pattern 3695 is marked 1822, which recurs until Pattern 4168, which has the date 1825; this date, in its turn, continues until 1827 appears for Pattern 4518. The two dates 1825 and 1827 alternate until Pattern 5058, which is marked 1831. Pattern 5447 has 1833 and Pattern 5767 has 1836.

77 Ex. inf. Reginald Haggar. There is a copy in the Solon Library, Stoke Technical College.

78 See H.Owen, *op. cit*, pp.326 and 327. Evidence at the 1891 Wages Arbitration. The employers stated the rates as 50/3½d. for throwers and 34/2½d. for turners.

79 An Edwardian edition of Cassell's *Dictionary of Cookery* gives the price of pineapples as 1/– to 2/– each, 'when available'. The same book prices strawberries at 4d. per lb.

80 Blue clay was the most popular of the West Country ball clays. Black and brown were other, inferior, varieties. The colours refer to their natural appearance only and are irrelevant to the colour of fired ware made from them.

81 The Murray Curvex machine, now widely used, dispenses with the use of transfer paper; but it has very strict limitations. It is still possible to see, even in the largest factories, the entire process being carried out exactly as described by William Evans, using the same equipment and skills. The engraver's art has remained completely unchanged and survives despite the emergence of quicker, cheaper and cruder ways of cutting coppers.

82 Hester Savory died in February 1803, eight months after her marriage, aged not quite twenty-six. Her tea service is now in the possession of a descendant of her brother, Mrs M.B. Moore of Tonbridge, Surrey.

Hester was the beautiful Quaker girl with whom Charles Lamb fell in love, although he was never to exchange a word with her. He wrote a touching poem on her death. (See E.V.Lucas, *The Life of Charles Lamb*, 1921, Vol.1, pp.101 and 291 and an article by Walter Powell in *Toronto Week*, December 1890.)

83 The weight of Spode Stone China dinner plates varies from fourteen to eighteen ounces, but New Stone ones can be as heavy as twenty-one. This compares with a weight of twelve to thirteen ounces for Spode earthenware plates of the same shape and size. China plates can weigh as much as twenty-three ounces.

84 Shaw's description is of interest: 'Stone China in imitation of the Oriental, is very thick, strong, semi-translucent, vitrescent, coarse texture, granular fracture, durable, but with a very soft glaze'. (*Chemistry of Pottery*, p.446.)

85 On 6th March 1800, Spode II wrote to Thomas Byerley: 'Having seen the specification of Messrs. W. and J. Turner's Patent, I think it would be desirable for a few manufacturers to meet on that business. I have wrote to several requesting their attendance at the Swan Inn, Hanley, on Tuesday next at 3 o'clock in the afternoon, at which time I hope you will make it convenient to attend.' (Wedgwood MS 2200-12.)

86 Ex. inf. Major R.St.G.G.Bartelot RA.

87 There are references, *c.* 1812 and *c.* 1830, in the Spode and Daniel MSS to George Bell, a bat printer. Another printer mentioned (not necessarily a bat printer) is Bruce, *c.* 1815 and *c.* 1836. A George Bell and a George Bruce were tenants of Spode III's executors in 1832, living at Cliff Bank and paying rent of £5.5s.0d. and £6.10s.0d. per annum respectively.

88 J.K. des Fontaines. *Underglaze Blue-printed Earthenware with Particular Reference to Spode*, 1969, ECC Vol.7, Pt.2. Every Spode devotee will be grateful to Mr des Fontaines for this profusely illustrated and very informative work but, as mentioned elsewhere (Note 13), I have particular cause since the results of his extensive researches among the Wedgwood MSS were generously made available to me. Regrettably, his paper was not available in printed form in time for detailed references to be made to it in this book.

89 The Orleans Light Bowls (Shape 305) were made to convert large Chinese porcelain jars into lamps for the Music Room of Brighton Pavilion. The jars bear the arms of the House of Orleans. The finished lamps—with elaborate metal mounts and very ornate pedestals—now flank the approach to the famous balcony of Buckingham Palace, in the Centre Room of the Main Front. They are illustrated by H.Clifford Smith, *Buckingham Palace, Its Furniture, Decoration and History*, 1931, plates 283 and 284.

The conversion was extremely costly. The record of payments for the Music Room furnishings shows one to Spode of £277.16s.6d. under the heading 'The Orleans Jars and Pedestals'. This is modest compared with £1417.10s.0d. paid, under the same heading, to Vulliamy (metal work). The sculptor, E.H.Bailey, received £141. It is not clear if more than the two lamps which survive were made.

Another combined effort resulted in some of Brighton Pavilion's most famous objects—the six pagodas which once graced the Music Room. These now stand in Buckingham Palace: four of them, fifteen feet high, in the Principal Corridor (see H.Clifford Smith, *Ibid*, plates 117 and 263, p.217). Again, the main part was Chinese porcelain but the richly painted and gilt pedestals were produced by Spode. For these he received £305.17s.6d. Vulliamy's share was £1406 and Bailey's £134. Richard Westmacott, who was also concerned, received £159.1s.4d. The largest payment made to Spode for supplies to Brighton Pavilion was £440 for 'Jars Bowls and Pedestals' which cost, in total, £5322. These were for the Banqueting Room.

I am indebted to Geoffrey de Bellaigue for identifying the Orleans Light Bowls and for advising me of relevant papers among the Royal Archives (RA 34223, 34224), details from which are published by gracious permission of Her Majesty The Queen.

References

Unpublished Sources

100 SPODE MSS. This collection is housed at the Spode Factory in Stoke-on-Trent, and documents contained in it are the authority for many statements in the text. Since this material is not generally available, there has seemed little point in supplying detailed references, but these have been lodged with the manuscript collection itself.

101 DANIEL MSS. Preserved by William Algar, a great grandson of Henry Daniel's youngest son, John. As with the Spode MSS, detailed references are not supplied for the various pieces, which are the authority for many statements in the text, but have been lodged with the manuscript collection itself.

HANLEY MUSEUM MSS. See Note 2
102 Petition of Staffordshire potters against increased canal freight charges, 1785.
103 Tittensor Road Mortgage, 8th November 1792.

INDIA OFFICE MSS. See Note 65
104 Minutes of Court of Directors, 29th March 1821 (B/172, p.1279).
105 Minutes of Court of Directors, 30th October 1822 (pp.588 and 614).
106 Court's Letters, xx, 1823.
107 Main Ledger, Export Goods and Stores, Commercial Dept, 18th September 1824.
108 Ex. Inf. S.J.McNally Esq.

WEDGWOOD MSS. See Note 13
109 18.16204.
110 13.11690A.
111 13.11659.
112 13.11798.
113 13.120081.
114 13.11844.
115 13.11717.
116 121.23534.
117 13.11815.
118 13.120083.
119 2203.12.
120 20834.29.

Published Sources

121 Act for enlarging the term of Cookworthy's Patent, Geo. III, 1775, Cap.52.

122 Newcastle Canal Act, Geo. III, 1795, Cap.87.

123 Champion's Specification, 15th September 1775. See Jewitt, *op. cit*, p.217.

124 W. and J.Turner's Specification, 6th February 1800, No.2367.

125 Warburton's Specification, 9th April 1810, No.3304.

126 Mason's Specification, 14th August 1813, No.3724.

127 *Art-Union*, November 1846, The Works of Copeland and Garrett, p.288.
128 Ibid, p.289.
129 Ibid, p.296.
130 Ibid, p.297.

131 *Gentleman's Magazine*, 1827, ii, p.470. Obituary Spode II.

132 *Pottery Mercury*, 18th February 1824.

133 *Repertory of Arts*, Vol. 39, 1821, pp.219 to 221.

134 *Review*, 8th January 1713, Vol.1, No.43.

135 *Staffordshire Advertiser*, 8 July 1797. (See also A.Hayden, *op. cit*, p.23.)
136 Ibid, 9th March 1811.
137 Ibid, 15th April 1815.
138 Ibid, 21 July 1827.
139 Ibid, 10th October 1829.
140 Ibid, 24th October 1829.
141 Ibid, 19th December 1829.
142 Ibid, 18th April 1868.

143 *Staffordshire Mercury* (Quoted, John Haslem, *op. cit*, p.127).

144 *The Times*, 29th August 1797 (Quoted in full, Arthur Hayden, *op. cit*, p.26).
145 Ibid, 4th July 1817.

146 *Proceedings of the Wedgwood Society*, 1957, No.2. Tom Lyth, 'Wedgwood Stone China', p.67.
147 Ibid, 1966, No.6. Una des Fontaines, 'The Darwin Service and the First Printed Floral Patterns at Etruria', p.79.
148 Ibid, 1966, No.6. J.K. des Fontaines 'Letters from Thomas Sparks, Engraver, to Wedgwood, 1815-1819' p.99.
149 Ibid, p.97. Wedgwood MS.3 (87-1).
150 Ibid, p.100. Wedgwood MSS. 16525.18 and 25470-34.

151 *Victoria History of the County of Staffordshire*, 1963, Vol.8, pp.115 and 183.
152 Ibid, pp.169, 222 and 246. See also Bevis Hillier. *The Turners of Lane End*, p.4.

153 ADAMS, PERCY W.L. *History of the Adams Family*, 1914, p.314.

154 AIKIN, JOHN *A Description of the Country from Thirty to Forty Miles round Manchester*, 1795, p.516.
155 Ibid, p.522.

156 CANNON, T.G. *Old Spode*, 1924, plate 20.

157 CHAFFERS, *Marks and Monograms*. Thirteenth Edition, 1912, p.645.

158 CHURCH, SIR A.H. *English Earthenware*, 1911, p.107.
159 Ibid, p.119.

160 DAVIS, DOROTHY *A History of Shopping*, 1966, p.201.

161 DODD, A.E. *Dictionary of Ceramics*, Second Edition 1967, p.195.

162 DUNLOP, O.J. *English Apprenticeship and Child Labour*, 1912, pp.66, 132 and 178.
163 Ibid, p.116.

164 EVANS, WILLIAM *Art and History of the Potting Business*, 1846, p.7.
165 Ibid, p.26.
166 Ibid, p.37.
167 Ibid, p.46.

168 GEORGE, M. DOROTHY *London Life in the Eighteenth Century*, Peregrine Books 1966, p.16.

169 GILHESPY, F. BRAYSHAW *Derby Porcelain*, Spring Books 1965, p.69. Letter from Joseph Lygo.
170 Ibid, p.70.

171 GODDEN, GEOFFREY A. *Illustrated Encyclopedia of British Pottery and Porcelain*, 1966, p.541.

172 GODDEN, GEOFFREY A. *British Pottery and Porcelain*, 1780–1850, 1963, p.80. (Solomon Cole's account.)
173 Ibid, pp.81, 151 and 152.
174 Ibid, plate 33.

175 GODDEN, GEOFFREY A. *Minton Pottery and Porcelain of the First Period 1793-1850*, 1968, p.15.
176 Ibid, p.39.
177 Ibid, p.156.

178 GRANT, CAPTAIN M.H. *The Makers of Black Basaltes*, 1910, pp.265 and 266.

179 HAGGAR, REGINALD G. *The Masons of Lane Delph*, 1952, p.14.
180 Ibid, pp.19 to 21.
181 Ibid, pp.31 and 32.
182 Ibid, pp.47, 62 and 89. (See also *Staffordshire Advertiser*, 2nd September 1815.)
183 Ibid, p.50.
184 Ibid, p.65.

185 HARGREAVES, THOMAS *Map of the Potteries*, 1st May 1832.

186 HASLEM, JOHN *The Old Derby China Factory*, 1876, p.34.
187 Ibid, pp.28, 29 and 201.
188 Ibid, pp.90 to 93.
189 Ibid, p.127.
190 Ibid, p.128.
191 Ibid, p.130.
192 Ibid, p.200.
193 Ibid, p.221.

194 HASSELL, JOHN *A Tour of the Grand Junction Canal in 1819*. First published 1819, Cranfield and Bonfield Reprint, 1968, p.62. For this valuable reference I am indebted to Norman Emery.

195 HAWLEY, T. *Sketches of Pottery Life and Character in the Forties and Fifties*, c. 1900, p.5.

196 HAYDEN, ARTHUR *Spode and His Successors*, 1925, p.109.
197 Ibid, p.111.

198 HILLIER, BEVIS *Pottery and Porcelain, 1700-1914*, 1968, p.63.
199 Ibid, p.83.
200 Ibid, p.177. See also Note 33.

201 HILLIER, BEVIS *The Turners of Lane End*, 1965, p.3.
202 Ibid, p.4.
203 Ibid, p.57.
204 Ibid, pp.73 to 75.

205 HUGHES, THERLE *The Spode Way to Dress a Desk*, Country Life Annual, 1969, p.44.

206 JEWITT, LLEWELLYN *The Ceramic Art of Great Britain*, Second Edition, 1883, pp.213 to 219.
207 Ibid, p.382.
208 Ibid, p.392.
209 Ibid, p.396.

210 JOHN AND BAKER *Old English Lustre Pottery*, 1951, p.22. Quoting J.M.Clarke, Director of the New York State Museum.

211 LAKIN, THOMAS *The Valuable Receipts of the Late Mr. Thomas Lakin*, 1824, pp.9 and 10.

212 LAMB, CHARLES *A Dissertation upon Roast Pig: Essays of Elia*.

213 MANKOWITZ, WOLF *Wedgwood*, 1953, p.27.
214 Ibid, p.67.
215 Ibid, plate v, pattern 81.

216 MANKOWITZ AND HAGGAR *Concise Encyclopedia of English Pottery and Porcelain*, 1957, p.24.

217 McKENDRICK, N. *Josiah Wedgwood: An Eighteenth Century Entrepreneur in Salesmanship and Marketing Techniques*, 1960, Economic History Review, Vol. XII, No.3, p.413. Letter from Josiah Wedgwood to Thomas Bentley, 2nd September 1771.

218 METEYARD, ELIZA *A Group of Englishmen*, 1871, p.4.
219 Ibid, p.20.
220 Ibid, pp.154 to 158 and 184.
221 Ibid, p.169.
222 Ibid, p.187.
223 Ibid, p.195.
224 Ibid, p.228.
225 Ibid, p.337.

226 OWEN, H. *The Staffordshire Potter*, 1901, p.16 et seq.

227 PLOT, DR. *Natural History of Staffordshire*, 1686, p.124.

228 PALISSY, BERNARD *The Art of the Earth*, 1580. Translation by H.Morley, *Palissy the Potter*, Second Edition, 1855, p.15.

229 SHAW, SIMEON *The Chemistry of the Several Natural and Artificial Heterogeneous Compounds used in manufacturing Porcelain, Glass and Pottery*, 1837, pp.254 and 417.
230 Ibid, p.438.

231 SHAW, SIMEON *History of the Staffordshire Potteries*, 1829, p.5.
232 Ibid, p.18.
233 Ibid, pp.58 and 220.
234 Ibid, p.63.
235 Ibid, p.66.
236 Ibid, pp.66 and 126.
237 Ibid, p.70.
238 Ibid, p.72 (See also John Ward, *op. cit*, p.553).
239 Ibid, p.151.
240 Ibid, p.153.
241 Ibid, p.155.
242 Ibid, p.156.
243 Ibid, p.166.
244 Ibid, p.170.
245 Ibid, p.172.
246 Ibid, p.173.

247 Ibid, p.178.
248 Ibid, p.180.
249 Ibid, p.181.
250 Ibid, p.182.
251 Ibid, p.203.
252 Ibid, p.214.
253 Ibid, p.215.
254 Ibid, p.216.
255 Ibid, p.217.
256 Ibid, p.218.
257 Ibid, p.219.
258 Ibid, p.221.
259 Ibid, p.223.
260 Ibid, p.226.
261 Ibid, p.227.
262 Ibid, p.229.
263 Ibid, p.230.
264 Ibid, pp.231 and 234.
265 Ibid, p.231.

266 SOLON, M.L. *A Brief History of Old English Porcelain*, 1903, p.220.

267 THOMAS, DR JOHN *Josiah Spode—his Times and Triumphs*, 1933, ECC, Vol.32, p.497.
268 Ibid, p.503.

269 TILLEY, FRANK *Teapots and Tea*, 1957, plate LI.

270 TOWNER, DONALD *The Leeds Pottery*, 1963. p.56.
271 Ibid, between pp. 58 and 142.

272 TURNER, WILLIAM *William Adams: An Old English Potter*, 1923, p.28. See also Llewellyn Jewitt, *op. cit*, p.454.

273 WARD, JOHN *The Borough of Stoke upon Trent*, 1843, p.43.
274 Ibid, p.53.
275 Ibid, pp.57 and 58. (See also Bevis Hillier, *The Turners of Lane End*, 1965, p.19 and Arthur Hayden, *op. cit*, p.111.)
276 Ibid, pp.57, 58, 158 and 501.
277 Ibid, p.67.
278 Ibid, pp.88, 102 and 176.
279 Ibid, pp.175 to 177.
280 Ibid, pp.335, 422 and 513.
281 Ibid, p.445.
282 Ibid, p.499.
283 Ibid, p.500.
284 Ibid, p.501.
285 Ibid, p.503.
286 Ibid, p.511.

287 WATNEY, DR B. *English Blue and White Porcelain of the Eighteenth Century*, 1963, p.8.
288 Ibid, pp.16, 64, 70 and 94. See also Eccles and Rackham, *Analysed Specimens of English Porcelain*, 1922.

289 WILLIAMS, S.B. *Antique Blue and White Spode,* Third
Edition 1949. (First published 1943.)
290 Ibid, p.13.
291 Ibid, p.60.
292 Ibid, p.91.
293 Ibid, pp.94 and 98.
294 Ibid, p.116.
295 Ibid, p.149.
296 Ibid, p.185.

297 YOUNG, ARTHUR *A Six Months Tour through the North of
England,* 1770, Vol. III, p.309.

Index

Index to patterns